Ronnie

Ronnie dedicates this book of her life to her children
Peter and Judy
'For all the times I was not there for you.'

Ronnie

The authorised biography of
VERONICA DUNNE

ALISON MAXWELL

ashfield
PRESS

Published in 2016 by
ASHFIELD PRESS · DUBLIN · IRELAND

ISBN 978 1 901658 97 2

British Library Cataloguing in Publication Data.
A catalogue record for this book is available from the British Library.

*The Friends of the Vocal Arts receive half the royalities from the sales of this biography
in recognition of their work promoting the Veronica Dunne International Singing Competition.*

Designed and typeset in 11 on 12.5 point Scala and Zapfino by
SUSAN WAINE

Contents

ACKNOWLEDGEMENTS

The creative and collaborative world of singing seems to imbue its enthusiasts with a special energy and positivity, and it has been a real pleasure to talk with all the people involved in this book.

I am deeply grateful to Ronnie, and to her children, Judy and Peter. Special thanks go to Paddy Brennan, archivist of the Dublin Grand Opera Society. His knowledge of opera is legendary, and he was kind enough to give my manuscript the once-over, suggest some changes and then declare himself satisfied – praise indeed.

To each and every one of you who have contributed to this biography in so many ways, Ronnie and I say a huge 'Thank you'. John Allen, Patricia Bardon, Seóirse Bodley, Richard Bonynge, Barra Boydell, Orla Boylan, Nicholas Braithwaite, Celine Byrne, David Callopy, Jane Carty, Vivian Coates, Brian Comerford, Joseph Dalton, Michael Donnellan, Paul Dorgan, Brian Doyle, Imelda Drumm, Gerald Duffy, Brianain and Joe Erraught, Tara Erraught, Angela Feeney, the late Edwin FitzGibbon, Edith Forrest, Ann Fuller, Austin Gaffney, Kevin Gaughan, Gerard Gillen, Deirdre Grier-Delaney, Kevin Hough, Mairéad Hurley, Kenneth Jones, Dieter Kaegi, Anthony Kearns, Deborah Kelleher, Paul Kelly, Courtney Kenny, Lucy Lane, Sheila Larchet/ Cuthbert, Lynda Lee, Anne Makower, Geraldine McGee, Veronica McSwiney, Miriam Murphy, Suzanne Murphy, Gemma Ní Bhriain, Jennifer O'Connell, John O'Conor, Tony Ó Dálaigh, Ite O'Donovan, Jack O'Kelly, Pat O'Kelly, Geraldine and Alec O'Riordan, Brian O'Rourke, Cara O'Sullivan, Tony Peacock, Colman Pearce, Richard Pine, Margaret Quigley, Howard Reddy, Nicola Sharkey, Fergus Sheil, Philip Shields, Sarah Shine, Conor Stapleton (Odearest), Sister Bernadette Sweeney, Simon Taylor and the National Concert Hall, Ronan Tynan, George Vaughan, Nyle Wolfe, Judith Woodworth, Finbar Wright, Alison Young, and Dearbhla Collins, Diarmuid Hegarty and Marcia Weldon of the Friends of the Vocal Arts.

Ronnie and I are very grateful to the Royal Irish Academy of Music whose generous sponsorship helped to ensure the publication of this book.

My husband, Dudley Foster, has shared all my near disasters and small triumphs. His encouragement and practical help deserve a whole page of love and appreciation. Jonathan Williams of the Jonathan Williams Literary Agency has been a true support and friend. Very special thanks to Susan Waine and John Davey of Ashfield Press who have produced a most beautiful book to honour a remarkable person, Veronica Dunne.

Preface

*T*HE GREAT LADY laid her hand gently on my arm, looked into my eyes and said, 'You may write my life if you wish.'

I was so overcome I could not speak. I had been helping Ronnie with a short article, and her offer was so unexpected, so apparently spontaneous, that I double-checked with her the next time we met. She reassured me that she was now ready to see her life in print and that I, whom she hardly knew, should write it. She was prepared to spend a great deal of time with me, and to offer all assistance, documents, photographs and memorabilia – everything that was relevant to such a book.

Tuesdays with Ronnie were a delight. Over the course of two years my little device recorded hundreds of hours of memories of family life and her operatic appearances, which she recalled almost to the day of performance: the venue, the work, the conductor, her fellow soloists and the orchestra. Fond memories, too, of her students and of watching their careers reach dizzying heights. Through Ronnie, I was led on a privileged journey to some of the great artists of the international world of opera. Singers, musicians, composers, teachers, family and friends were eager to relate anecdotes about Ronnie and her extraordinary life; all stressed her generosity, kindness, humour and dedication.

The writing of this biography has been a revelation. Ronnie has touched the lives of many people in an exceptional way; I am fortunate to be among them.

ALISON MAXWELL,
Maynooth, January 2016

SELECT BIBLIOGRAPHY

Allen, Thomas, *Foreign Parts: A Singer's Journal*, Methuen Publishing Ltd., London, 1965.

Fleming, Brian, *The Vatican Pimpernel: The Wartime Exploits of Monsignor Hugh O'Flaherty*, The Collins Press, Cork, 2008.

Kennedy, Michael, *Barbirolli, Conductor Laureate, The authorised biography*, Granada Publishing Limited, London, 1972.

Leonard, Maurice, *Kathleen. The Life of Kathleen Ferrier 1912-1953*, Futura Publications, London & Sydney, 1989.

Major, Norma, *Joan Sutherland. The Authorized Biography*, Little, Brown & Company, London, 1994.

Nelson, Havelock, *A bank of violets: The Musical Memoirs of Havelock Nelson*, Greystone Books, Antrim, 1993.

Pine, Richard and Charles Acton (eds), *To Talent Alone: The Royal Irish Academy of Music 1848-1998*, Gill & Macmillan Ltd., Dublin, 1998.

White, Harry and Barra Boydell (eds), *The Encyclopaedia of Music in Ireland*, University College Dublin Press, Dublin 2013.

Smith, Gus, *Irish Stars of the Opera*, Madison Publishers Ltd., Dublin, 1994.

——, Gus, *Love and Music: The Glorious History of the Dublin Grand Opera Society 1941-1998*, Atlantic Publishers, Dublin, 1998.

Foreword

by JOHN O'CONOR

VERONICA DUNNE is one of the most beloved people in Ireland. Just to mention her name will bring forth a wealth of memories from everyone with whom she has come into contact – and a genuine smile of true affection for this wonderful lady who has influenced my life so much, as well as that of many others.

Ronnie – I have never heard anyone call her Veronica – is a legend on so many fronts: as one of the greatest Irish singers of all time, as one of the greatest singing teachers in the world, as someone who has opened her heart and home to so many young singers who could not afford to live elsewhere, as a generous and hospitable hostess, as well as having one of the most raucous laughs around and a fund of stories ranging from the enlightening to the bawdy. An evening spent with Ronnie is one to be cherished, providing you haven't invited anybody who is too prim and proper! She is irrepressible, hilarious, intense, delightfully irrational at times, charming, enthusiastic, effervescent, emotional, passionate, tempestuous, resilient, tough – and utterly adorable.

To anyone who has never met her, this book will give you an idea of the aura that surrounds her and why those of us who have had the immense pleasure of knowing her are completely under her spell. She is indeed one of Ireland's greatest treasures and long may she continue to bewitch us all.

Prelude

AWAKENED BY MUSIC, the child crept to the landing in her bare feet and edged down the stairs. Her perch was a step just out of sight from the hall. Pulling her nightdress tightly about her knees, she imagined the scene in the room below: Billo and her parents in the glow of the fire, in thrall to the opera on the wireless. A creak of floorboards made her look up.

'What are you doing?' May asked.

'Listening,' whispered the four-year-old. She huddled closer to the bannisters and the sounds.

Veronica Bernadette Dunne was born on 2 August 1927. Her parents, William and Josephine, had considered themselves a complete family with their two children, William and May, when along came this new baby, demanding attention. It was with relief that the hard-pressed Josephine handed the child over to Kathleen, live-in housekeeper, and now nanny to this bundle of ferocious energy.

A few months before Veronica's arrival, the family had moved to Clontarf, Dublin, about two miles along a coastal road from Ballybough, Dublin where William Dunne worked with the firm of Farmer Brothers, Builders. Number 154 Howth Road was a new bungalow that had been left on the firm's books. William, a master builder, extended the house upwards to create a bathroom and three bedrooms: two for his children and a spare room for guests. He and Josephine had a bedroom on one side of the ground floor. Kathleen slept on the other side. Off the hall was a kitchen and breakfast room. Double doors divided the dining and drawing rooms which could be opened up to become one spacious room.

The couple were very sociable. Every weekend Josephine's sisters, Rose and Virginia (Ginny), and two or three friends gathered around the table for the Sunday roast. Ginny ran Balfe's Furniture Shop on Ormond Quay, and she and her husband Michael and teenage daughter Rosie always looked forward to the excursion out to the Dunnes. Josephine was an excellent manager and cook, very particular about how food was prepared and presented. With the jovial company and free-flowing talk, Veronica often felt like voicing her opinion, but in an era when children could be seen but certainly not heard, she knew she had to button her lip or invite trouble.

Josephine's own childhood had been difficult. An arranged match had been made between Joseph Hetherington, an elderly Protestant widower, and a young, beautiful local girl. The couple had three daughters, Josephine, Rose and Ginny, but the union was not a happy one. The girls had a lonely upbringing because their mother became increasingly unhappy and withdrawn.

Josephine resolved to do better. She and William had a loving marriage. They shared views on the strict Catholic way to raise children, but the practice proved more complicated than the theory. The arrival of a son and heir, William (Bill), excited great rejoicing; nothing was too good for him. A long gap of ten years preceded the much-anticipated arrival of their daughter, May. Four years later, there was Veronica.

Fourteen-year-old Bill was enchanted by the new addition to the family. He gazed down on the baby in the cot: the eyes so alert and blue, the tiny, clutching hands which sought out his fingers, the throaty, gurgling giggle. Later she tried to say his name and it came out like bubbles: Bill-lo, Bill-lo, Bill-lo, and the name stuck.

His sister wanted nothing to do with the interloper. May was cosseted and over-protected by her mother following an unfortunate incident when she was two. Josephine had arranged for Santa Claus to pay a surprise visit to the house. The appearance of the strange man with his bristly beard, outlandish garb and huge booming voice so terrified the child that she was left with a pronounced squint in one eye and had to undergo an operation, a serious procedure in those days, which was not altogether successful. Josephine never forgave herself, and spent years bringing May to specialists and on pilgrimages, and in time the defect was corrected. Meanwhile, Veronica was left in the capable care of Kathleen.

Kathleen was always there, wringing the clothes through a mangle, pegging them out on the line, scrubbing the kitchen floor, burnishing silverware, stoking fires, baking soda bread, and when the little girl buried her head in her apron to howl over the latest calamity, it smelled of flour and love. The two formed a close bond in the kitchen side of the house, content to let the others get on with their own lives.

Veronica feared nothing, except her father's displeasure. Her mother's displeasure was all too familiar as boisterous escapades in tree climbing, wall jumping or chases with her dog Rex invariably resulted in scrapes, cuts and clothes torn beyond repair. But when she entered a room, her father's eyes softened. She would wait until permitted to speak, and then unburden herself of her latest concern to which he would listen with patience and amusement before offering a solution to her problem.

There was one problem he could not fix. When Veronica was four, Kathleen sat her down at the kitchen table and tearfully told her that she was leaving to get married. The child was bewildered. Her father said she should be happy for Kathleen and she tried, very hard, but it was a bad, sad day when she ran to the kitchen and found a stranger by the sink. The realisation sank in: from now on, she was on her own.

After Kathleen, there was a succession of maids. One of them, Mary, was on her hands and knees cleaning out the fire grate when Veronica leapt onto her back, hollering like a Red Indian. Mary reared up, dislodged the child and gave her a nasty clout on her leg. But it was Veronica who was chastised by her mother, for frightening the servant. It was too much. She went in search of her brother; at least he would understand.

Billo laughed and hugged her, and later, when all was forgiven, he commented to the family that the name Veronica was far too straight-laced for such a tomboy. Her father agreed, recalling the song he chanted to rouse her for school: 'The wron, the wron, the king of all birds, St. Stephen's day was caught in the furze, Although he was little, his honour was great, Jump up my child and give him a treat.' Ronnie she became.

Ronnie and Rex went on adventures with the children in the neighbourhood. Six or seven of them would buy Marietta biscuits and red lemonade from Newman's Shop, and run across the field to the quarry at Stiles Road where they would play tip and tig. The shop was managed by two sisters; Mary was fat and Rose was thin with fuzzy white hair. Her father bought his newspaper there, and found the two women so disagreeable that he privately dubbed them Vinegar Pot and Sour Grapes.

Ronnie could not sit still. She was always out and about, never at home. When Josephine wanted her to come in for tea, she sent Rex to fetch her. He would visit the local houses one by one, eventually find her, seize the edge of her clothing and drag her back – many a torn dress resulted from that. It seemed to Ronnie that it was impossible to get on the right side of her mother, or even receive an affectionate gesture, whereas stay-at-home May was such a goodie-goodie, she was her mother's pet.

May was never in her gang, never took part in the plays Ronnie presented in the Dunne's garage. With her friends – the Meegans, the Cooks, the Crowleys, the O'Connors and the Egans – Ronnie

Ronnie, her mother
Josephine and sister May

sourced boards for a rudimentary platform. They 'borrowed' sheets
for curtains and strung them on cords across the stage. Old bicycle
lamps were the spotlights. Ronnie made up the plays and told
everyone what to do as they went along. She, of course, was always in
the spotlight. They charged a penny entrance from whatever parent
had been cajoled into coming, and used the money to buy more
lemonade for picnics at the quarry.

Ronnie delighted in taunting her sister. She would hide one of her
Sunday gloves just before church, or put jam in the toe of her shoe.
Despite such misdemeanours, there were occasions when the
children were deemed to have behaved relatively well, and William
would bring them to the Corinthian Cinema in town to see Cowboys
and Indians (where Ronnie learnt to holler), Laurel and Hardy and
Charlie Chaplin films. The whole family attended the Abbey Theatre
where actor F.J. McCormick was a particular favourite of her father's.

All three children were taught the value of good manners and to
show proper respect for everyone, pauper or prince. Tip Donnelly

was an elderly man who had fallen on hard times. He wore a long coat and a battered homburg hat and visited the Dunne's house once a week. When Ronnie answered his knock, she'd call to her mother, 'Dip Donnelly's at the door,' and a big plate of stew or roast, whatever the family was having, would be warmed on the range for him. Tip Donnelly had a seven-day cycle, visiting each of the neighbours in turn without being a burden on any of them.

For many years, William had been employed by the highly regarded building firm of Farmer Brothers, which had extensive premises under the bridge at Spring Garden Street, Dublin 3. Mr Farmer never married. He had the greatest of respect for William's workmanship and integrity, and when he died, left him 51 per cent of the business. William and Josephine struggled financially to buy out the extended family, and there were quiet celebrations when that was eventually accomplished. William kept the name Farmer Brothers, his firm specialising in large projects such as schools and churches.

Early in the 1930s William got an important break: he secured the contract to build the Church of Our Lady of Perpetual Succour in Foxrock, County Dublin. Designed by Robinson and Keefe Architects to accommodate upwards of 900 people, it was constructed and faced using local granite. Skilled craftsmen in the carpentry workshop of Farmer Brothers fitted out the interior with carved wooden pews, architraves and timber mouldings. The bell tower is 20 metres high surmounted by a 3.3 metre gilt bronze cross, and to this day the entire edifice commands an imposing presence at the crest of the hill on the corner of the Dublin–Wexford road.

William worked long, hard hours. If he had a project in the country he would rise at five in the morning and have breakfast prepared by the housekeeper. At six o'clock, his driver Paddy Coughlan would be waiting by the black Austin to drive him to the site, and home again at night. The firm was successful, and William was able to indulge his great love of horseracing. He and Josephine were keen race-goers and horse owners. At one stage William had a string of ten horses with trainer Tom Taaffe in Rathcoole, County Dublin. One of his proudest moments came in 1938 when his daughter Veronica led in his winning horse, Laceaway, at the Curragh Racecourse in County Kildare. Laceaway was by a famous horse called Runaway out of Interlace. When Laceaway went to stud, William arranged for all her foals to have the prefix 'Ronnie'.

Ronnie with chimpanzee at London Zoo

Ronnie, c.1935

Ronnie leading in her father's winning horse Laceaway at the Curragh Racecourse in County Kildare, October, 1938

May and Ronnie attended school at the local Holy Faith Covent in Clontarf. They were usually dropped down by Paddy in the morning and collected by their mother in the afternoon. Josephine ensured they were always well turned out, with a change of clothes every day, not easy in the 1930s. Washing, drying and ironing were a daily chore for the maid, and the kitchen was perpetually draped with garments for each of the five family members. Complete outfits were purchased for Christmas and Easter, and new dresses every summer.

There were quiet, reflective times when Josephine relaxed her parental guard. On Saturdays the girls went to school in the morning while their parents were out all day at the races. That evening was bath night. The fire in the drawing room would be lit. If Josephine had time, she massaged almond oil into May and Ronnie's scalps and then wrapped towels around their heads for half an hour. After their bath and hair wash upstairs, they changed into fresh flannelette nightgowns and came down to dry their hair by the fire. May's chestnut red hair was long and lustrous. Ronnie's shoulder-length hair was auburn and wavy. Josephine would spend hours stroking through all the tangles with hairbrushes from India, especially bought for them by William. Both girls squealed if their mother had to use the nit comb – essential after a trip to the cinema where it was presumed that the heads of other children would be crawling with vermin.

Rex died. Nine-year-old Ronnie cried and cried for two days and would not leave her room. Later in the month, William bought her a pony, a bay of fourteen hands. Ronnie called him KitKat, after her favourite chocolate bar. He was kept at Brian Berry's riding school in Kilbarrack, about four miles from Clontarf. The stables became her second home. There she learnt to ride, jump, care for her pony and swear like a trooper. Ronnie went hunting and relished the sound of the horn, the excitement of the chase, the challenge of conquering whatever was thrown in her path. Horse riding became a passion.

Every Tuesday night when the girls were old enough, they were allowed in the drawing room in their nightgowns for the live opera performances from Milan on the mahogany-framed cabinet radio with the names of faraway places inscribed on the yellowy dial. William would be spellbound, listening to works by his favourite composer, Puccini – *La Bohème, Manon Lescaut, Tosca, Madama Butterfly*. As the glorious sounds, sometimes haunting, sometimes tempestuous, filled the room, Ronnie would catch her breath, holding on to the last note until it faded away. Trailing up the stairs to bed, her mind would be filled with song and images of busty maidens on parapets.

May and Ronnie

These images were stimulated by visits with their parents to grand opera in the Olympia Theatre, Dublin. The three Dunne children would be scrubbed down and dressed up in their best clothes and the whole family driven into town by Paddy. In the gilded auditorium they were ushered with all due ceremony into sumptuous, red plush seats. There they would eagerly await the tuning up of the orchestra, a flicker of movement behind the curtains, a glint of golden light from the stage, the swell of music, and finally the great whoosh of heavy brocade, revealing the magical world beyond. The singing, the costumes, the fairy tale sets – Ronnie was entranced. One of the operas was Verdi's *Il Trovatore*, which featured the famed British baritone Dennis Noble; little could Ronnie imagine that one day she would share the stage with him.

The child loved music; that was plain to see. It was decided she should 'learn the piano', a doom-laden phrase. Once a week, Miss Carroll from Carlow arrived at the house to give lessons to Ronnie and May. Miss Carroll's patience was short, and her pencil, long and sharp, was in constant use, smacking away the slightest mistake. Ronnie became adept at snatching her fingers from the keys just before Miss Carroll pounced. Every weekday, her mother locked her in the drawing room for an hour to practise. Ronnie got into the habit of easing up the sash window and jumping down to play in the garden, before climbing back into the room to pick out a few desultory scales. One morning, she had just recommenced practising when a voice from behind said, 'A pity you didn't do that an hour ago!' She froze, and swung around to find her tight-lipped mother. That was the end of the lessons.

When May was twelve, she went to boarding school at the Dominican Convent in Wicklow town where she was very happy, probably glad to get away from her pesky sister. Every second Sunday the family drove down and took her out for lunch at Hunter's Hotel. With May gone and Billo at work with his father, Ronnie and her mother were left in the house. Their relationship did not improve. Although Josephine was a kind person and a conscientious mother, she felt it was her duty to curb the high spirits of her younger daughter, for her own sake. But from her early experience of losing Kathleen, Ronnie had developed a strong sense of independence and a rebellious nature. Mother and daughter were constantly at odds; neither could understand or appreciate the other.

Ronnie was very fond of her older cousin Rosie Balfe, who took her on trips to the cinema. When Rosie announced she was getting married and moving away to Sligo, Ronnie swore she would never speak to her again, but Rosie smiled and promised they'd always be friends. Ronnie was eleven when Billo married and left home to live in Stradbrook, a large house nearby provided by his father. Ronnie then acquired a bedroom of her own but she was saddened by her brother's absence, and Rosie invited her to Sligo for a whole month in the summer. They went swimming every day at Rosses Point. In the evening they sang songs, and Ronnie learnt 'The Hills of Donegal'.

The Dunnes enjoyed hosting musical evenings. William was a baritone, Billo had won many Feis Ceoil competitions with his fine tenor voice, May was a pretty soprano, and family and friends would all do a turn. Ronnie normally listened to all the fun from her usual step on the stairs, but that Christmas she was permitted to stay up and was entranced as her father sang Balfe's air 'The Heart Bowed

Down': *The heart bowed down by weight of woe, To weakest hopes will cling, To thought and impulse while they flow, That can no comfort bring.* Her mother, normally so correct, was gazing at him in loving attention, tears welling in her eyes and sliding down her cheeks. After the song finished, there was a pause when no one seemed to know what to say, then one of her uncles got up to imitate Maurice Chevalier with 'Every little breeze seems to whisper Louise'. May and Billo sang, and one or two others, then Billo turned to Ronnie. 'Why don't you have a go?' he asked. She knew only one song really well, so 'The Hills of Donegal' it was.

At the end, Billo was looking at her in amazement. 'My God,' he said, 'this one's got a voice.'

2 Early lessons

RONNIE CLIMBED the narrow flight of stairs to the little room over Gill's Music Shop on Nassau Street. Mr Rooney, her new teacher, awaited her. He was a kindly man who gave private tuition there in his studio and at the Royal Irish Academy of Music. He had trained many fine singers, including Billo, who had arranged the lessons.

Mr Rooney believed in simplicity and patience. 'The most important thing is breathing,' he said. 'Everyone takes a big breath before they start to sing. No, it disturbs the cords – these two little pieces of flesh. You don't think of breathing when you're talking, but you still breathe. So pause. Your lungs are two sponges; all you have to do is pause, and they fill automatically. I call this "the pregnant pause" before you start to sing. Listen. Listen to the music. Prepare for your lungs to fill, open your mouth and let the sound float out.'

Ronnie practised breathing, feeling her diaphragm expand. She learned to keep the air circulating in the way Mr Rooney described. 'It's like a U-turn,' he told her. 'You turn and go back out again with the sound. Always come from above onto the lower notes, like a little bird landing.'

Hubert E. Rooney was steeped in music. As a young man in the early 1900s he had taken the unusual step of travelling to Paris to study with the Polish-born teacher Jean de Reszke. De Reszke, considered to be the greatest tenor of his generation, regularly performed at The Royal Opera House, Covent Garden. In 1904 he retired from professional singing to become a teacher. Students came to him from all over the world. Hubert Rooney accompanied the finest of these to support his singing lessons. He imbibed the maestro's Italian *bel canto* tradition – a lyrical style of operatic singing characterised by sustained and seamless *legato* phrases and rapid, intricate passages requiring great agility and precise placing of the voice. Such finesse takes many years to learn. It was this method that Hubert Rooney imparted to his own students.

Some of his compositions for children and adults were printed as early as 1903, and eventually numbered many hundreds. He collected and arranged Irish songs and melodies. His anthologies include *The Well-known Songs of Ireland* (1905) and *The Pigott Album of Irish Songs* (1920s). He contributed articles to learned publications, and in 1929 his *Three-part Sight Reading Exercises* was published. Always fascinated by Plain Chant, for many years Rooney trained and conducted the Dublin Bel Canto Singers in church services, concerts and radio broadcasts.

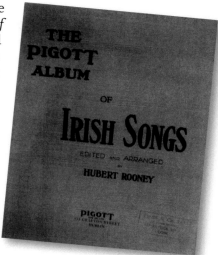

Breathing exercises, scales, arpeggios. It was only as Ronnie began to grasp a degree of technique that she was allowed to learn songs. 'Snow Queen', her first piece, came from Hubert Rooney's musical fairy play *Slumberland* which had been performed in the Gaiety Theatre in 1913. Having mastered that, Ronnie was allowed to progress to 'The Lark in the Clear Air' and 'The Sally Gardens'.

The day she was introduced to Schumann's lieder was the day she entered into another realm. She had never heard such music before. During the war, the BBC broadcast radio programmes that featured such artists as Richard Tauber, Isobel Baillie and Dennis Noble, but no German singers or composers were allowed on the airwaves. Schumann filled her soul as well as her lungs. Although her sight-reading was not great, she had a good ear, and never tired of practising 'Die Lotosblume', 'Der Nussbaum' or 'Widmung' at home with her own faltering accompaniment on the piano. She sang in German because Mr Rooney, a fluent French speaker, insisted that all songs be sung in their original language.

The hour-long lessons became two hours. Mr Rooney nurtured Ronnie's voice with care; it was a delicate yet powerful instrument that relied as much on emotion as it did on craft. He came to regard Ronnie almost as a daughter. He and his wife were, sadly, childless. They lived in a lovely old house in Killiney, Co. Dublin, where he went swimming every day, come hail or shine. Before lessons he attended morning mass in Clarendon Street and Ronnie never heard him speak ill of anyone.

As her voice developed, she began to tackle operatic arias – 'Voi che sapete' from *The Marriage of Figaro*, 'O mio babbino caro' from *Gianni Schicchi*, and *Madam Butterfly's* 'Un bel dì vedremo'. She was probably too young for such material, but she had a big voice. Downstairs in Gill's Music Shop customers would halt in their tracks and listen; she could even be heard in the street. Ronnie did not understand why Mr Rooney would not allow her to enter Feis Ceoil competitions. He maintained it was because he didn't want anyone to boast in later years that they had beaten Veronica Dunne, which seemed an odd thing to say.

At this time Ronnie was a day pupil at Eccles Street Dominican Convent. During her first year she began doing really well at school, especially at maths. Class reports were favourable and her parents were delighted. She bused in and out of Dublin quite happily, and was never late for her singing lessons. Her second year continued in this vein until the Easter term, with its heavy emphasis on religion. The solemn atmosphere was augmented by a decade of the rosary between every class and much Catholic instruction. The girls, however, were far more interested in discussing the size and quantity of Easter eggs they might receive. One of her friends told her a rhyme that had cracks in it: 'One month married, all goes well. Three months married, tummy begins to swell. Six months married, tummy begins to crack. Nine months married, out pops Jack'. Ronnie delighted in the little ditty, imagining a Mickey Mouse cartoon with eggs cracking open and chicks jumping out. She had repeated it a couple of times before she was summoned to go to the Reverend Mother.

'I believe there's a funny story going around.'

'Yes,' said Ronnie.

'Can you tell it to me?'

Happy to oblige, she rattled it off.

Reverend Mother's face grew stern. She demanded to know the originator of this tale, and Ronnie got a twisted feeling in her stomach; there was going to be trouble, but her father had taught her never to snitch on her friends. 'Oh,' she said, 'no one in particular. Just, well, everyone really.'

'In that case,' said the nun, 'instruct your mother to come and see me tomorrow'.

At home Josephine Dunne threw her eyes to heaven. 'What in the name of goodness have you done now?'

'Nothing. I did nothing.'

Next morning she attended school as usual. The Dunne's driver, Paddy Coughlan, drove her mother to Eccles Street where she was ushered into the presence of the Reverend Mother in the parlour. Ronnie was called from class. The nun instructed her to write down 'the lovely little tale you told me yesterday'. Ronnie did as she was asked.

Her mother read the note, looked at Ronnie, read the note again, and looked over at the nun. 'I don't think the child knows anything about the facts of life,' she said.

Reverend Mother pursed her lips. 'Remove your daughter from the school immediately,' she said. 'We don't wish to have her here.'

Ronnie collected her books and went out to the car. She was

ordered to sit in the front with Paddy, as if her mother found her presence abhorrent.

William Dunne saw the note and he was livid. 'As a punishment, you are to eat all your meals with Mary in the kitchen'.

'But Daddy,' said Ronnie, 'you told me always to tell the truth and I told the truth. What have I done wrong?'

'You're a disgrace to the family' was all he'd say. That was in April. He didn't speak to her again until her twelfth birthday on 2 August!

It was too late to find another school, so it was arranged that a tutor come to the house twice a week. Ronnie refused point blank to study. Her mother didn't know what to do. May was away in boarding school. Billo tried to reason with her without success, at least but, he was still talking to her.

The child was wretched, but damned if she'd let anyone see it. Eventually William Dunne relented, and she was permitted to join the family for Sunday lunch and, little by little, for other meals until things returned to something like normality. She had been bloodied and scarred, but remained resolutely unbowed. She would never forget that feeling of being unfairly castigated and rejected by the one person she loved above all.

Every August, Josephine and her two daughters flew to the Isle of Man for a holiday. They stayed at the Majestic Hotel in Douglas and the girls were active all day with games, horse-riding and swimming.

On the morning of 3 September 1939 Ronnie came back from the pool and bounded into the lounge to find her mother. Grave-faced adults told her to shush. It was 11.15 a.m. The Prime Minister of Britain, Neville Chamberlain, was about to speak on the radio:

> This morning the British Ambassador in Berlin handed the German Government a final Note stating that, unless we heard from them by 11 o'clock that they were prepared at once to withdraw their troops from Poland, a state of war would exist between us. I have to tell you now that no such undertaking has been received, and that consequently this country is at war with Germany.

There was a shocked silence. An Englishman in the group declared it was beyond comprehension; the Germans were a civilized, cultured race – how could they bring such calamity on Europe again? All thoughts of holidays banished, the guests prepared to leave. Next day, the Dunnes flew back to Ireland and an uncertain future.

Ronnie got a place at the Loreto Convent in St Stephen's Green, Dublin. She was still a keen rider but had outgrown KitKat and was given a new pony, Connemara Boy. Brian Berry had moved his stables from Kilbarrack out to Tallaght, County Dublin, and although it was on

May, Ronnie and Josephine boarding a plane to the Isle of Man, 1939

the other side of the city and much farther from Clontarf, Ronnie kept Connemara Boy with him. She discovered that a fellow pupil, Nuala Gately, loved horses as much as she did, and that she also had a pony stabled at Brian Berry's Riding School. Day pupils normally went home for lunch at 12.30 and returned to the school at 2 pm for lessons. The new friends hatched a plan. The following morning Ronnie wore her riding britches and boots under her long gymslip, so only the boots were visible. Instead of going home for lunch, the two took a bus out to Tallaght and rode their ponies all afternoon. It was a great lark. The teachers didn't notice and their parents didn't know. No one at the stables raised any questions. Why not do it again, and again? Soon, the girls were going AWOL two or three times a week.

This continued for several months until a nun drew Ronnie aside to say, 'You're missing school a lot.'

'Oh yes,' said Ronnie. 'My mother's very ill. She's in a wheelchair and I have to wheel her out nearly every day.'

'You poor child,' said the nun. 'Kneel at the statue of the Blessed Virgin every day, and we'll all pray for your mother.'

Coincidentally, Josephine Dunne had to have a serious operation shortly thereafter. She took quite a while to recover, not helped by her daughter's disastrous school report that term. As soon as she felt well enough, she arranged to meet with the nuns; a meeting that Ronnie dreaded. Once again, she was called in to a Reverend Mother's office, and told to sit quietly until her mother arrived.

When Josephine appeared, the nun clasped her two hands warmly. 'It's wonderful to see you, Mrs Dunne,' she said. 'It's a miracle you're so much better – we've been praying for you.'

Sweet Jesus, thought Ronnie, where's all this going?

Josephine was taken aback. 'Thank you, Reverend Mother, that was good of you, very good indeed. Now tell me, what are we going to do about Veronica's studies?'

'She does have a lot of catching up to do,' replied the nun. 'Perhaps some extra classes?'

It was decided that Ronnie would stay back after school to make up for lost time. Nuala Gately did not fare so well. Her absences were discovered and she was soundly punished, but she never divulged her co-conspirator. Ronnie did not stand up for her friend. She did not tell her parents. The school never found out. She had got away with it. She recalled her father's old song about the wron, the wron, the king of all birds: *Although he was little, his honour was great.* She knew she had not behaved honourably, and she felt utterly miserable.

A kind nun, Sister Considine, noticed her distress. 'You're not very happy here, are you?' she said.

'Not really. I don't feel I'm getting anywhere.'

'Why don't you go to boarding school?' she suggested. 'The routine might suit you.'

At home, her mother's comment was, 'So you want to go to boarding school now, do you?'

'Yes.'

'I think that's a very good idea.'

Ronnie was thirteen when she went to her fifth and, thankfully, final school. Mount Anville Convent in Goatstown, County Dublin was run by the nuns of the Sacred Heart Order. She did settle into the routine, but her experiences during the past few years were preying on her mind. She knew she was capable of achieving high grades, but she would not work. She made friends, learned some German, and did not to get into too many scrapes. Not once was she homesick.

Before bed, the girls would brush each other's hair for half an hour while a nun stood outside the dormitory, and then she would think of those Saturday nights by the fire and the fresh laundered smell of flannelette.

Her only free afternoon in the convent was Thursday; the one day Mr Rooney could not take her for lessons. She was taught singing by Mrs Dunlop, and also piano, and each year passed the grades required. However, her voice was not universally appreciated, and she was ordered to refrain from singing at Hymns because she drowned out the others. She was permitted to practice in the concert hall where she would let fly, the sound resonating in the large, empty space with no one to stop her.

Ronnie became fond of one of the nuns in Mount Anville. Mother Bodkin (whose brother had been the eminent Judge Matthias Bodkin) was unusual in that she had entered the convent later than most and had a great sense of fun and also of fairness. As Mistress of Studies, she was second in seniority to the Reverend Mother.

Ronnie the golfer

The girls were not allowed outside the convent perimeter. On Sundays their mothers would visit with sweets or cakes which had to be handed up to the nun for sharing around, and essentials like toothpaste or soap which they could take back to the dormitory. It was during the war and there was no fuel for private cars, so every week Josephine travelled by bus as far as The Goat Inn, then walked up to Mount Anville where she would be shown into the parlour to wait for Ronnie – these visitations were referred to as 'Parlour'. If the weather was clement, they might take a turn around the grounds. On one occasion, Josephine brought a fruit cake, together with shampoo and soap and a small box of talcum powder.

After Parlour, Ronnie clasped the toiletries to her chest and hurried to the Assembly Hall where the other girls were saying a Novena to a statue of Mater Admirabilis. She slid into a seat beside her friend Lucienne Albertas, who was curious about her haul. Ronnie showed her the talcum and eased off the lid so they could have a sniff. As Lucienne's head bent low over the box, Ronnie couldn't resist giving it a little shake and Puff! the powder went up into her face and all over her gymslip; rubbing, of course, only made it worse.

It wasn't long before Mother Bodkin collared her. 'I hear you've been smoking,' she said.

When Ronnie protested that the ash was, in fact, talcum, the nun was sceptical, so she ran to fetch the offending article.

'This is how it happened,' she said, holding out the box and Puff! the powder cascaded all over Mother Bodkin and her habit. She was

Ronnie on Connemara Boy
1944

as white as a sheet! The nun laughed and laughed, and every time she saw Ronnie after that, she'd say with a smile, 'Don't you go doing that again!'

During the summer holidays Ronnie went out to Dudgeon's Riding School in Belfield, County Dublin. Connemara Boy was now kept there and she spent many happy hours putting him through his paces and mucking out his stable. Show-jumping, hunting, gymkhanas, point-to-points – she loved them all, and won many rosettes and trophies for her efforts. She made friends with Mr and Mrs King whose daughter entered the same competitions. They had a double horsebox and were happy to take Ronnie and her horse along to events up and down the country. But they lived in Swords and Connemara Boy was the other side of the city in Belfield. Nothing for it, but Ronnie would have to hack the twenty-five miles if she wanted to avail of the Kings' offer.

It was early morning as fifteen-year-old Ronnie led Connemara Boy from his stable. She checked that she had her map and a bottle of water. She swung into the saddle and guided the horse from the yard out onto the Merrion Road. As they went through Merrion Gates and along the coast road to Sandymount, the sea reminded her of all the times they had taken poor May on pilgrimage to cure her squinty eyes. Poor May indeed! Through the Dublin traffic then, keeping the horse reined in among cyclists and cars, lorries and drays. Under Pearse Street Bridge, past the Five Lamps and all the way out to Fairview. On the Malahide Road and out by Cloghran she had a clear road to Swords.

Five hours later, a weary horse and rider ambled into the Kings' farmyard. Mrs King pressed a glass of milk into the girl's hand and watched as she gulped it down. Ronnie put Connemara Boy into a stable, slipped off saddle and bridle, and gave him a bran mash and a clean bucket of water. As the horse buried his muzzle into the malty grain, she gathered a fistful of straw and rubbed him down vigorously, forehead to fetlocks. A final pat and a kiss on the nose and Ronnie had the stable door bolted and was haring out the gate to catch the first of two buses back to Clontarf. If she didn't get home by teatime, her mother would be furious. Next morning she was up at six to catch the early bus to the Kings'. The twenty-five-mile hack back to Dudgeon's would have to be completed the following day, but she was happy to be setting off for another competition. Ronnie made that journey several times over the next few years, and always enjoyed it.

Immediately after the war, she decided to enter the jumping competitions at the Royal Dublin Horse Show. Her expectations were high, for wasn't she the great little horsewoman? The thing was a disaster from start to finish. On the first day Connemara Boy planted his feet firmly on the wrong side of the fence while she flew over it. The next day the crowd unnerved him and he shied. On the third day he ditched her and sailed over the fence by himself! Thoroughly fed up, she retired in disgust to watch the rest of the jumping from the competitors' stand.

While all this was going on, singing was still number one on the agenda. With no opportunity for proper singing lessons during term time, both Ronnie and Mr Rooney were keen to take full advantage of any holiday time she had, and her studies with him continued both in Nassau Street and at his home in Killiney.

Ronnie always thought that she was as strong as any horse, yet from time to time she became extremely tired and got dizzy spells. She didn't tell anyone, and in time these feelings always passed. But in her final year at Mount Anville, the nuns became so concerned they put her to bed and called the doctor. He diagnosed anaemia and sent Ronnie home to recover. She was still convalescing when the year ended, and she never returned to the convent.

With Ronnie at home and finished with school, Mr Rooney

realised that she would have to pursue her training at a much higher, intensive level if she were to reach her full potential. There were no facilities on the island of Ireland for such training. He discussed the situation with Josephine and William. He suggested that she live in his house for a year or so. They could then concentrate on technique, musicianship, repertoire, languages and grooming for the world stage. Ronnie was enthusiastic, but her parents did not like the idea.

'In that case,' said Mr Rooney, 'there's only one thing for it: she must go abroad to study, and the place to go is Milan, the home of opera.'

Right, thought Ronnie, Milan it is.

3 Preparations

I T WAS 1945. Ronnie was eighteen, and she was in a hurry. Somehow she had to convince her father that her whole life was in the balance. With no funds of her own, there was only one thing for it.

'Daddy,' she said. 'I'm going to sell Connemara Boy. I want to study in Italy.'

William Dunne could see she was in deadly earnest. Anxious about her venturing so far away on her own, he discussed the situation with Billo, who was now in business with him. They decided that if she was determined enough to sell her beloved horse, they would have to let her go.

She got a good offer of £125 for the horse on the proviso that the vet, Maxi Cosgrove, check him out and give him the all-clear, which he did. On the appointed day, the new owner handed over the cash. Her father made her give back £5 luck money, and Ronnie was mightily relieved when it was graciously returned. She said goodbye to Connemara Boy with a sore heart. She kept her saddle and bridle as mementos, but her riding days were over.

It was all very well to announce that she was going to study abroad, quite another thing to put it into effect. For a start, she would have to find somewhere to stay. Perhaps her great ally, Mother Bodkin, could help.

'Milan!' The nun was horrified at the very thought. 'You can't possibly go there. Do you not know they've been through a terrible war?'

When she saw the child was serious, she wrote to the mother house to inquire if Ronnie could stay there. The news was not good. The convent had been bombed, almost demolished, there was little food, and the advice was on no account to travel anywhere in Italy.

A frustrating few months followed. In July 1946 Ronnie received an invitation to lunch from the parish priest of Kill, Father Campion. He thought she might be interested in meeting Delia Murphy, renowned singer and collector of Irish ballads. Ronnie had often heard her recording of 'I'm a rambler, I'm a gambler' on the radio but the nasal voice and jiggy tunes drove her crazy!

She borrowed her sister May's little Austin car to travel the long, winding roads of Kildare. At Father Campion's house she was introduced to Delia and to her husband, Dr Thomas J. Kiernan, who had just returned from five years serving as the Irish Minister Plenipotentiary to the Holy See in Rome. They had brought along a friend who was on holiday from Rome, Monsignor Hugh O'Flaherty. Ronnie took to him immediately. Behind his thick glasses he had a warm twinkle in his eye, and he spoke in a quiet, measured way. During lunch, she noticed that he ate very sparingly. Father Campion quietly explained that he'd been through five years of war and austerity and his system could not tolerate food that was in any way rich.

After the meal, Father Campion called on her to sing. She kept it simple with 'Danny Boy' and the Neapolitan song 'Core 'ngrato (Catarì, Catarì)'. They were so impressed, they all insisted she must pursue a career in operatic singing. On hearing that her teacher had wanted her to go to Milan, they urged her to consider Rome; it had escaped the worst ravages of war and had some of the finest opera houses in the world. Ronnie was very excited by the prospect, and the Monsignor offered to help in any practical way he could.

When Delia Murphy sang, Ronnie was bowled over. The records did not do her justice. Delia was a real artist, a storyteller, and her beautifully controlled keening voice gave a great depth of meaning to 'The Blackbird' and 'The Spinning Wheel' – the old Irish songs which she loved so well.

Monsignor O'Flaherty was as good as his word, and a few days after that lunch he paid a visit to William and Josephine. He pointed out that current conditions in Rome were far from easy, but if Ronnie was determined to study there, he would keep an eye on her, and see her at least once a week for a progress report. She could get accommodation at a French-run convent near the Vatican and a monthly allowance for her upkeep could be sent to Father Finian Cronin at St. Isidore's, the Irish Franciscan College in Rome. The Dunnes were reassured.

Permission to take money out of the country had to be agreed with the Department of Finance. Ronnie went to Government Buildings on Merrion Street to see Sarsfield Hogan, Secretary of the Department of Finance. She explained her situation.

'Well,' he said, 'the most you can take out at any one time is £125.'

'But that's precisely what I've got!' she exclaimed. 'And my father wants to send out £50 a month for me to live on.'

Sarsfield Hogan leaned back in his chair. 'If I agree to this,' he said, 'I suppose you'll be like all the others – John McCormack and Margaret Burke Sheridan and so on, and not come back to pass it all on.'

'What do you mean?'

'I mean, you won't come back and teach the young people of Ireland to sing.'

'As a matter of fact,' said Ronnie brazenly, 'that's exactly what I intend doing!'

'Do you promise?'

She had absolutely no intention of teaching, but at this stage she would have promised anything. 'Of course I do,' she said. Little did she know!

A couple of weeks later, Ronnie took the bus into Arnott's of Henry Street to get lightweight imitation leather bags, the old suitcases being too heavy for modern aeroplanes. She was advised on size and type, and then carried her purchases to a printer on the Quays to have her initials embossed on the front. Choosing the colour and size was easy: gold, about 6 inches tall. And the initials? Why, 'V.D.' of course.

She collected the cases a couple of days later. Thrilled at how smart they looked she arrived home at lunchtime to show them off. Her father nearly choked on his chop. 'Josie,' he said, 'would you take a look at what Ronnie's brought back.'

She gasped. After a few moments she gathered herself sufficiently to say, 'Err, they're lovely, but ... I think you should have your middle initial there as well. It'll look bigger and better with the three.'

'Oh fine,' Ronnie agreed happily. So back on the bus to the printers. 'Would you mind putting V.B.D. on my luggage, please?' He smiled. Everyone in the shop smiled. 'Not at all,' he said, assuring her they'd be ready by the end of the week.

Nineteen-year-old Veronica Bernadette Dunne, shortly to be let loose on her own in the city of Rome, did not know the first thing about the facts of life. Her mother was too embarrassed to discuss that sort of thing; she assumed Ronnie would have picked it up at school, or from other girls. The most she had ever brought herself to say was: 'Don't let a man touch your private parts.' However, the initials incident could not be ignored. As she helped her daughter pack, she mentioned that after the war there had been a terrible illness called Venereal Disease, V.D. for short, which was why it was better to get the extra letter. Preoccupied with what to bring and what to leave behind, Ronnie merely shrugged. If V.D. was anything like measles, she certainly didn't want that on her cases.

September 1946. Ronnie's parents drove her to the new airport

out at Collinstown, County Dublin. It was the first time she had flown on her own. They cried, she cried. She walked across the tarmac to the DC propeller plane and turned to wave, then resolutely climbed into the passenger cabin and walked up the slanting aisle to a seat near the front. She stayed overnight in London, and early the next morning boarded the plane that would take her to Italy, with three refuelling stops. At the military airport in Paris and again in Marseilles the passengers were locked in huts for a couple of hours since no customs posts had yet been set up. From Marseilles they flew to Genoa and another long wait, and finally on to Rome. It had been a gruelling, twelve-hour journey, but at last she was on her way to a new life.

May and Ronnie, 1946

4 Rome
1946 to 1948

THE TALL FIGURE of Monsignor Hugh O'Flaherty in his black soutane and wide-brimmed hat was a welcome sight. He strode across the tarmac of the Military Air Force Base in Ciampino and seized her suitcases. He had been thirty-one years in Rome and had seen many young Irish girls arrive only to return to Ireland several months later, pregnant. His first words to Ronnie were: 'Do you see that plane? If I catch you with an Italian man, you will be back on the next flight home. Welcome to Rome. Come on now, we'll have you at your quarters in jig time.'

The Suore di Santa Dorotea della Frassinetti, a monastery run by French nuns to accommodate students, was situated on what is sometimes referred to as the Eighth Hill of Rome, the Gianicolo. Ronnie had a lovely room overlooking the city and there were orange and lemon trees in the garden. On her first morning she went down to breakfast to find hard stale bread, black coffee made from burnt orange peelings, no milk, sugar or butter, but the cherry jam was tasty. Lunch was a bowl of spaghetti swimming in olive oil with a

Monsignor Hugh O'Flaherty

sprinkling of cheese, and an apple for desert. For dinner there were two slices of thick garlicky sausage with obscure ingredients, served with cold potatoes, again doused in olive oil.

Olive oil, garlic, slippery pasta and gobbets of meat – they churned around and around in Ronnie's system, giving her stomach cramps and diarrhoea. Her discomfort was compounded by dehydration since it was expressly forbidden to drink the tap water for fear of dysentery. Although she felt pretty wretched, she refused to tell anyone, knowing full well that if her parents got to hear of it she would be hauled back to Ireland.

Each day she caught a bus that passed the monastery and went as far as the Monteverdi Bridge. From there she travelled by old buses or military lorries into San Silvestro, the centre of Rome. These vehicles were always jam-packed with people hanging from every handhold. Having paid her fare to the driver at the front she had to run the gauntlet of a phalanx of randy Italian men so that she could disembark at the back – not a pleasant experience for they wasted no opportunity of having a good grope of anything in a skirt. Her friends would later joke that with those buses you got on as a virgin and got off pregnant. It was a far cry from the sedate double-deckers in Dublin.

As she wandered through Rome her appreciation of the wonderful sights was blighted by the constant and pressing need of a toilet. There were stinking metal urinals placed along the streets for men but absolutely no facilities for women. The only place to go was a café, but to use their toilets she had to order a coffee, and she couldn't do that every half-hour.

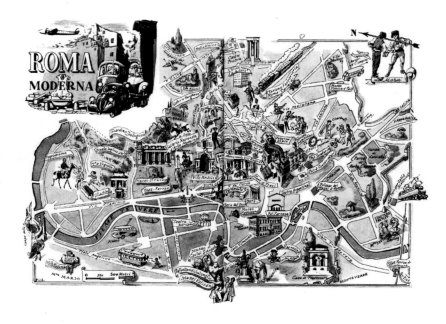

She walked everywhere: down the long and fashionable Via dei Condotti, around the walls of the Coliseum, up to the Palatine Hill and the crumbling Forum with its echoes of Julius Cesare and Mark Antony, through Trastevere with its cobbled streets, meandering laneways and women calling to each other as they pegged out their washing on ancient balconies. She threw her last threepenny bit into the Trevi Fountain with a fervent wish that her stay in Rome would bring her heart's desire.

She ran up and down the Spanish Steps many times, and one day decided to explore the church at the top – the Istituto Sacro Cuore della Trinità dei Monti. Inside the chapel she gazed at extraordinary ceilings and works of art, then made a discovery in a niche beside a cloister. It was none other than the original Mater Admirabilis, a replica of which had been placed in the assembly hall of the convent at Mount Anville for the girls to pray to every day. The demure young Virgin Mary in her rose pink dress and white shawl looked so different in this setting, waiting patiently for whatever the future might bring. When first painted in 1844 the fresco had been declared too garish for display and was hidden under a cloth, and so it might have remained had not Pope Pius IX been curious. It was found to have mellowed to such a thing of beauty that the nuns declared it a miracle.

Ronnie needed her own miracle. She was urgently trying to find a singing teacher, but this was proving difficult because all the best teachers had been lured to the land of prosperity, the United States of America.

Meanwhile, the Monsignor decided that this raw Irish lassie needed educating in the ways of presenting herself in high society. The ability to feel at ease and talk with important people was a skill she should acquire for when she became famous, as he believed she would, and he started to bring her along to diplomatic receptions. The first was about ten days after she arrived. General Supervia (whose mother had been the opera singer Conchita Supervia) hosted a dinner for senior Allied personnel, including Field Marshal Montgomery. It was a very glamorous affair, with all the men in splendid military uniforms and their wives outdoing each other in silks and sparkles. It took place in a grand hotel on Via Condotti, and glory of glories, there was food she could actually recognise and enjoy.

As she relished each and every one of the eight courses on offer, the gentleman on her left observed her in some amusement. He was a good-looking South African major who had come up from Sicily with the Fifth Army. He enquired if she liked Italian ice cream. 'I don't know,' she said, 'I've never had any.' He offered to bring her out for some after the meal. When Ronnie sought the Monsignor's permission, his eyes widened in disbelief. How on earth could she think of ice cream after such a meal? However, he consented, saying that she had to be back at the hotel in plenty of time so that he could escort her to the convent and return to the Vatican before the eleven o'clock curfew. Ronnie did not arrive back until a quarter to eleven.

The Monsignor scratched his head in what was to become a familiar gesture. 'Do you realise now I will be late back to the Vatican and I'll have to climb over a big wall in order to get home?'

'Monsignor,' she replied, 'with your long legs, you will be well able to do that.'

This unlikely pair became firm friends. The Monsignor introduced her to his many acquaintances, so she not only had him looking out for her in Rome, she had a whole retinue of priests and, it seemed, the entire Irish community.

Programme from Teatro dell' Opera

Ronnie resolved to go to as many operas as she could. The problem was that many of them began at 9pm and could last for three or four hours. Curfew in her lodgings was 9.30pm, so the Monsignor arranged that when she was going to be late, she could stay at the pensione of a Swiss woman on Quattro Fontane. It transpired that this lady was one of many who had helped to hide Allied servicemen during the war, and in that very house. It was so convenient to all the theatres that Ronnie stayed there many times.

The first performance she attended was in Rome's premier opera house, Teatro dell'Opera. She paid for her ticket and received the programme and libretto free. She was shown into a seat so high in the gods, she could almost stretch out and touch the beautiful, frescoed ceiling. Around the three sides of the auditorium were layers of gold-encrusted boxes arranged like the amphitheatre of the Coliseum. A dizzying way down she could see tiny people meeting and greeting and taking their places; women in décolleté gowns, men in uniform.

She studied the cover of the programme with its imprint of a heavenly band of angels, and turned to the first page. *La Favorita* by Gaetano Donizetti, with Gino Bechi, Ebe Stignani, Giocomo Lauri Volpi, Giuseppe Flamini, Nino Mazziotti and Maria Huder, conducted by Gabriele Santini. The lights dimmed, the audience hushed. Santini raised his baton. A delicate, melodic passage rippled from the orchestra like a gentle wave. At last the music ceased. In silence the heavy curtain slowly lifted on a massive set of Romanesque arches in the Kingdom of Castile. A monastery garden, and there were the doomed lovers, Fernando and Leonora. Giuseppe

Flamini as Baldassarre opened his mouth. His voice floated out and hung in the air. Ronnie held her breath. She was in Rome; she was at the opera. One day, she would sing in such a place. One day, it would be her on that stage.

That dream seemed a little closer when Ronnie heard that a conductor, Giuseppe Morelli, had begun to give singing lessons. He agreed to take her and immediately had her singing arias from *Il Trovatore* and *Aida* which almost wrecked her voice. She knew he wasn't right for her, but how to get out of it?

One day before start of lessons she said, 'Maestro, I have to go home tonight to Ireland. I'm going by train, so I just wanted to fix up with you.' She paid him, and he told her to hurry, or she'd miss the train. 'Yes,' she said, 'I've a taxi downstairs waiting for me. Thank you very much for everything.'

Ronnie was getting to know many of the Irish people living in Rome. While visiting Major John Fagan and his Italian wife, Maria, she was introduced to their friend, the Italian conductor Vincenzo Bellezza. He spoke of Margaret Burke Sheridan in glowing terms. 'Ah Peggy,' he said in Italian, 'I conducted her in many performances. Her Cio-Cio-San in *Butterfly* was exquisite.'

Ronnie's father was a great fan of Margaret Burke Sheridan. He had a recording of her with the tenor Aureliano Pertile singing the duet from *Madama Butterfly*, and the aria 'Un bel dì'. Ronnie adored the record, and listened for every phrase, every nuance. She was amazed that these two singers could sing right through a long recording session with no stops or breaks, and still attain perfection. 'Un bel dì' was one of the arias she had begged Hubert Rooney to teach her. She knew, too, that Burke Sheridan had scored a huge success at her début as Mimi in Puccini's *La Bohème* in Rome's Teatro Costanzi (the original Teatro dell'Opera) in 1918.

Margaret Burke Sheridan 1889–1958. An Post stamp issued in 1989 which features a scene from *La Bohème*

During the Second World War, Burke Sheridan lived in Dublin and Ronnie became fascinated by her. She would catch glimpses of the diva wearing a large hat with a veil, a coat with a luxuriant fur collar, and high, high heels adorning her lovely legs as she strolled down Grafton Street. Everyone would bow to 'Maggie from Mayo' as if she were royalty. Occasionally the Dunnes went for tea in the Gresham Hotel and there she would be, holding court. She was so beautiful; her eyes shining, her mouth in a smile ready to sing. And now, here was this conductor who actually knew and had worked with her.

Maestro Bellezza believed he could help Ronnie in her quest. He introduced her to Contessa Soldini Calcagni, a highly respected teacher who lived near Piazza di San Lorenzo. The Contessa was a kind, elderly lady who gave Ronnie an hour's lesson every morning. She concentrated on technique and antique arias from the sixteenth and seventeenth centuries that are good training for the voice, but were no longer performed. It was slow-going and frustrating, and Ronnie knew she would have to expand her repertoire for auditions and potential roles.

She became friendly with another young student, Gianella Borelli who herself became a big star. Gianella paid for her own lessons by playing the piano for the Contessa's star pupil, Caterina Mancini. Ronnie often hung around outside the closed music room door as Caterina practised the same scales and techniques as herself, and by careful listening she learnt how to improve her own practice sessions. She also listened to Caterina studying arias from Mascagni, Puccini and Verdi. She realized that to sing in Italian she must learn the language properly. Gianella told her of an impoverished duchess who lived in a large palazzo on Via Condotti. The duchess spoke English fluently and would be only too glad to have a student at two hundred lire a day, which was no hardship to Ronnie, but desperately needed by the duchess.

Although bombed on several occasions by the Allies, Rome had been a quasi 'open city' and most of the buildings were left intact. But during the German occupation between September 1943 and June 1944, even wealthy citizens were reduced to scrounging for scraps. Jews were deported to extermination camps. Male civilians were rounded up and forced into slave labour. Escaped prisoners of war were hunted down and shot. Those suspected of helping them or resisting the imposed military law were tortured for information and then executed. The Allies liberated the city on 4 June 1944 but conditions remained difficult. Much of Italy and Europe had been laid waste in the hideous tug of war, and the conflict dragged on for another year.

While Ronnie was there, the countryside beyond Rome was still devastated. People lived in makeshift tents and daily converged on the city in search of food. Some took up precarious residence in hill caves above Via Flaminia; others slept rough on the streets. Everywhere there were beggars. Ronnie was crossing the Ponte Cavour one evening when she saw a woman leaning against the parapet, a baby pulling vainly at her flaccid breast for nourishment. Homeless, jobless, hopeless people everywhere. Any money she had to spare she gave to them.

She still suffered digestion problems. Food was scarce and her weight plummeted. Monsignor O'Flaherty arranged for her to go to the Volpe Palace every day where she served mugs of tea, spam sandwiches and Danish pastries to Allied soldiers. Although the palace and gardens were very beautiful, Ronnie came to associate the place with the smell and taste of spam. Nevertheless, it kept her going.

Almost every Friday she lunched with the Monsignor. She climbed the worn stone steps to his apartment in the German College in Vatican City and was admitted by Maria, his housekeeper. The drawing room was sparsely furnished with a couch, an armchair and a glass-topped cabinet in which his medals and honours were displayed. The Purple Heart, the Légion d'honneur, the OBE and other medals intrigued her. He was reticent to speak of why these awards had been granted or of his wartime exploits. What he did talk about was his love of golf and Gaelic football. A native of Caherciveen, Hugh O'Flaherty was an avid Kerry supporter. Once he showed Ronnie his secret transmitter, a big black box with earphones and a microphone. He said he had used it to listen to football matches from Ireland during the war, and to make clandestine contact with London. He had kept it hidden from the Germans, of course, on pain of death.

Lunch was invariably soup, followed by pasta, and water, never wine. The Monsignor did not drink or smoke. Afterwards there was tea prepared by the doughty Maria. No less than six teaspoons of tea went into the pot for good measure with lukewarm water splashed on top. It was as thick as porter, and bitter; the Monsignor was so grateful for having a housekeeper that he could not bring himself to correct her in any way. He had many visitors. Some were fellow clergy, but others were the grateful parents of American or British soldiers whom he had helped; once there was a Maharani in a beautiful sari who spoke of her son's merciful escape from the clutches of the Gestapo.

Ronnie and the Monsignor walked the streets of the city he loved, and as they walked he told her the story, little by little. During the early years of the war, he had visited prisoner of war camps around Italy to locate British soldiers who had been declared missing in action. When he did so, he was able to reassure their families at home through Radio Vatican. Mussolini fell from power in 1943 and thousands of these POWs were released. Fearful of recapture, they made their way to the German occupied city of Rome to seek help from the one person they knew, the Monsignor. Initially, there was just a question of harbouring a few men, but as the number of Allied soldiers seeking help swelled, he had developed an elaborate underground movement with the aid of priests, nuns, escapers and a network of courageous sympathisers throughout the city who gave safe haven to these soldiers and members of the Jewish community in their own homes. Despite stringent and closely monitored rationing, the safe houses had to be kept supplied with provisions, and the Monsignor made regular forays from the Vatican into the city.

The commander of the German SS, Colonel Herbert Kappler, was no fool. He knew the POWs were being hidden and he had a shrewd idea of who was responsible. A massive reward was offered for any information leading to the capture of the Monsignor. 'He very nearly caught me, too', he told Ronnie with a smile. In the winter of 1944 he had to visit Prince Filippo Andrea Doria Pamphilj, who was involved in the underground. While he was there the Gestapo raided the prince's palazzo. The Monsignor fled to the cellar and, as luck would have it, coal was being delivered. So he stuffed his soutane and clerical hat into a sack, covered himself with soot, climbed up the ladder, crept out behind the SS trucks and walked away. The coalman was just one of many disguises he'd used. He had even dressed as a nun, a very, very tall nun, and got away with it. The Monsignor never spoke of how many he had helped. Years later Ronnie learnt that 6,500 escapers, and countless Jews and other persecuted people, survived the war owing to the efforts of his underground movement.

Ronnie was mesmerised by the Monsignor's stories, and by his great love of the city. He seemed to know every street and alleyway, square and monument, church and building of note, and had written a guidebook for Vatican visitors. Everywhere they went together, all doors were open to him, from the old noble families in their palazzos to slum dwellers striving to survive. He was treated like a god, not just by Romans, but also by British, American and French soldiers. Every Saturday he loaded up his battered truck with food and clothes and delivered them to those in want, never questioning their faith or their origins. He visited German prisoners in jail and tried to help them make contact with their families at home, many of whom were missing, perhaps dead. 'It is sad, Ronnacio,' he said. 'They do not know who is left.' The actor Gregory Peck memorably portrayed Monsignor O'Flaherty in the 1983 made for TV movie, *The Scarlet and the Black*.

Once a month Ronnie made her way over to the Franciscan college of St. Isidore's on Via Degli Artisti to collect her allowance from Father Finian Cronin. If she was fortunate, she ran into Father Hubert, Superior of the Franciscans in Rome, who was a wonderfully droll character with a very red nose and great interest in the excellent wines served in the local bodega. He carried an umbrella with him, winter and summer – you can never be too careful, he used to say.

Through Major Fagan she met an Irish couple, Colonel Eyre and his wife Kate. Over the next couple of months her new friends became concerned that Ronnie was not getting enough to eat. They would take her out for meals and, surreptitiously, order double portions just for her. Eventually they decided that she should leave the monastery. Since they had a large apartment, the Eyres suggested she live with them. Monsignor O'Flaherty was not keen because they were not Italian speakers, so it was agreed that it should be a temporary measure until she found somewhere else.

The Eyres lived in a substantial pink stucco building at No.7 Via Niccolò Paganini. From the ground floor a lift clunked up three storeys to arrive in the hall of the apartment. Off the hall was a study with folding doors that opened onto the large drawing room, notable for the fact that it possessed a fireplace, reputedly the only fireplace in Rome. Ronnie's bedroom was next to the double room occupied by the Eyres. Down the hall were the dining room, kitchen and bathroom. A staircase led up to a pretty roof garden and a small apartment occupied by the butler and cook – a displaced Czechoslovakian couple.

Many dinner parties was held in that apartment. One evening the guest list included Frank Biggar, Secretary to the Irish Minister to the Italian Republic, Michael MacWhite. Accompanying him was Laura Sarti and two of her friends, a dentist and his wife. After the meal, the ladies withdrew for their coffee and left the men to their brandy and cigars. As Colonel Eyre and Frank Biggar were engrossed in a conversation in English, the Italian dentist adjourned to the drawing room with the ladies. By way of amusement, Kate Eyre suggested a séance. Ronnie had no idea what that was all about, or that Kate was a clairvoyant.

They sat at a round table, hands spread out, fingers touching. Kate went into a trance. Then she intoned, 'There's somebody here who wants to talk to ...' They started to recite the alphabet: A, B. On B the table tilted, and so it went on until the name Bigger was spelt out.

'This is all nonsense,' Ronnie laughed; 'it's a spoof.' The table started shaking and the others glared at her to be quiet.

'Go into the study,' said Kate in a strange voice, 'look in the drawer of the bureau, and you will find a photograph of me with the King.'

Ronnie fetched the photograph of King Victor Emmanuel III of Italy standing with a tall gentleman, and when she showed it to the others they said it was the previous owner of the apartment. But the séance wasn't finished. It spelt out the name Rosaline Taylor and the table started to gyrate so fiercely that Ronnie got frightened. Let me outta here, she thought, this is for the birds! She pulled her hands away and fled to the dining room.

'Frank,' she said, 'a woman named Taylor wants to talk to you'.

He went ashen. 'My God,' he said. 'She's been dead ten years!' He ran into the drawing room with Colonel Eyre close behind. They gave Frank a stiff brandy and the Colonel started playing tricks with the chair and laughing, making light of the whole thing. But Frank was not the better of it for a long time.

Following a concert in the Teatro Argentino conducted by the legendary Arturo Toscanini one evening, Ronnie returned to the apartment. As she was taking her customary bath, she heard the butler walk down the stairs, and started to feel the pressure of eyes upon her. She glanced around. No one there, but the sensation of being watched intensified. She pulled the towel from the chair to cover herself and began to sing 'Ave Maria, gratia plena, Maria' very loudly. People from the apartment below yelled '*Zitto! Zitto!*' to shut her up. The water grew cold. She scrambled from the bath and flung on her nightdress wet and all as she was. Running into the hall, she noticed the dining room light was on, and the table had been laid for just one place for breakfast, instead of the usual three. A drawer of the sideboard was hanging open. All very peculiar. She scurried along to the kitchen, but nobody was there. In her room she jumped into bed and drew the blanket over her head.

Then she heard shouting from outside. Peering through her window, she saw Colonel Eyre and his wife, *and* the butler and his wife gesturing to her to open up. The porter had locked the front door and they had forgotten the key. But if they had all been out, who had she heard on the stairs?

Petrified, Ronnie didn't even trust the lift, but flew down the three flights of stairs, wrenched open the door and blurted, 'There's something funny going on in this house'.

'Don't be silly', Kate said as they stepped into the lift. Up in the hall, Ronnie told how she'd heard footsteps and the table had been set for one.

'Oh,' said Kate, 'that often happens. It's nothing – just a little ghost.'

Gradually the story was revealed. The previous owner of the apartment lived alone. He had died a violent death just after the war when many scores were settled. The three bullet holes in the ceiling over the fireplace were regarded as something of a novelty; Ronnie was not so sanguine. The Eyres had been more than hospitable, but she could not feel comfortable in the apartment after that night.

Next morning at the Contessa's she related the story to Gianella, who invited her to meet her parents, just a short distance away. Signor and Signora Borelli invited her into their modest home and it was quickly decided she would move into a small spare room as a paying guest for the equivalent of £1 a day. Signor Borelli was as strict with her as he was with his own daughter and she had to be back for dinner every evening. She picked up many Italian customs, yet his habit of sucking in spaghetti through a gap in his front teeth was quite beyond her. So there she was, living with an Italian family and conversing with them in their own language. She had learnt some German and French in Ireland, but she organised extra French lessons for herself in Rome, which was a bit of a waste because the French pronunciation was so Italianised. She spent that Christmas in Rome, her first away from home and family.

Ronnie appeared on stage in Rome on 6 June 1947 at a concert organised by Contessa Calcagni for her students. It was a nerve-racking experience, but all the messages and good wishes from home encouraged her, and some made her laugh. Margaret (also known as Mairéad) Pigott, head of music in Radio Éireann, had a great belief that Ronnie was in the right place to develop her beautiful voice. 'Ronnie, m'love!' she wrote. 'Tis my fondest wish that your singing may equal that of all the birdies in Erin's Isle this day'. Ronnie sang her little heart out, and did her best to charm the Roman birdies.

She attended every opera, concert and recital she could get to, and she kept all her programmes. Each day she would scan the newspapers for dates and times of performances, and she became adept at buying cheap tickets for Teatro Argentino, Teatro Quirino, Santa Cecilia Academy and Terme di Caracalla. First and second performances were always the dearest, so she attended the third or fourth. In Rome, the opera season started just before Christmas and finished at Easter. There were different operas on every night in the same theatre, and they could be loud, boisterous affairs, with the audience clapping and cheering or shouting insults to the singers on stage – it was great fun.

During a performance in Viterbo, north of Rome, she watched the crowd take such a dislike to the tenor in a Donizetti opera that they booed until the curtain had to come down. The manager walked onstage to announce, 'Don't worry. We have another singer who'll take over.' Whereupon the tenor reappeared, shoved the manager out of the way and said, 'You think I'm bad – wait til you hear the other fellow!'

The operas in Teatro Dell'Opera featured famous and lesser-known singers. Ronnie saw *Tosca*, conducted by her new acquaintance Vincenzo Bellezza, with Mercedes Fortunati and Mario Del Monaco; *Manon* with a very young Giuseppe di Stefano who made his début in the opera, and later sang with the Dublin Grand Opera Society; *Rigoletto* with di Stefano as the Duke; *La Sonnambula* with Alda Noni; *Otello* with Francesco Merli, Gino Bechi, Renata Tebaldi and Maria Huder; *Salomè* with Tito Gobbi and a young Sesto Bruscantini in a minor role; and *Turandot* with Giacomo Lauri Volpi. She also saw Boris Christoff make his début in the minor role of Pimen in *Boris Godunov*, and later in *Lohengrin* with the meatier part of King Heinrich. She was so impressed with Tito Schipa in *Werther* that she went backstage to seek his autograph. As he signed it, she tentatively asked how long it took to be a singer. 'My dear girl,' he replied, 'it takes for ever. I'm over sixty and I'm still learning.'

Programme from Teatro dell' Opera

While Ronnie was gaining a fantastic appreciation for opera, she remained in lamentable ignorance of other aspects of life. She noticed billboards on buildings advertising doctors and treatments for '*malattia venerea*'. She wondered what that was, so asked the Monsignor.

'You mean to say,' he said, 'you've been in Rome all this time, and don't know what venereal disease is? No? Well, let me put it this way: when people get married, they have children. But when people go with ladies of easy virtue, they are liable to get that disease.'

She was not much the wiser, but decided to let it go. It must have something to do with men and women, but as for herself she just liked having a good time. At home she'd been to the pictures and dinners and dances with boys but it had never gone further than a chaste peck on the cheek, and she didn't see why it should.

It was nearly a year later before Ronnie was enlightened. She had become friendly with Joan Fitzpatrick, a nurse who worked with the Blue Sisters of the Little Company of Mary, dedicated to caring for the sick and the dying. Joan had to have her appendix removed and Ronnie visited her in hospital. Inspecting her friend's scar she asked, 'Is that how they take out a baby?'

Joan nearly split her stitches laughing, and she pleaded to be left alone for a minute. When Ronnie returned, Joan sat her down and described how babies are delivered and, more importantly, conceived. The twenty-year-old was scandalised; humans were no better than the dogs in the street! She was extra careful around Rome after that.

Slowly her dismay receded. She started painting her nails and toenails and going to the hairdresser once a month. She found a dressmaker, Suzanne, who worked for a couturier. They went shopping together and had long debates over material, colour and pattern. It was the era of Audrey Hepburn, Gina Lollobrigida and Sophia Loren, of short cocktail dresses with figure-hugging jackets and the romantic swirl of full-length gowns. Ronnie was just eight stone and she could wear anything. Suzanne made her a pale pink silk taffeta evening dress in the 'faith, hope and charity' style, that is, sleeveless and strapless and supposed to stay up on its own. She wore it for singing engagements and for going to dances. Another outfit was a little pleated jacket and skirt worn with high platform heels for effect. Walking along the Via Sistina or through the Borghese Gardens, it felt good when men whistled and called, '*Bella Signorina!*'

The Monsignor was most particular that Ronnie should dress elegantly and appropriately: a plain back sheath dress for receptions; a beige suit for visiting; a beautiful evening dress, white with a little flower detail, for dinners. She was blossoming into a stylish and accomplished young woman. She worked hard to develop her voice and technical ability, and to expand her repertoire. She was learning two of the main operatic languages, experiencing live opera with incredible music and singers, and she was discovering her own femininity. She had made many friends and learned to cope on her own in a foreign land. Every day was a day of purpose. Yet the aftermath of war was ever present. The city and its people had endured great suffering, some of which could never heal.

In the spring of 1947 Monsignor O'Flaherty asked Ronnie to accompany him to caves on the Via Ardeatina for a commemoration. He told her of an event that had taken place there during the Occupation, and this time he did not spare her the details.

On 23 March 1944 partisans ambushed a column of the German 11th Company, 3rd Battalion, SS Police Regiment 'Bozen' in the centre of Rome, killing thirty-three men. Adolf Hitler declared that reprisals must be carried out immediately, at a ratio of ten Italians to every German. Colonel Kappler was charged with fulfilling this quota. He selected 271 men imprisoned for suspected anti-fascist activities, 57 Jews and, to make up the numbers, a few men casually picked up off the street. The youngest was a boy of fifteen.

One day later, 333 men were secretly trucked to disused quarries near the Via Ardeatina. In groups of five, they were herded into caves with their hands tied behind their backs and ordered to kneel so that a soldier could kill each one with a single bullet to the back of the head. Some of these soldiers were not experienced in the ways of warfare, so a copious supply of cognac was provided to strengthen their nerve. The caves quickly became clogged with the dead and dying. As each group came in, they had to kneel over the bodies of those gone before – shopkeepers, students, lawyers, teachers, musicians, a priest, a boy, and five members of Monsignor O'Flaherty's underground movement. The process was repeated 66 times. After the slaughter, the bodies were piled in heaps, and the rock face of the caves blasted by dynamite, concealing the atrocity. Relatives were eventually informed of the deaths, though not where, or why, or how. The bodies were discovered only after the liberation of the city.

It had taken three years for the rocks to be removed and the area made safe. On the day the caves were officially reopened, the people of Rome gathered at the site to grieve. The Monsignor was eager to be among them to pray and offer what comfort he could. The scene was imprinted on Ronnie's memory:

> We arrived in late afternoon to find the place crowded with people. Upon entering the cave, we saw row upon row of coffins, and on each coffin was placed a photo with the name and age of the person inside. Candles were burning and the back wall was covered with wreaths of flowers. The stench was oppressive. The Monsignor and I walked in silence, looking at each photo in turn. I was overwhelmed by the tragedy of the scene and my tears began to flow; I noticed that the Monsignor was crying too.

It was hard, after that experience, to attend lessons, have a casual coffee, stroll through the beautiful piazzas. Everywhere she saw buildings riddled with bullet holes, roads rutted by tanks. But her bright young Italian friends shrugged disarmingly and said, '*Beh, cosa si può fare?*' ('Well, what can you do?')

May Dunne arrived in Rome for a holiday in Italy with Billo's wife Molly and a friend, Enda Gaffney. May had not seen her sister for over a year and was worried by how thin she looked, but Ronnie made her promise to say nothing to their parents. While May and Enda stayed in Rome, Ronnie and Molly went down to Capri for a few days. They travelled through the countryside by bus and Molly was dismayed by the war damage, especially the charred and flattened ruins of Montecassino, the vast monastery on the hill outside Cassino. In Naples they boarded an ancient boat for Capri and got a close-up view of the warships and submarines moored in the Bay. They stayed in the Grand Hotel Quisisana, which was indeed grand on the outside, but the interior revealed its chequered history, having been commandeered first by the Germans and later as a rehabilitation centre by the Allies. But it was cheap at £1 a day all in, the view was fabulous and the girls sunbathed all day and wandered around the old town in the evening. It was so restful just to enjoy herself and unwind that Ronnie almost forgot scales and scores and schedules, but when it came time to say goodbye to her sister and friends in Rome she was ready for work again.

However, as the days lengthened into summer, the city began to sizzle. In July temperatures soared to 110 degrees Fahrenheit – hotter than the Sahara Desert. Ronnie gratefully accepted her parents' gift of a return ticket home with KLM through Amsterdam. The flight had come from the Middle East and, as Ronnie embarked, the air in the cabin was already thick with cigarette smoke and the heavy perfume worn by some of the passengers. Ronnie found it hard to breathe in the fug and felt queasy. She was relieved when the lights of Amsterdam appeared spread out like diamonds on a carpet of night. As the plane descended, it suddenly lurched to one side and hit the ground with a thud, reared up and bit into the ground again. The lights went out. Overhead bins spewed bottles, cases and clothes. Ronnie gripped the edges of her seat and braced, prepared for the final, calamitous jolt. But there was nothing. Silence. The plane appeared motionless. She heard the other passengers' gasps of relief. They were on the ground, safe. It all happened so fast that shock set only in after the event. On a crackling intercom the Captain announced that they had had to make a forced landing in a field beside the airport. After some time, they were collected by buses and driven to accommodation. Next morning, Ronnie caught an Aer Lingus flight home, and was never more glad to see the familiar sight of Collinstown Airport and her mother and father there to greet her. She spent a month at home and returned to Rome and her studies in September 1947.

After a bitterly cold winter, the Monsignor sent her off to Florence to see more of Italy. He happened to know an Irish woman there, Mrs Quinn, who kept a *pensione*. The bus journey seemed endless as they drove through village after village of shelled-out buildings populated by poverty-stricken people. It was dark when she arrived in the city and she hurried to the address she'd been given, Piazza della Santissima Annunziata, No. 3. She was shown up to her sleeping quarters at the top of the house and left to settle in. The small room was clean and adequately furnished with cupboard and washstand, but it was the narrow bed in the corner that caused concern. There was something in it. A tall, pointy thing about two foot high camouflaged by grey blankets. Could it be a person? Or an animal? It didn't seem to be moving. Keeping a safe distance, she reached out and gingerly lifted an edge of the covering to expose a thin metal rod.

She touched it; it was hot! All the blankets came off then and on the bed was a tripod contraption from which was suspended a brazier of smouldering coals. She had to laugh. When she thanked Mrs Quinn, the brazier was removed and Ronnie had a toasty bed to curl up in.

Next morning, she found Florence to be something of a building site, with rubble and workmen's carts and makeshift scaffolding. Most of the bridges into the city had been bombed; only the Ponte Vecchio remained operational. But many of the buildings had been spared, and she wound her way in and out of churches and galleries and marvelled at works by Giotto, Fra Angelico and da Vinci. It was in the Piazza della Signoria that she found the spirit of Italy. There, in all its vulnerable nakedness, stood the giant statue of Michelangelo's *David*, proclaiming defiant survival against the crushing might of history.

Accademia di Santa Cecilia programme cover, 1948

Three of opera's biggest stars performed in Teatro Argentina in February 1948 – Beniamino Gigli, Rina Corsi and Alda Noni. Ronnie listened entranced as they performed pieces by Pergolesi, Gluck, Cilea, Rossini, Donizetti, Verdi and Mascagni. In April she attended a concert in the Accademia di Santa Cecilia when the brilliant young conductor Herbert von Karajan conducted works by Haydn, Richard Strauss and Beethoven to huge acclaim.

Ronnie sang at several recitals during the year, and on St. Patrick's Day 1948 entertained the guests at a reception given by the rector of the Irish National Church of St. Patrick and Assistant-General of the Augustinians, Very Rev. Fr. Ambrose Doyle, O.S.A. This was attended by J.P. Walshe, Irish Ambassador to the Holy See, Michael MacWhite, Irish Minister to the Italian Republic, and practically all the Irish religious superiors in Rome, including Ronnie's old friend, Father Hubert from St. Isidore's. It was a special delight that Monsignor Hugh O'Flaherty was there to cheer her on. Shamrock distributed to all the guests by the American airline TWA added to the festive occasion.

The opera world was intrigued by the young star from America, Maria Callas. In the summer of 1948 reviews of her performances in Verona and Venice had been favourable, but reserved. When it was announced that she would be singing *Turandot* in Rome at Terme di Caracalla in July, however, tickets were snapped up and Ronnie was fortunate to get one. The production, conducted by Oliviero De Fabritiis, included the cast of Galliano Masini, Giuseppe Flamini, Vera C. Montanari, Mario Borriello, Nino

Teatro dell'Opera programme
with Callas in *Turondot*

Mazziotti, F. Delle Fornaci, Blando Giusti and Gino Conti.

The monumental ruins of the third century Terme di Caracalla created a dramatic backdrop for Puccini's most exotic opera. From start to finish, Callas commanded the stage. Her gorgeous red and gold embroidered kimono, with its sweeping train, belied the bulk of her body, and striking make-up emphasised her large, expressive eyes. Her voice filled the arena effortlessly, even reaching Ronnie in the back row.

Boy! Here was a woman who had it all: powerful big voice; incredible flexibility, astonishing high notes, and she had all the passion and power to portray the 'dragon lady', Princess Turandot. Ronnie was smitten. From that night on, she did her utmost to see Callas wherever she performed in Italy and, like a star-struck fan, would hang around the stage door afterwards to get her autograph.

Home leave 5

RONNIE WAS NOT WELL. She felt so tired and weak that doing even ordinary things like walking down the street became an effort, but it was her dizzy spells that were alarming. Reluctantly, after two years in Rome, she decided she would have to return to Ireland to regain her health.

In Dublin, family and friends were shocked by the change in her: she was so thin, pale and listless. The doctor diagnosed severe anaemia, the same condition that had afflicted her in Mount Anville and which would affect her from time to time all her life. She was put on a course of iron injections, one a week. Her mother Josephine was calm and reassuring. 'You'll be alright,' she told Ronnie. 'You weren't being given good food in Rome, that's all.' She cooked nourishing meals with plenty of dairy produce, meat and vegetables with spinach four or five times a week, and encouraged Ronnie to drink the water from boiled cabbage which, she said, was full of iron.

At first Ronnie just wanted to sleep, all day if she could, but as she grew stronger, she looked out at the rain streaming down the window panes and was frustrated at not being in the sunshine of Rome learning her craft. She resumed her lessons with Hubert Rooney in Nassau Street. As soon as word got out that she was back in Dublin, she received numerous engagements to sing in concerts and recitals. Mairéad Pigott (Margaret) was always keen for her to do live broadcasts with Radio Éireann, as was Dermot O'Hara, who worked with the Radio Éireann Symphony Orchestra. Her appearances caused quite a stir among opera devotees up and down the country. The music critic for the *Irish Press*, John O'Donovan (who wrote under the initials JO'D and was referred to within the business as GOD), stated that 'Irish audiences suddenly woke up to the fact that Ireland was producing sopranos as well as tenors! In various performances ... Veronica's lovely quality and great range won her a large and ardent circle of admirers'.

She had not fully recovered from her illness on 2 August 1948 when she celebrated her twenty-first birthday quietly at home with

Ronnie in her wonderful
ocelot coat

her family. She felt they had already done so much for her that she did not want a big fuss made of the occasion. She was given a beautiful ocelot coat by her parents that she wore everywhere for the next few years with great pride and panache.

Her friendship with Peter McCarthy deepened. The McCarthys and the Dunnes shared a love of horses. Ronnie's father, William, and Peter's father, Peter, both owned and raced horses, and met up at race meetings. Ronnie and Peter went out two or three times a week, either to the races or to dinner dances at the Gresham Hotel or for elegant meals in Jammet's Restaurant.

It was the spring of 1949 before Hubert Rooney finally deemed Ronnie ready to enter the maelstrom of competition. The Southport Music Festival in Lancashire was a prestigious event with two categories that suited her voice, the Soprano Solo (Open) and the Operatic Soprano Solo. Together they prepared her pieces: 'Die Lorelei' by Liszt and 'The Bubble Song' by Shaw, and Micaëla's aria from Bizet's *Carmen* for the Operatic Solo. At the end of September that year she flew over and stayed in a hotel on her own for the week of the competition. She gained two very valuable experiences – one by coming first, the other by coming third, and she quickly found out which she preferred. For her first place in the Soprano Solo, the adjudicator, John Booth, noted on his marking sheet:

> Here is a high standard of artistry. She makes effective use of *diminuendo* to finish her phrases. Warm quality is allied to pleasing facial expressions. The picture is outlined and vividly coloured. Has a wide range of tonal variety. Her play with words and phrases is a feature of her work.

Booth did suggest that her voice was a mezzo rather than a soprano; he found her highest notes 'rather hard'. In later years Ronnie realised that because her teachers had not exploited her top range, she had never felt confident that there were four or five achievable notes above her highest. When she herself became a vocal teacher, she always developed her students' voices top and bottom to give security of range. However, coming home on the plane from Southport, she proudly clutched her first award and a cheque for the princely sum of £1.10.0.

A couple of months later, it was with mixed feelings that Ronnie returned to the scene of her old school, Loreto College on St. Stephen's Green. In the hall she was greeted by the nuns, not as a pupil but as a soloist with the Radio Éireann Choir and Symphony Orchestra under the guest conductor, Edward Appia. The concert of sacred music, which was also broadcast on Radio Éireann, included the first performance in Dublin of the *Mass in D Major* by Giovanni Battista Pergolesi, more famous for his moving *Stabat Mater*. While the acoustics in the hall were far from perfect, Robert Johnston in the *Irish Times* declared the performance to be a fine rendering of the Mass. 'Miss Dunne,' he wrote, 'sang with great control and with purity of tone. Her duet with Miss Eva Tomshon (contralto) was beautiful.'

Later that year Ronnie was chosen by Radio Éireann to represent Ireland in Paris in the Marshall Aid Musical Production, 'This is Ireland'. One morning in December, wearing her warm ocelot coat, she flew to Paris for three days to record a special edition of Irish songs. With her were Patrick Thornton, baritone, Joseph McNally, tenor, and the commentator, Terry O'Sullivan. In March 1950 the programme received worldwide acclamation when it was broadcast to Europe, U.S.A., Australia and New Zealand.

Lieutenant Colonel James M. Doyle, the enterprising Director of the Army School of Music and former Musical Director of Radio Éireann, was delighted when Ronnie agreed to tour with the Army No. 1 Band as part of a fund-raising campaign for The Army

VERONICA DUNNE

*Photo—*Studio 1.

LIEUT.-COL. J. M. DOYLE
Director
ARMY SCHOOL OF MUSIC

Benevolent Fund (Western Branch). She had a fine time junketing around Connacht with the band during February and March 1950. The tour was not without its moments of hilarity. At one venue, her luggage was thrown into the back of a lorry and somehow, somewhere, it must have fallen out, for her evening gown, shoes, make-up, all she needed for the next performance, vanished. The Irish Army was deployed to scour the country in an effort to retrieve it, which they never did. Ronnie had to scrounge around to find something halfway wearable, and no one was any the wiser.

Local newspaper reviewers were enthusiastic in all the towns they visited. After her performance in Mullingar it was noted that:

> Veronica Dunne is taking the country by storm at the moment. One can easily understand why. She has such a beautiful voice. There is great depth and sweetness in it. Her first aria was 'They call me Mimi', from Puccini's *La Bohème*. Then Verdi's 'Ave Maria' from *Otello*, and back to Puccini with 'Oh, My Beloved Father' (*Gianni Schicchi*) and a number from *Turandot*. For a change we got 'Padraic The Fiddler' (Larchet), and 'The Last Rose of Summer' (arrangement Rooney). I think it was the nicest song recital I have ever heard.

Galway, Sligo, Tuam – everywhere they went was a sell-out. She

and Jim Doyle struck up a valuable friendship, and afterwards he sent a message saying: 'For Veronica, An unsolicited testimonial to a good trouper and a fine artiste – from 'the brutal soldiery'.

On 21 April Ronnie faced an entirely different challenge: Verdi's *Requiem,* performed at the Phoenix Hall, Dublin with a simultaneous broadcast on Radio Éireann. It was an ambitious project for Our Lady's Choral Society, the Radio Éireann Symphony Orchestra and the soloists: Ronnie, soprano; Patricia Lawlor, mezzosoprano; Joseph McNally, tenor; and Michael O'Higgins, bass. Jean Martinon's superb skill as a conductor drew all these elements together to reflect the dramatic qualities and emotional depths of Verdi's music. Robert Johnston in the *Irish Times* noted that:

> The performances by all concerned were of consistently high quality, and bore striking evidence of detailed preparation, as well as of the rare rapport between Jean Martinon and his forces .... Michael O'Higgins's singing of the bass solo parts was all that could be desired. He is undoubtedly the complete artist. Veronica Dunne's singing on an equal level was notable for golden tone, exemplary enunciation and intensity of feeling.

It was appreciated by everyone in the Irish music world that Ronnie was on the cusp of becoming a great talent. She was engaged by the Dublin Grand Opera Society to make her operatic début as Micaëla in Bizet's *Carmen* at the Gaiety Theatre on 29 April 1950.

As Micaëla in *Carmen* with Frans Vroons, April 1950

Rehearsals went well, but on the evening of performance she arrived at the theatre in a high state of nervous tension. Her father and mother, brother and sister and a party of family and friends were ensconced in the middle row. There, too, was her teacher, Hubert Rooney, and even Kathleen, her beloved nanny. All awaited her entrance with pride, and some trepidation. Offstage, she tried to stop shaking, bit hard on her tongue to produce saliva in her dry mouth, and told herself to breathe; she had been training for eleven years for this moment. Rousing music, curtain up, sauntering soldiers. She gripped her little basket, and prepared to meet her fate.

With Frans Vroons and Kenneth Neate alternating the role of Don José, and Patricia Black as Carmen, the production, conducted by Vilém Tauský, garnered much praise.

However, one critic did comment that Lillas Pastia's tavern under the ramparts of Seville looked more like Ye Olde English Inn under the ramparts of Birmingham, and the DGOS should reconsider Micaëla's wig, whose blonde plaits were of incredible length and hay-rope thickness.

In June, she featured on Robert Johnston's regular radio programme, *Organ, Violin and Song*, for a selection of J.S. Bach arias to commemorate the bicentenary of the composer's death. More appearances and broadcasts followed, and by September she was both ready and eager to return to Rome.

Rome
1950 to 1951

6

ROME, THE CITY SHE HAD COME TO LOVE. Monsignor O'Flaherty was delighted to see Ronnie back and keen to hear her plans. Her enforced absence had served her well. She had gained valuable experience, and now knew exactly what she had to do to develop her voice and her operatic career.

She found a new vocal coach in Maestro Francesco Calcatelli, who lived close to the Trevi Fountain. She engaged Maestro Frederighe to broaden her repertoire, focusing on such roles as Susanna in

Ronnie arriving in Rome with fellow Irish student, Barbara Quinn, 1950

Mozart's *The Marriage of Figaro*, Marguerite in Gounod's *Faust*, Norina in Donizetti's *Don Pasquale* and Mimi in Puccini's *La Bohème*. Sessions with both teachers lasted for two to three hours every day, the first starting at eight in the morning. A third coach was required for instructions on the stage moves for operatic characters, and producer Maestro Riccardo Picozzi was engaged. With Frederighe singing along, Picozzi directed her on where to go and what to do. She was determined to be ready for anything.

The Borelli's son had grown older and needed his own bedroom, so Ronnie got digs with Signora Leardini on Via Sardegna, near the Hotel Flora. Every morning she walked along Via Veneto to Via Sestina and down the Spanish Steps to her lessons. On her way back, she often paused at the foot of the Steps to gaze at the enormous diamonds glinting in the Bulgari windows; whatever way the sun hit them, they threw out gorgeous facets of light. She got friendly with a fellow student, Viera Magrini. When funds allowed they would bag seats in Caffè Greco and, over *espresso lungo*, try to spot all the writers, artists and musicians drifting in and out. Viera was much better at this than Ronnie – she seemed to know everyone.

Pope Pius XII declared 1950 to be a Holy Year. He invited the faithful to the Eternal City and granted a complete indulgence to those who prayed in the four major basilicas of St. Peter, St. Paul outside the Walls, Basilica di Santa Maria Maggiore and St. John Lateran. The Irish responded in their thousands, including a great number of the Dunnes' acquaintances, who were given assurances by Josephine that her daughter would be delighted to show them around. With three intensive classes a day, these visitors were an intrusion on Ronnie's carefully worked out routine. However, she was as friendly and helpful as she could be, which was much appreciated, and she was treated to some welcome and very fine meals.

Viera Magrini introduced Ronnie to Frederico, a young lieutenant in the Italian army. Not only was he good-looking, he was well connected, and could get tickets for theatre boxes any time he liked. So every Sunday afternoon they would go to the opera together. Ronnie, ever mindful of the Monsignor's admonition that she should never date an Italian, would sneak in and out of the theatre for fear of being recognised. At Christmas Frederico sent a little Bambi statue to her digs with an invitation to a New Year's Eve party. He arrived in a magnificent black sports car and off they zoomed to the Magrini's fabulous house up in Monte Parioli. They had a wonderful time, but the next day she discovered that Gianella Borelli and her parents had been expecting her at their house, which left her feeling embarrassed and disloyal. Her friendship with the lieutenant fizzled out.

Friday lunches with the Monsignor were still an important fixture in her life, as were the receptions and cocktail parties they attended together. When she was talking animatedly to someone or flirting a little, he would look over at her and laugh; you could never take yourself too seriously with Monsignor O'Flaherty around. Sometimes when he was busy he asked her to help him out by showing someone around Rome. She spent a day with Olivia de Havilland, who seemed very religious, and another with the parents of an ex-serviceman he'd rescued. Once a month he was out of town for the whole day. Ronnie was curious about where he went.

Ah, Ronnacio,' he said with a wry smile, 'you might not believe me.' He was visiting his old adversary, Herbert Kappler of the Gestapo. Kappler had been arrested and found guilty of war crimes in 1947, largely because of his involvement in the Ardeatine Caves massacre. He was sentenced to life imprisonment in the military prison of Gaeta, 75 miles from Rome. His one request was for Monsignor O'Flaherty to come and see him, and for many years the Monsignor was his only visitor. Their talks ranged through politics, religion and philosophy. Eventually Kappler converted to Catholicism, and found a little peace.

Ronnie was soon to discover a new sensation. She met a group of Swedish students one afternoon in Teatro Argentina. They were members of the Scandinavian Circle that sponsored its cultural students with apartments, studios and a house on Via Condotti where they could meet up, display their work and perform. The music students put on a recital once a month and Ronnie was invited along. She took her seat in the long, narrow hall and enjoyed a quartet and a solo soprano. Then on walked this hunk – tall, blond, blue-eyed – and as the piano accompaniment for Schumann's *Dichterliebe* rippled gently through the hall, she leaned forward. 'Im wunderschönen Monat Mai' he sang in a sweet, clear tenor voice. She couldn't take her eyes off him, so much so that she moved her chair until he was right in front of her, singing to her and her alone, and the blossoms of May fluttered into her heart.

After the concert he was quickly at her side, and told her his name was Karl Shoenson. Someone mentioned that Wilhelm Furtwängler was holding rehearsals at the Argentina, and they went along with another couple. They paid the porter a small bribe and crept up into a box where they crouched on the floor, hidden from view. Ronnie shared a manuscript of Beethoven's *Ninth Symphony* with Karl and they followed the score together, very closely indeed. Occasionally they'd peep over the edge of the box to watch the conductor, and were amazed by the frenetic beating of his baton. Below them, his little troupe of supporters – the family of three women who accompanied him everywhere – were knitting and doing embroidery in the otherwise empty auditorium.

Ronnie started going to the opera every night with Karl and his friends, and sometimes just the two of them went to concerts in the afternoon or off on picnics. Karl was wonderful company and interested in all the things that fascinated her. And he definitely wasn't Italian – his behaviour was impeccable, almost too impeccable. After a concert or a day out he would escort her to her digs. She'd wait for a tender word or, better still, a kiss, yet it never happened. He returned to Sweden a few months later, but they exchanged letters. When he wrote to say he was coming back for a visit, she was thrilled. He came to pick her up at Signora Leardini's house, and brought along his boyfriend! They all went to lunch together, and the boyfriend took a fancy to her. He kept rubbing his leg against hers under the table, and he was even better-looking than Karl, but she'd had it with the Swedes.

Furtwängler was one of many outstanding conductors in Rome at the time – Toscanini, Kleiber, von Karajan. On an extraordinary night in the Accademia di Santa Cecilia, Ronnie heard the beautiful Swiss soprano Lisa Della Casa sing Mozart's *Exsultate Jubilate* and had the rare privilege of seeing Herbert von Karajan conduct Beethoven's Fifth Symphony. The symphony was sweeping along majestically when, after a few minutes, his baton paused in mid-flight. '*Da capo*,' he hissed at the orchestra. They shuffled their scores, and started from the beginning, much to the bemusement of the audience. Not every conductor included the *da capo* and the players had evidently been unprepared for von Karajan's strict adherence to Beethoven's notation.

Ronnie's studies were progressing well. During many long hours of intensive work, Maestro Frederighe became increasingly drawn to her. She was young, gifted, vivacious, and a sympathetic listener. His life was very troubled. As a Belgian Jew, he had been lucky to escape persecution in his own country but his wife had died in a Nazi concentration camp. Their daughter, whom he visited every Sunday, was in foster care in Frascati, twenty kilometres south-east of Rome. Ronnie regarded the kind, middle-aged man as a friend and mentor, but she could see he was falling in love with her, and she didn't know how to handle it.

After about ten months he asked if she would like to come and visit his daughter. What could she say? They agreed to meet the next day at the railway station. Overnight she worried and worried. She was not in love with Frederighe, and she knew that the next step after meeting his daughter would be a proposal, which she would have to turn down. That would not be fair on him or the little girl. In the morning she rang to say she was very sorry but she couldn't come because the Monsignor had asked her to meet some people. Frederighe was very pleasant and said he quite understood. They worked together for nearly a year after that, and the subject was never referred to again.

Magda Olivero starred in *La Bohème* at Teatro Dell' Opera in January 1951. Olivero had retired from singing ten years previously, on her marriage, but was coaxed back to the stage by her great admirer, Francesco Cilea, who was gravely ill. He begged her to sing again the title role in his opera *Adriana Lecouvreur* in February. Before that, she sang Mimi in Rome as her comeback. The performance was not universally praised, but Ronnie was mesmerised by the warmth of the Italian soprano's voice and her great acting skills. Olivero is famous for saying: 'One has to find the exact facial expression for what one is saying and singing. If one just sings, without putting in any heart or soul, it remains just beautiful singing and not a soul that sings!'

Ronnie attended all remaining performances of *La Bohème* and made copious notes in her copy book about each intonation, every look and move, all the emotions displayed. It was on these details that her own early portrayals of Mimi were based. Olivero reprised her role as Adriana in Brescia the following month, and after 'Poveri Fiori' there was such an outpouring of applause that the aria had to be encored. Sadly, Cilea did not live to see the tremendous success of his opera; he had died the previous November. Olivero returned to Rome in May with Massenet's *Manon* and she was on top form. Ronnie particularly enjoyed the seduction scene where she threw aside her cloak to reveal a stunning low-cut gown while singing 'N'est-ce plus ma main?' What man could resist? Certainly not Count Des Grieux, who fell into her arms. Ronnie drew a quick sketch of the gown, thinking it would be fabulous to wear something similar if she were ever lucky enough to sing the role of Manon.

Caterina Mancini, Contessa Soldini Calcagni's star pupil, performed at Teatro dell'Opera in Verdi's *Ernani* with Gino Penno, Paolo Silveri and Boris Christoff in February. As she watched the dramatic coloratura soprano give it her all on the Rome stage, Ronnie had to smile. She remembered the hours she had spent outside the Contessa's doors, listening to her going over and over her scales and technique. Here it was in effect – the ease and flexibility, the power of her voice that had been moulded and formed through sheer hard

Teatro dell'Opera interior

work and dogged determination in a small room off the Piazza di San Lorenzo.

Francesco Calcatelli arranged that Ronnie should sing at a student concert on 15 March 1951, commemorating the fiftieth anniversary of Verdi's death. Under the auspices of the Corsi Superiori di Studi Romani, it was held in the Borromini Room of Chiesa Nuova, and she shared the billing with three other groups – a string quartet, a vocal quartet and a tenor. Ronnie's four Verdi songs – *Il mistero*; *Brindisi*; *Stornello*; and *Deh, pietoso, oh Addolorata* – received a warm response.

She was much encouraged, for she had organised her own solo recital in April, engaging the services of a fine pianist, Giorgio Favoretto, official accompanist to RAI Radio. She chose a varied selection of pieces by Bach, Brahms, Duparc, Debussy, Handel and Pergolesi to display her range and versatility. Many of her Irish and Italian friends attended, as did a contingent of clergy. Monsignor Tom Ryan from Loughrea, County Galway, who was teaching English to Pope Pius XII at the time, came along with Monsignor O'Flaherty, so she was assured of an enthusiastic reception. Favaretto was so impressed with Ronnie's voice and her sensitive approach to the music that he arranged for her to sing at a dinner given by Count Guido Chigi Saracini, founder of the music academy in Siena, the Accademia Musicale Chigiana.

The Count was enchanted, and immediately offered Ronnie a

62

scholarship to study in Siena for a year. It was an exciting proposition, but when she broached the subject with Maestro Calcatelli he wouldn't hear of it. He insisted that everything she needed was already in place for her in Rome and she was making excellent progress. It may have been that he didn't want to lose his star pupil, but Ronnie felt he had her best interests at heart and she bowed to his advice. And yet, a year in a distinguished music academy was, she felt, an opportunity missed.

In Ireland, the Dublin Grand Opera Society (DGOS) had been working on a scheme to bring Italian opera singers to sing in the Gaiety Theatre. They learned that the Italian government wished to promote their cultural standing abroad, and had initiated a special subvention to impresarios and agents that covered the fees of their artists engaged overseas. It was just the spur that the chairman of the DGOS, Colonel Bill O'Kelly, needed. He and other members of the committee visited Rome where they met the Italian impresario, Cardenio Botti. His agency, O.P.E.R.A., supplied singers, producers, conductors and designers, and also organised concerts, festivals and operatic tours – anything the Society required Maestro Botti could provide.

Bill O'Kelly and his colleague Bertie Timlin returned to Rome in October 1951 to finalise their plans. There, they contacted their 'man on the ground' Veronica Dunne. With her knowledge of the city and fluent Italian, she was invaluable as guide and translator, and she introduced them to many singers and associates in the operatic world. She accompanied them to meetings with Maestro Botti, and was very impressed by his knowledge and acumen. As well as being an accomplished musician, he had trained in one of the leading agencies in Milan, and his own business in Rome was flourishing. He undertook to provide a clutch of singers for the spring season of 1952, sponsored by the Italian government. Bill O'Kelly wished to hear the proposed artists before they travelled, and to have the final say. With Ronnie he attended operas and concerts, and they then travelled to Bergamo, where he and Bertie Timlin bought tickets for Maria Callas singing Violetta in Verdi's *La Traviata*. Callas was due to open the season at La Scala, Milan on 7 December as Duchess Elena in Verdi's *I vespri Siciliani* in a new production to mark the centenary of Verdi's death.

With much regret, Ronnie knew she could not attend this anticipated performance. She had important singing engagements of her own to fulfil in Dublin in November and December.

7

A star has triumphantly arrived

Requiem, Giuseppe Verdi's powerful and exciting masterpiece, with its dramatic soprano role, was the perfect work to display the growing maturity of Ronnie's voice. It was performed at the Capitol Theatre, Dublin on 4 November 1951 with Our Lady's Choral Society and the Radio Éireann Symphony Orchestra under the baton of Italian conductor Francesco Mander. Her fellow soloists were Maura O'Connor, mezzo-soprano; Joseph O'Neill, tenor; and Michael O'Higgins, bass. Audiences and reviewers had looked forward to her return on the Dublin stage with keen interest. The previous year, her performance in the same *Requiem* at the Phoenix Hall in Dame Court, Dublin had been praised for 'the sheer joy' of her singing, 'the excellent and telling quality of her voice', her 'exemplary enunciation' and 'ease in the high register'.

Reviews of the current production were mixed, owing to the limitations of the Capitol in presenting such a large-scale work. *Requiem* is a celebration of the human voice, complemented and coloured by orchestral instruments, but the necessary configuration in the small theatre skewed this concept. Soloists and choir were all piled to the back of the stage and the orchestra in the foreground produced such a volume of sound that it almost drowned out the singers. Yet the plaudits for Ronnie were glowing. Many commented on how much she had benefited from her training in Rome, singing now with great assurance, mastery and warmth. Music critics commended her 'clear, telling tone and superb vocal quality' and observed that her 'singing and interpretation in the Absolution were a joy to hear'.

Things had not gone so well in the lead-up to the performance. She had returned to Dublin in October and immediately began

64

preparing for the work. At the second rehearsal she made a slip in one of the quartets. Francesco Mander turned on her and snarled in Italian, 'Can you not read?'

The following morning, Maestro Mander was about to commence rehearsals when Renzo Marchionni, the first violin, stood and said to him, 'The orchestra will not play today until you apologise to the soloist. You cannot speak to a singer like that.' The great conductor, famed throughout Italy, had no option but to mumble his regret, and rehearsals proceeded.

Renzo Marchionni, originally from Florence, was one of a number of superb musicians from war-torn Europe who had been attracted to join the newly formed Radio Éireann Symphony Orchestra in 1948. He was a quiet, studious man, dedicated to his art, highly regarded by such conductors as Sir John Barbirolli. Ronnie and he got on well and chatted in Italian. He lived in Clontarf, quite close to the Dunnes. His wife could not speak English and was lonely, so Ronnie introduced her to her mother. Josephine took the young woman under her wing, invited her home, plied her with tea, taught her conversational English, and prayed for her to have a little baby. Renzo remained as leader of the Radio Éireann Symphony Orchestra until 1959, and was friends with the Dunnes all his life.

Verdi's *Requiem* was followed in quick succession by three major works in which Ronnie was engaged to sing: Bizet's *Carmen*, Gounod's *Faust* and Handel's *Messiah*. All were scheduled for December, and all were under the baton of Lieutenant-Colonel J.M. Doyle. During that frantic month of preparation and performance, Ronnie was reassured by the friendly and supportive presence of her old comrade-in-arms. Jim Doyle was much in demand as a guest conductor of the Radio Éireann Symphony Orchestra, and directed Ronnie on many memorable occasions. Rehearsals for both *Carmen* and *Faust* took place during the same week, and Ronnie happily flitted from one to the other. There were a couple of 'sitzprobe' run-throughs with the singers sitting on stage and integrating their scores with the orchestra before the full dress rehearsal.

Carmen opened the DGOS season on 3 December 1951 for four performances, alternating with three performances of *Faust*, which opened the following night. Ronnie sang Micaëla in *Carmen*, and once again direct comparisons were drawn between this and her previous appearance in the role, as in this review in the *Evening Herald*:

> Veronica Dunne has improved immeasurably since she made her operatic debut with this Society .... I said of her first portrayal two

years ago that we had a star in the making. After this second portrayal it can be stated that a star has triumphantly arrived. Miss Dunne made a deep impression in the first act, and in the third gave a brilliant rendering of the principal aria. Her smooth, effortless singing was a continuous delight. I have never heard this aria better sung.

Patricia Black, who sang the lead, did much more for the DGOS than merely sing. She and fellow soprano May Devitt were the backbone of the Society, often called upon to make costumes, paint scenery or whatever was required – the company could hardly have functioned without them. Patricia had played Carmen at the Gaiety many times and again made the part her own with the 'force of her personality and the attractive quality of her voice', while the 'Don José of Frans Vroons was brilliantly effective' (*Irish Independent*).

Ronnie's delightful Micaëla sparked much anticipation for her first appearance playing the lead in Gounod's grand opera *Faust*. She clearly had the voice, but did she have the emotional depth to carry the demanding role of Marguerite, the carefree young maiden made pregnant and abandoned by Faust and who, with her baby, was turned into a social outcast? It was an enormous responsibility for a

(Below) As Marguerite in *Faust*. DGOS, 1951

(Below right) As Micaëla in *Carmen* with Frans Vroons (Don José). DGOS, 1951

young singer at the start of her career, but it was one that Ronnie relished. In the *Evening Press* Robert Johnston wrote:

> Veronica Dunne's first appearance as Marguerite ... was undoubtedly the finest performance of the evening. Not only was her singing of the highest order throughout, but her acting had a full appreciation of the importance of detail. All the shades of emotion which make the character such a complex one were most subtly suggested, and it was done without any underlining. Obviously Miss Dunne is destined for a great success as an operatic artist.

Joseph O'Neill in the *Irish Independent* observed that the considerable courage Ronnie had shown in accepting the part was indicative of her courageous approach to her art which, coupled with her musical ability and voice, had 'supported her in her great adventure. There was an amazing security in her performance which aroused admiration.'

That admiration was expressed at the final curtain as wave after wave of applause reached the young star on stage. The Irish audience sensed they were witnessing the start of a great operatic career, and for one of their own. Not since Margaret Burke Sheridan had so much been expected of a singer, and been so amply rewarded. It was one of the most exciting evenings of Ronnie's singing career; a vindication of her parents' and teachers' belief and support, and the long hours of coaching, learning and travelling. Her great adventure was really beginning, and she was in demand all over Ireland. She finally began to make a little money earning a flat fee of about £20 for concerts, £8 for broadcasts and £30 per appearance with the DGOS. These fees made no allowance for expenses, however. Opera seasons were short, and she was still living at home and being supported by her family.

Handel's *Messiah* was, and is to this day, performed annually by Our Lady's Choral Society. By 1951 the choir was a mere five years old, yet had already gained considerable experience at home and on overseas tours. In Wales, it had been described as 'the choir that loves to sing', and in 1950 had received much acclaim with its performance of the *Messiah* in Teatro Argentina, Rome with the Santa Cecilia Orchestra. This had been followed by the Verdi *Requiem* in the Théatre des Champs Elysées with the Paris Conservatoire Orchestra under Jean Martinon, who would later conduct the Radio Éireann Symphony Orchestra. Ronnie loved singing with the choir. They were dedicated, knowledgeable, ambitious, and, under their musical director, Oliver O'Brien, they produced the most wonderful sound.

On 23 December Handel's *Messiah* drew a huge crowd to the Capitol Theatre, Dublin to hear Ronnie, soprano; Owen Brannigan, bass; Joseph McNally, tenor; Maura O'Connor, mezzo-soprano; and the hundred-strong choir. It was described as 'a truly impressive and satisfying performance'. One critic wrote that, of the quartet of soloists:

> Veronica Dunne was out on her own. After her recent remarkable successes in Verdi's *Requiem* and Gounod's *Faust* she again gave a fine display of versatile artistry. She certainly knows how to control her strikingly clear and full voice. This was particularly evident in 'I know that my Redeemer liveth' and 'Come unto Him all ye that labour'.

Relieved that she had got through an arduous month, Ronnie relaxed at home. May had married a paediatrician, Dr Michael Curtin, who secured a highly sought-after position at the Boston Children's Hospital in the Unites States of America. When they travelled, they left their daughter Carolyn in the care of Josephine and William, so it was a time filled with excitement as the proud grandparents, Billo and Molly, Ronnie and Carolyn celebrated a family Christmas together.

Early in January it was back to Rome for Ronnie. Maestro Calcatelli had entered her for one of the most important singing competitions in Italy, the Concorso Lirico Milano.

Milan, Rome, Dublin, London 8

THE CONCORSO LIRICO MILANO COMPETITION is held every year to identify young, exceptional talent, and to produce operatic performances of the highest calibre in which to display these artists. In 1952 vocal coaches from all over Italy put forward their finest students, many of whom were already very experienced. The task of the judges was mammoth. Eight hundred singers (two hundred in each of the four voice categories) were permitted to compete for just eight professionally produced operas. It would require several auditions to arrive at the fortunate few to perform in Milan's Teatro Nuovo later in the year.

Sunday, 7 January 1952. Ronnie hurried through Piazza della Scala, Milan, pausing to gaze in awe at the greatest opera house in the world, its billboards proclaiming the imminent appearance of Maria Callas in the title role of Bellini's *Norma*. She shivered. She had not slept the night before, and the journey up on the unheated Rome train had seemed interminable. From the address, she knew her destination was just around the corner in a studio attached to Teatro Nuovo. They had been very specific about the timing of her appointment; she must be neither early nor late. On the pavement outside a plain building she checked her watch, and pushed through the door into a poky room. Almost immediately she was shown into a hall where a panel of austere men were seated behind a table. To one side were a pianist and a piano. There was nothing else; no stage, no other furniture.

Ronnie had been instructed to prepare twelve arias, and bring three along to the audition. The sheets of music shook as she handed them to the pianist and glanced towards the judges. They sat implacably, and nodded for her to begin.

She started a little shakily with 'Sì, mi chiamano Mimì', but as the lovely aria from *La Bohème* gathered momentum, she took courage, and remembered to move, to intonate, to act the part of the impoverished young seamstress. At the end there was no reaction from the judges, just a rustle as the pianist changed the score to 'Depuis le jour', the lyrical song of happiness from *Louise* by Gustave Charpentier. She ended with Nanetta's aria from Verdi's *Falstaff*.

It was over. Ronnie was directed from the building through a back exit and was momentarily disorientated. She realised that at very moment another young hopeful would be singing her heart out in the bleak hall, fighting for the priceless prize of getting noticed. There was little chance the judges would hand such an opportunity to a chit of a girl from Ireland.

All the talk around Rome was of the English contralto Kathleen Ferrier. She was on a tour of Europe and would be appearing in Teatro Argentina on 2 February. Before her recital, Kathleen received the news that her father had suffered a stroke and was close to death. She wanted to return home at once but there were no flights because London was fogbound. The audience knew nothing of this, and the Argentina was packed. Accompanied by pianist Giorgio Favaretto, who had played for Ronnie, Kathleen sang a varied selection of songs, including Orfeo's glorious aria, 'Che farò' from Gluck's *Orfeo ed Euridice* (Orpheus or Orfeo, the legendary musician, poet, and prophet in ancient Greek religion and myth, is traditionally sung by a contralto). The crowd adored her; they wanted more and more. In the audience, Ronnie was moved to tears when Kathleen sang as her encore, 'I once loved a boy, a bold Irish boy'.

The Roman public had a cavalier attitude to their opera. They did not sit on their hands and then clap politely as befitted a great occasion, instead they either viewed it entirely casually or as a participatory sport in which the principals required raucous comments at inappropriate moments. Kathleen found their behaviour appalling. 'They arrive three-quarters of an hour late,' she wrote, 'get up and walk in and out, and chatter all the time' (Maurice Leonard: *Kathleen: The Life of Kathleen Ferrier 1912-1953*, 1989, p.173). Ronnie had become used to such ways but knew they could be bruising, and after the recital she made a point of going up to say how much she had enjoyed the recital. Kathleen smiled and signed her programme with a flourish.

At the end of the month Ronnie was amazed to learn she had got into the second round of the Concorso Lirico. She knew what to expect this time and in some ways it wasn't as nerve-racking, but having got this far she had more to lose. She sang arias from Mascagni's *L'amico Fritz* and, fresh from her success in Dublin, Marguerite's spinning wheel aria from *Faust*, 'Il ne revient pas'. She never got to see any of the other contestants at the auditions or know how many were knocked out in each round. While in Milan she attended the stupendous performance of Maria Callas and Ebe Stignani in *Norma* at La Scala. The title role of Norma, the Druid priestess, is regarded as one of the most difficult in the bel canto repertoire. It demands exceptional vocal control, a wide range, variety of tone and extraordinary acting talent. Callas displayed all these, and she added her own unique dramatic intensity to its most famous aria, 'Casta diva'. Immediately after the performance, Ronnie was at the stage door to collect yet another Callas autograph.

Vatican Radio invited Ronnie to make a guest appearance in March. Father Henry Nolan, in charge of the English-speaking section, was an old friend. Many years previously, he had taken boys on pilgrimage to Lourdes, and there he had heard a young boy soprano sing 'Ave Maria' so beautifully it made the hairs on his arms quiver. It was Bill Dunne, Ronnie's brother. 'So,' he laughed when he saw her, 'nice to see you kept it in the family.' She told him that not only had Billo won many competitions for his fine baritone, May was a lyrical soprano and her father's tenor voice was renowned.

She was planning her return home at Easter where several engagements were lined up. She hadn't heard anything from Milan, and presumed that was the end of it. But early in April there was a letter to say she had made it into the penultimate round. She could hardly believe it. How many singers out of the original two hundred were left – thirty, twenty – and she was one of them?

In Milan, it was back to the hall with the same judges and the same pianist. This time she chose two arias from *Turandot*. Her last piece was her childhood favourite, 'Un bel dì vedremo', and she called on all her reserves of love and hope and musicality to let Butterfly soar high into the sky and far out to sea for the first glimpse of that ship. She sang in homage to her father, and to Hubert Rooney.

On her return to Rome she heard that Bill O'Kelly of the DGOS needed a favour. No provision had been made by Maestro Botti towards the cost of airfares for the Italian artists contracted to go to Ireland. Instead, arrangements had been made for a two-day trek by train and boat across half of Europe and on to Dublin. Bill wondered if Ronnie could possibly accompany them, smooth out any difficulties; she was, after all, bilingual and well used to travel. What could she say? Even as she agreed, she knew the journey would be dreadful. All went as planned from Rome to Paris and on to Calais where they boarded a boat across the Channel. But when their visas were examined in Dover, it was found they were not valid for landing on English soil. Endless negotiations with the authorities ensued, and Ronnie had to use all her charm and Irish wit to get them through. Eventually, they were allowed to travel by train from Dover to London to Holyhead, there to get the boat to Dublin.

There were further difficulties in Dublin. Although digs had been secured for the singers, hotel and restaurant workers were on strike. With nowhere to eat, the situation seemed dire. Ronnie's parents came to the rescue. Josephine cooked many meals for them, but on the evening that William brought home packets of dried spaghetti, an exotic ingredient for Dubliners, the young Italians took over the kitchen and set to work with heaps of enthusiasm and little culinary skill. In a great pot of boiling water the pasta quickly turned to mush and bubbled all over the stove and onto the floor, some even winding up on the ceiling. But they made a decent *sugo* tomato sauce and dolloped everything into bowls. William uncorked the wine and everyone slurped their way through the meal with much merriment.

These 'glamorous stars' were causing quite a stir among the opera-

The Italians making themselves at home in Howth Road, Clontarf

going public. Expectations were high, particularly as their own Veronica Dunne was going to be with them, and performances at the Gaiety were sold out. On 29 April 1952 Ronnie sang Mimi in *La Bohème* for the first of many times in her career. Magda Olivero was very much in mind as she prayed all would go well.

The Italians won many friends that night. Handsome and romantic Giuseppe Zampieri was an ideal Rodolfo, and Giulio Fioravanti's Marcello and Sandra Baruffi's Musetta were beautifully performed, but the highest acclamation was reserved for Veronica Dunne. The *Evening Herald* noted that 'she brought to the role the very ecstasy of youth. The notes were beautifully shaped; the Puccini melodies lay easily on the clear, spring-like voice. This was a Mimi of heart-touching quality, notably in the 'Farewell' aria of the third act'. The *Evening Mail* declared it a 'Triumph for Dublin singer in *Bohème*'. She 'added lustre to the part and her singing and acting showed a maturity surprising in one with so little experience of grand opera'. At the final curtain, conductor Karl Rankl turned to receive the applause of an enthusiastic audience, and all the principals were called back again and again, with Ronnie singled out for a standing ovation and showers of bouquets.

Five performances of *La Bohème* alternated with four nights of Donizetti's comic opera, *Don Pasquale*, in which she sang the part of Norina. The conniving young widow was a perfect foil to the doomed Mimi, and Ronnie delighted in displaying her sense of fun in light, bel canto singing. 'Her acting had all the playfulness and guile that the character of Norina demanded' noted the *Evening Mail*. That her performance attracted such good reviews was all the more commendable as she was paired with an Italian tenor whose voice, according to one reviewer, was 'lacking in any lyric beauty' and whose acting was 'wooden'. But old favourites of the DGOS, Bruce Dargavel, Ronald Stear and Barry O'Sullivan were highly praised and the production declared a success.

The glamour and box office interest that the guest artists generated boded well for future seasons. There was a discrepancy, however, between the Italian singers who sang in their own language and the excellent, unpaid chorus of the DGOS who performed all the operas in English. Ronnie's facility with both languages was a bonus: she could easily sing in Italian with the soloists and switch to English with the chorus. In later years, operas were performed entirely in their original language.

Shortly after the last performance of *Don Pasquale* on 24 May, Ronnie performed at a Prom concert with the Radio Éireann Symphony

Orchestra at the Gaiety, and then travelled with them for a concert in Sligo. It was there that she received the news that she was a finalist in the Concorso Lirico, and would have to return to Milan by the next day if she wished to compete. Sligo to Milan in a day – it was impossible.

At home in Dublin, her parents booked the first flight out the following morning. Billo jumped in his Jag and hared over to Sligo. After Ronnie had finished her concert, they belted back along the twisting country roads. In Mullingar, seventy miles from Clontarf, the car broke down. It was two o'clock in the morning. All was lost.

Somehow, Billo managed to find a taxi. They arrived home as dawn was breaking. Ronnie just had time to take a quick bath, change her clothes and grab her suitcase and passport before her father sped her to the airport where she caught the first of two connecting flights. She arrived in Milan at three in the afternoon, went to her hotel, changed and headed straight out to Teatro Nuovo where rehearsals were already underway. She had not slept for thirty-four hours.

Four of the operas were to be cast that day: *Cavalleria Rusticana*, *Pagliacci*, *L'amico Fritz*, and *La Bohème*. She almost wept when she learned she was one of five sopranos shortlisted for Mimi, the role she had just sung with the DGOS. One by one the contestants took to the stage, Ronnie watching everything intently. Eventually, she was asked to sing the duet from Act 3 with a baritone competing for the role of Marcello, and then to perform Mimi's farewell aria, 'Donde lieta uscì'. One shot, and one shot only – that was all she needed and she gave it her all. There was a short break. When she was invited to sing in the quartet, she knew it was a good sign. Ronnie was chosen for the role of Mimi for six performances starting on 13 July 1952. Ugo Rapalo conducted the production, with Gianni Piluso as Rodolfo, Bruna Boccalini as Musetta and Lino Puglisi as Marcello.

An hour before the first night in Teatro Nuovo there was a knock on Ronnie's dressing room door. The woman who was assisting her said it was the claque, and she had to pay them

La Bohème cast list

something or they would wreck her performance. Ronnie was flabbergasted, and she hadn't much money. She searched her bag and came up with the equivalent of about £15, and had to pay the same on each night.

The claque's practice was, and still is in some places, an insidious form of blackmail. A small group of people demand money from the soloists every night. They then position themselves throughout the theatre, about four in the gods, two or three in the back rows, two in the middle and four up at the front. During a singer's performance they start the applause and encourage the audience to join in. If they have not been paid, they create a disturbance. In one notorious incident in Naples Enrico Caruso was hissed and booed during his singing of the Donizetti aria 'Una furtiva lagrima' in *L'elisir d'amore*, because he had refused to pay. Ronnie learned later that Tebaldi, Callas, Gobbi – everyone paid, fearful of the consequences if they didn't.

That night in the theatre there was standing room only. As she stepped on stage, Ronnie could feel the heat emanating from the crowd, the hungry expectancy. The evening passed in a blur. At the end, the audience rose and whistled and applauded again and again.

Next day, she awaited the reviews anxiously. The critics were kind in her home town where she had become a big fish in a rather small pond, but how would a partisan press in the heartland of Italian opera view the performance of an unknown Irish girl in one of Puccini's greatest works?

'*Voce d'Irlanda esordiente Mimì*' (translated as 'The Voice of Ireland ushers in Mimì') was the bold headline in Milan's prominent newspaper *Corriere Lombardo* on 14 July 1952:

> The theatre was packed out ... and the public did not regret their ready response to the *Associazione Lirica e Concertistica*. It was the best presentation yet staged at the Nuovo .... In the role of Mimì was Veronica Dunne, who, in our opinion, was clearly the best of the evening. We might be able to register a reserve or two about her Italo-Irish pronunciation, even though her diction was one hundred per cent. Beyond question, this young singer possesses the sweet and fresh voice of a lyric soprano; she uses it with great taste, shows a good 'school', and her skill of interpretation is very high. Let her avoid certain affected mannerisms which are not in the best tradition and she will be fully convincing in the role of the dear little flower girl. 'Donde lieta uscì' was sung most movingly and persuasively in a tone of restrained grief .... The audience decreed the show a stunning success, which culminated in many curtain calls.

LA "BOHÈME., ALLA STAGIONE D'AVVIAMENTO

Voce d'Irlanda esordiente Mimì

La Bohème, l'opera cara al cuore del pubblico italiano come forse nessun'altra, per la delicata poesia che si espande dalla dolce melodia, e per la suadente teatralità, ha richiamato ier sera al Teatro Nuovo una grande folla di spettatori: il teatro era tutto esaurito. Nè gli spettatori si sono pentiti d'esser accorsi al richiamo, chè l'edizione dell'opera pucciniana predisposta dall'Associazione Lirica e Concertistica è sembrata complessivamente degna, vocalmente, e teatralmente convincente. Diremmo, questo, il miglior allestimento finora apprezzato al Nuovo.

Il quartetto dei protagonisti si valeva del tenore Gianni Piluso quale Rodolfo: egli è stato ammirato per la vocalità chiara, per la dizione nettissima e per la facilità negli acuti, anche se i suoi mezzi sono apparsi di non grande volume e meno percepibili nel registro basso. Comunque, il Piluso è un cantante che sarà bene non perdere d'occhio. Accanto a lui, come Mimì, era Veronica Dunne, che ci è parsa la migliore della serata. Potremmo fare qualche riserva circa la pronuncia italo-irlandese ch'ella ha esibito, pur in una dizione chiarissima; ma dobbiamo riconoscere che questa giovane cantante possiede una dolce e fresca voce di soprano lirico, e ne usa con grande garbo, con buona «scuola» e con e interpretativa già notevole. pena ella eviterà certe smancattiva tradizione, potrà to, nei panni cciniana,

The next day Milan's other newspaper, *Corriere d'Informazione*, agreed: 'Veronica Dunne has a voice of wide range, rich in expression, and she gave us a most moving interpretation of the part. She sang throughout with a delightful naturalness, besides presenting a very charming dramatic figure on the stage.'

David Webster, General Administrator of the Royal Opera House, Covent Garden, attended all performances of *La Bohème*. He realised that he had he found a singer of huge potential; Veronica Dunne had the complete package – voice, acting, command of the stage. She was invited to audition for his guest conductor, Sir John Barbirolli.

The day before her audition, Ronnie flew to London and joined her parents who, as it happened, were staying at the Park Lane Hotel for their annual excursion to the Ascot races. Ronnie had never been to Covent Garden, but she found her way around to the stage door and was told to wait. The manager and the pianist came down and brought her along a labyrinth of dusty corridors, past dressing rooms, up steps, through the wings and onto the vast empty stage. The pianist led her over to an upright piano, they briefly established the tempo of the piece, then he waited. Her heart pounded in her chest, her mouth went dry. She chewed on her tongue for saliva. Breath, she thought. The most important thing in singing is breathing.

The auditorium was dark. Way at the back she could dimly discern a row of men's faces. The spotlights were trained on her. She resolved not let her nerves get the better of her; there would be just one bite of this apple. With a slight nod to the pianist, she went for it: 'Sì, mi chiamano Mimì'. Her voice flowed over the rows of empty seats and up into the laps of the gods.

When she had finished, she saw that the men were huddled in conversation. The pianist motioned that she should stay where she was. After a few minutes, she was asked to sing the first act duet with an Australian tenor, John Lanigan, who had auditioned earlier. To her surprise, she enjoyed it. They sang and acted well together, and at the end she reached, and held, top C. The men got in a huddle once again, then thanked her for coming. She had been there less than an hour. Over dinner that evening her parents enquired how it had gone. 'I honestly don't know,' she replied. There was no point in getting their hopes up, or her own.

Back in Dublin, she did several live broadcasts with Radio Éireann, and was delighted that she would be singing with the DGOS again in December, but she could hardly make a living in Ireland.

9 *Royal Opera House, Covent Garden*

THE ENVELOPE ADDRESSED to *Miss Veronica Dunne, 154 Howth Road, Clontarf, Dublin* bore an English stamp and postmark. Her hand trembled as she drew out the letter and spied the crest and logo of the Royal Opera House, Covent Garden. It was an offer to join the company for nine months at a flat rate of £10 a week; £20 a week in production; £30 a week on tour.

'Well,' said her father, ever practical, 'that'll hardly pay your way.'

Nevertheless it was the break they'd been hoping for, and enquiries were made about finding digs in London. Ronnie heard of two Irish girls looking for a flatmate in Herne Hill and she decided to go for it. Although six miles from the city centre, it was easy to take the tube or get the No. 6 bus at Waterloo Bridge, the conductor calling the stops along the way: 'Helephant and Castle' and 'Ern 'ill'. They had the ground floor to themselves, with a drawing room, a kitchenette and bathroom, a double room for the girls and Ronnie's single. Rent was £10 a month each, and they paid the wonderfully named Mrs Coffin half a crown a week each for cleaning the rooms. A man who had been in a concentration camp during the war occupied the top floor. The girls could hear his racking cough all night; the poor fellow must have got little rest, but neither did they.

Peter McCarthy telephoned to make sure she was settling in all right, and his lovely Irish voice at the end of the line gave Ronnie warm feelings of happiness and home. He visited, too, going over on a Friday night and leaving on Sunday. While she was working he might go to the races with his pals and then they would all attend her performance. Peter didn't pretend to know a thing about singing or opera but they were so mad about each other it did not seem to matter.

The singers' day in the opera house began at ten o'clock in the morning. When not in a production, there were three hours of work with a coach and other singers in the morning, and a further three hours in the afternoon with a répétiteur, learning new roles or perfecting familiar ones. Rehearsals for a specific production started at ten o'clock with a producer who directed every detail. In the afternoon there was more coaching, and orchestral and ensemble rehearsals could go on until seven in the evening. Ronnie flew back to Ireland for a day in late September to fulfil an engagement to appear in a charity concert in Drogheda with tenor James Johnston.

In Covent Garden, Ronnie had to hit the ground running. She was immediately plunged into rehearsals for Richard Strauss' *Der Rosenkavalier*, to sing the role of Sophie. She had never seen the opera, never even heard of it. For the first time in her professional career she was not prepared in any way and it was terrifying. With exactly three weeks to learn the music, the words, the acting and the stage moves, the oil was burned way beyond midnight every night in Herne Hill, and days were taken up with coaching and rehearsals with the cast, orchestra and conductor, Peter Gellhorn. At least Ronnie was familiar with the four other soloists; she had seen Constance Shacklock, Sylvia Fisher, Howell Glynne and Ronald Lewis perform on the Gaiety Theatre stage.

ROYAL OPERA HOUSE
COVENT GARDEN

OPERA SEASON

1952

Outside the theatre, billboards announced some of the productions for the forthcoming winter season: *The Magic Flute*, *A Masked Ball*, *Tosca*, *Aida*, and *Der Rosenkavalier* featuring Veronica Dunne on several nights, including 7 November. Splashed across another billboard was the announcement that Maria Callas was making her London début on 8 November in the La Scala production of *Norma*.

Wednesday, 29 October 1952. Dozens of telegrams, flowers and messages of good luck were delivered to the dressing room with the name *Veronica Dunne* inscribed above the star on the door. A large contingent of family and friends travelled from Dublin to be present at Ronnie's Covent Garden début, among whom were the Brennans, whose son Paddy would inherit their great love of music and would go on to make his own, unique contribution to the history of opera in Ireland.

Excited by the good wishes and feverishly trying to get ready, Ronnie was in a whirl, but her dresser and make-up artist formed an oasis of calm. The costumes were laid out, from the clips for her wig right down to her underwear. Her nervousness mounted when she learned that the great Margaret Burke Sheridan was seated in a box close to the stage.

Der Rosenkavalier is a comic opera with four main characters: the aristocratic Marschallin, her young lover Count Octavian Rofrano (written for a mezzo-soprano), her boorish cousin Baron Ochs, and Ochs' prospective fiancée, Sophie. Ochs designates Octavian to act as his 'Rosenkavalier', his 'Knight of the Rose', to present a silver ceremonial rose to Sophie to formalise their engagement. The twist in the tale is that Octavian and Sophie fall for each other. On stage, Ronnie managed to control her voice but her entire body was shaking. When Constance Shacklock as Octavian passed her the rose, Ronnie caught her hand and they both shook and shook. In her frightfully British accent, Constance murmured, 'Don't do that, dear. Stay still.'

The shakes were not noticed; the performance was a triumph. The soloists were called back time and again, especially the new young star from Dublin. One reporter heard an Irish voice behind him exclaim: 'I never thought she could look so glamorous'. He turned to find Josephine Dunne revelling in her daughter's success. Later, in a dressing room crowded with family and well-wishers, still more bouquets arrived and Ronnie felt like a child at Christmas as she read the messages and posed for photographs.

She had passed her first test before discerning English opera-goers, but a far greater task lay ahead. She had been chosen to take the lead in *La Bohème*, due to open in three weeks. On the days she was not performing as Sophie, she was in rehearsal with Sir John Barbirolli. Renowned as a singers' conductor, he was always sensitive to vocal timbre and range. At rehearsal, when the orchestra threatened to drown out the singers he would say: 'Gentlemen, if you wish to play loudly, go down to the Festival Hall!'

There was a clutch of excellent young sopranos in the company, including Adele Leigh, Sylvia Fisher and Blanche Turner, and despite a healthy rivalry, all were friendly towards Ronnie and the other newcomer, Australian Joan Sutherland. While Ronnie had succeeded at her first audition and was deemed ready for productions, it was on Joan's fourth attempt that she had finally been accepted as a 'Utility Soprano', and then with some hesitation. The dramatic power and high quality of her voice were unquestionable but she was ungainly and self-conscious on stage. However, she was getting extra coaching

As Sophie in *Der Rosenkavalier*. Covent Garden, 1952

from a dashing young Australian pianist, Richard Bonynge, and the two were seldom apart.

Although often competing for the same roles, bright and pretty Adele Leigh and Ronnie became great friends. At lunchtime she and Adele, and Joan on occasion, hurried along to Lyons Corner House on Coventry Street where they had their main meal of the day, sausage and chips at one shilling and ninepence. This was a real treat as Ronnie's ration card allowed her to buy only one chop, one rasher and one sausage *per week* to cook at home.

Dublin butcher F.X. Buckley was a friend of the Dunnes who knew all about the terrible rationing in Britain. He parcelled up a great joint of beef and sent it over to Ronnie with his very best wishes. This turned out to be a well-meaning but misguided gesture, because it took so long getting through the postal system that by the time it arrived at the door in Herne Hill it was a putrid mess fit only for the bin, much to Ronnie's chagrin.

Der Rosenkavalier and *Norma* were to run concurrently. The arrival of Maria Callas created a huge wave of publicity, spurred by her recent triumphant appearance in the same role in Milan and her reputation as one of La Scala's greatest and most volatile artists. Yet at rehearsals there was no sign of temperament. She worked herself to exhaustion to achieve as near perfection as possible, and expected the same of

Norma: Maria Callas in dressing room, and on stage with Joan Sutherland (Clotilde) and Ebe Stignani (Adalgisa). Covent Garden, 1952

those around her. Her eyesight was so deficient she wore thick-lensed glasses, and walked through her moves many times to familiarise herself with the sets before the glasses were discarded during performance. She was a real inspiration to the young singers in the company, especially Joan Sutherland (Clotilde), who sang with her.

Callas in Covent Garden. Opening night on 8 November could have been sold out many times. People converged on Bow Street in the biting cold with the vain hope of buying tickets from those lucky few who possessed them. Inside, the great and the fortunate moved towards the auditorium, and among the elegant gowns of the ladies and the men in formal black tie there was Ronnie, ocelot coat on her arm, caught up in the thrill of knowing that one of her idols would be singing in the same arena at which she had performed the night before.

Callas was magnificent. From the moment she stepped onto the stage the place was electrified. Her voice was powerful and insistent, her acting intense, and she and Ebe Stignani complemented each other majestically. It was one of the greatest nights Covent Garden had ever seen. At the end, the audience went wild and Ronnie cheered and cheered with the best of them. Afterwards, she and other members of the Company queued for autographs outside the great lady's dressing room. When it came to her turn, Callas looked at her in puzzlement. 'Not you again?' she said, remembering the slip of a girl in Italy. 'Yes,' replied Ronnie, 'but this time I'm singing here, too.'

The party in the Crush Room with its crystal chandeliers and plush red carpet was a glittering affair with everyone wanting to get a word, a touch, a glance from the star. Ronnie was asked to chat with the wife of Italian conductor Vittorio Gui, who knew no English, and then one distinguished guest approached. In 1919 Margaret Burke Sheridan had caused a near riot at her début in Covent Garden with *Madama Butterfly*. Now, thirty-three years later, she wished to speak with the Irish girl who hoped to take to this stage with another Puccini role. 'You are not ready, my dear,' she told Ronnie, not altogether kindly. 'You must come back to Italy with me and train and train. In two years, I will turn you into a *real* singer.'

Ronnie's confidence was shaken. Perhaps this doyenne of opera was right. Here was a woman who had sung all the great roles at La Scala, Rome Opera and Covent Garden. Opera lovers worldwide adored her. Princes threw themselves at her feet; kings tried to lavish her with honours. Her recordings were legendary. Toscanini had dubbed her 'The Empress of Ireland', and Puccini had coached and groomed her for *La Bohème* – she *was* Puccini's Mimi. And she was saying that Ronnie was not up to it. Should she turn tail and run back to Italy? But what of her parents? They had already invested so much financially and emotionally; they had been with her on every step she had taken and now that she seemed set fair in her career, they were so very proud.

Ronnie looked across the room at Callas and Stignani, the greats. Perhaps she had no business aspiring to count herself among them. Then her gaze rested on Sutherland and Leigh, not great yet but getting there. And that's what she was. She was getting there by her own efforts and in her own way. She belonged in Covent Garden; she had earned it.

Margaret Burke Sheridan was not pleased when she realised Ronnie would not bend to her will, and over the next few days telephoned on several occasions, insisting that she needed extra training. Ronnie just wanted to talk about Puccini and his opera, and eventually a meeting was arranged in Harley Street where Burke Sheridan was staying.

Late on Monday afternoon Ronnie stepped into the frosty dusk of Bow Street after hours of intensive rehearsals for *La Bohème*. Full dress rehearsals were scheduled for the following day with opening night on Wednesday and really she should be resting, but she was enthralled by the prospect of spending time with the former diva. Their discussions on Puccini were far-ranging. They pored over the score, Burke Sheridan explaining the composer's intentions regarding interpretation, and his regret that in some of his early notations the phrasing was not more fluid. Ronnie listened intently with no more than a cup of tea to sustain her. It was nearly ten o'clock when she caught the tube back to Herne Hill, her head buzzing with new information and fresh insight into the character of Mimi.

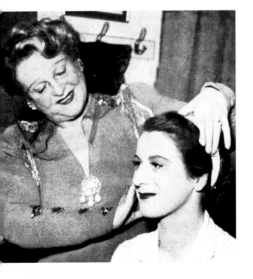

With Margaret Burke Sheridan before Ronnie's début as Mimi

Wednesday, 19 November 1952. Rehearsals on the day of performance were almost unheard of, but Sir John was not happy and had called the singers back in the morning for still more work. John Lanigan as Rudolph (also known as Rodolfo when sung in Italian), Jess Walters (Marcel), Inia Te Wiata (Colline), Kathryn Harvey (Musetta), Geraint Evans (Schaunard) and Ronnie gathered on stage. They went over and over sections of the opera, Ronnie revealing her inexperience by singing at full strength instead of sparing her voice. The conductor finally let them go at three o'clock in the afternoon. They had a couple of hours' break before it was time to prepare for the performance, starting at seven o'clock. Ronnie was almost too tired to be nervous, and concerned that her voice was tired, too. As her make-up was being applied, Margaret Burke Sheridan came to the dressing room. A photographer

Sir
John Barbirolli

With Margaret Burke Sheridan
in the dressing room, Covent
Garden

caught the wistful smile of the Irish star of the past as she handed a good luck token to the Irish star of the future.

During the performance the audience were so enthusiastic that Barbirolli felt compelled to address them from the rostrum before the beginning of the final act. 'You have spoilt for me the first and third acts of this beautiful opera by applauding in the wrong places,' he said. 'An opera ends when the music ends and not when the singers stop singing. If you have any affection, or should I say respect, for me and the music, you will reserve your applause until the music ends.' The singers hadn't minded the spontaneous applause – they relished it, and for Ronnie it was like being in the steamy, exciting atmosphere of Italian opera houses again. However, the English audience was suitably subdued, and

In last night's "Boheme" London gave a warm welcome to a young and attractive Irish soprano, Veronica Dunne, a somewhat shy Mimi, and to Australian-born lyric tenor, John Lanigan, as Rudolph. — J. H. H.

Veronica Dunne, who sang Mimi, receives a good-luck doll from Margaret Sheridan, former international opera star.

As Mimi in *La Bohème*. Covent Garden, 1952

Ronnie honoured by the Irish Club in London

they spared their many and prolonged ovations for the final curtain.

'London gave a warm welcome to the young and attractive Irish soprano, Veronica Dunne, a somewhat shy Mimi, and to Australian-born lyric tenor, John Lanigan, as Rudolph', observed the *Daily Graphic* of 20 November. The critic in the *Daily Telegraph* commented that: 'Covent Garden had an outstanding Mimi in Veronica Dunne, a newcomer from Ireland. Her voice, which she uses with taste and intelligence, has a charming lyrical freshness and in the top registers a generous dramatic quality. John Lanigan was a well-matched Rudolph, with a firm sweet tone and easy delivery.'

The Times was not so enamoured. Sir John Barbirolli was 'very well aware that he had a small-voiced cast, and it is to his great credit that his careful balance allowed so many of the words to come over .... Mimi, in the person of Miss Veronica Dunne, had most cause to be grateful for his tact, for though her voice was pleasant in quality it was not big enough for this theatre even for one simulating an affliction of the lungs. Her intonation was not impeccable, and neither her dress nor her manner was endearing enough to justify Rudolph's love at first sight.' Such a critique could be damning but audiences paid scant attention and continued to attend and enjoy the opera, despite extreme weather conditions.

On the evening of 5 December 1952, Ronnie took the train from Herne Hill to Victoria Station to catch the bus for Covent Garden. A noxious smell pervaded the station and caught in her throat, and as she hurried up the steps yellowish black smog was pressing down towards the platforms. When she emerged onto the street, it closed around her like a shroud. She stretched out her arm and her hand disappeared in the murk. She heard a low murmur of voices around her and muffled coughing but she could see nothing. In an eerie, nightmarish world she shuffled forward, groping her way along damp walls and chilled iron railings, gingerly testing for the pavement kerb with her foot. She feared she would become lost to wander around this icy, god-forsaken city for ever.

Even Londoners hardened by many a pea souper in the past were appalled by the dense, acrid fog which blanketed the city. The 'Great Smog of '52' went down in history as the worst air pollution event in Britain. Buses and ambulances were forced off the streets, cars were abandoned, work ceased, and it was later estimated that thousands of people died prematurely from respiratory failure during those four, awful days.

The fog invaded the theatre. It was not the first or the last time that performances were so affected, but it was the worst. From the stage Ronnie could not see the conductor, just a thin wavy beam from a light attached to his baton. The only chance of keeping accurate time was by watching the prompter in his box at the front of stage as he followed the conductor's beat and relayed it to the singers. Ronnie hoped that with the aid of floodlights, the intrepid audience could actually view the opera.

It was in these difficult circumstances that Ronnie had one of the busiest seasons of her life for she had commitments in both London and Dublin and had to fly back and forth between the two cities. On 5, 13 and 22 December she appeared in *La Bohème* at Covent Garden. On 3, 8 and 12 December she sang Suzel in Mascagni's *L'amico Fritz* at the Gaiety Theatre. Uncertainty about flying and the fog was stressful, but she thrived on the work.

In Dublin, her partner was the Italian tenor Alvinio Misciano whose charm and lyricism were ideally suited to the romantic comedy. The conductor was none other than Giuseppe Morelli, whom she had diplomatically rejected as a singing teacher all those years ago in Rome. 'Did you ever catch that train?' he asked when they met again. 'No maestro,' she laughed, 'but you got the message!'

Later that month she joined Dutch tenor Frans Vroons for a recital at the Olympia Theatre, where they and their accompanist, Kitty O'Callaghan, were given such a warm reception they gladly sang encore after encore.

'Did you ever catch that train?' Ronnie as Suzel in Mascagni's *L'amico Fritz* at the Gaiety Theatre with (from left) Noel Reid, Gianella Borelli (Ronnie's friend from Rome), the Italian tenor Alvinio Misciano, conductor Giuseppe Morelli, Veronica Dunne, Arturo La Porta and Brendan Cavanagh

A quiet Christmas at home was exactly what Ronnie needed. It was only as she stepped away from the exhilaration of auditions and training, rehearsals and performance that she realised how draining the last year had been. She had a mere week to recharge her energies, for in January another extraordinary challenge with Covent Garden lay ahead.

Peter telephoned, anxious to take her out before she returned to London. After a meal in the Gresham Hotel, during which he appeared nervous and she talked too much, too quickly, he reached into his pocket and produced a ring that filled the room with sparkles. All the hard work and dedication, all the excitement and successes of her life and career were now completed by this one declaration of love. In a haze of euphoria they drove to his parents for formal approval, and then on to the Dunnes in Clontarf.

In her excitement, Ronnie burst through the front door with the news. 'Mummy,' she exclaimed, 'I'm engaged!'

Josephine's smile froze on her face. She stared at the ring so proudly displayed, at the girl with her shining eyes, at the man hovering behind, then she turned heel and walked out of the hall. The couple were stunned. William quickly ushered them into the sitting room for a celebratory drink. From that moment, Josephine refused to have anything to do with her daughter's wedding plans, or to have any discussions about the forthcoming marriage. Her only tight-lipped comment was that Ronnie was making the biggest mistake of her life.

Orpheus

10

SIR JOHN BARBIROLLI wanted everything to be perfect. Each time he saw his dear friend Kathleen Ferrier, she was a little more frail. She was just forty-one, and there was nothing anyone could do to halt her cancer. This illness was never mentioned in public; only her closest allies knew of it. Her glorious contralto voice was richer than ever, her desire to perform undiminished.

In August 1952 Barbirolli had proposed a plan to fulfil one of her greatest wishes, to sing Orpheus in Gluck's *Orfeo ed Euridice*. Kathleen was entranced by the idea and Barberolli persuaded David Webster of Covent Garden to build an entirely new production around her – a risky venture, considering Kathleen's precarious health. Between their various work commitments, Sir John and Kathleen worked on the score note by note, line by line, and adapted it to an English version entitled *Orpheus*, to be ready for performance in February 1953.

Determined that it should be the finest production Covent Garden could stage, Barbirolli ensured that only the very best people were involved: Frederick Ashton as producer and choreographer; Sophie Fedorovitch as scenery and costumes designer; and for the dance sequences, the Sadler's Wells Ballet with their principal dancer Svetlana Beriosova. The two singers chosen to accompany Kathleen were Adele Leigh as Amor and Veronica Dunne as Euridice.

Early in January, Ronnie returned to London to continue singing in *La Bohème*, to start rehearsals for *Orpheus*, and to show off her new diamond ring. Reaction from the other girls was all she could have hoped with many congratulations and tinges of envy, but when Sir John heard of her plans, he was horrified. She should on no account get married, he said. She was at the beginning of what promised to be a great career. She must be single-minded. Marriage would at best be a distraction, at worst a disaster. She fared no better with David Webster, who was furious. It was he who had discovered her. He had hoped that she would soon be a box office star, a real asset to the company, and here she was, putting it all in jeopardy.

Ronnie was dazed. She had assumed they would be as happy for her as she was for herself. She was in love. She would get married. Why should anything change? Her singing could only be enriched by a fulfilling personal life. Her resolve hardened. They were all so wrong. She would show them.

Kathleen Ferrier's arrival was a red-letter day for the company. Everyone wanted to see her, to hear her, to watch her. She was a tall woman with a most beautiful face, warm dark eyes and sallow skin. She remembered Ronnie immediately and thanked her for her kind comments after the Rome recital. Her good humour, jokes and limericks made every day a pleasure for the cast, none of whom realised she was ill. On one occasion she was knocked to the floor by a lead-weighted curtain, but she picked herself up, and laughed. There were ten rehearsals, and Kathleen strove to be on time for all of them.

Yet the struggle for normal life was becoming increasingly difficult. She attended hospital daily for radium treatment. Severe pain in her back and legs made every movement an agony. Journeys to and from rehearsals along frozen, slippery pavements and up the steps to Covent Garden were torturous. When she stepped on stage, a miracle occurred. As she became rapt in the music, all vestiges of pain were sloughed off and she moved with ease and sang perfectly. But her condition was worsening and there was grave anxiety about whether she would be able to perform. Barbirolli, David Webster and Ferrier's medical consultants knew that to cancel would have broken her heart. Her one goal now was to sing; it was her divine gift and she wanted to use it to the end. They decided to let the production go ahead, but reduced the planned four performances to two, with a two-day break between.

As well as rehearsing, Ronnie was on stage pouring her soul into Mimi. Never had she felt more in control, more in sympathy with the little seamstress. Her own happiness deepened her appreciation for Mimi's longing and despair and her performances that January produced rave reviews. These gave her the confidence to approach Christopher West about Act 4. Under his direction, as Mimi lay dying on the bed, Rudolph pulled the curtains and remained on the other side of the stage. Ronnie felt it would be more effective if he were close by the bed. She happened to mention Margaret Burke Sheridan, and the change was made.

Preparations for *Orpheus* were going well. The sets and costumes that Sophie Fedorovitch had designed were classically Grecian and simple. Barbirolli was delighted with the cohesion between the three singers and with the artistry of the Sadler's Wells Ballet. After a dress rehearsal with Svetlana Beriosova, he bounded up on stage exclaiming, 'Perfecto! Perfecto!'

Tuesday, 3 February 1953. Just before the performance, Ronnie and Adele were touched by Kathleen's thoughtfulness as she gave each of them good luck presents of Arpège perfume. The auditorium was filled to capacity, and from the first few notes the audience was swept up in Gluck's melodic music, the ballet and the singers. As they took their curtain calls, Ronnie and Adele had been so enraptured by the supreme quality of Kathleen's voice that they stood to either side of her and joined in the tumultuous applause. A review in *Opera* magazine noted that the 'natural beauty' of Kathleen Ferrier's voice 'is supported by so high a musical and dramatic intelligence that she expresses the very heart of the Orpheus legend, the poignancy of human loss on the one hand and the consoling power of music on the other, in terms of the purest vocal and theatrical art' (March 1953).

Friday, 6 February 1953. Kathleen was unusually sombre before the performance. David Webster and her physician hovered in the

As Euridice with Kathleen Ferrier (Orpheus), Adele Leigh (Amor) and the Sadler's Wells Ballet Company. Covent Garden, 1953

Ronnie with Kathleen
Ferrier in *Orpheus*

wings, but the first act went without a hitch. During the second act, however, Ronnie realised that something was very wrong. Instead of taking her correct position, Kathleen was leaning against a piece of scenery and singing from there. Disregarding her own stage directions, Ronnie moved to her side.

'Ronnie,' she whispered, 'I can't stand the pain.' Ronnie held out her hand, palm upwards in the classical manner. Kathleen gripped her arm. With that support, she was able to drag her leg along and leave the stage on cue. In the wings, the pain was so intense that she vomited, but her determination pushed her back to finish the opera. When it was over, she collapsed in agony. Her physician could do little but give her a shot of morphine. With the help of Ronnie and Adele she insisted on returning to the stage to take her final bow and was showered with flowers and wave upon wave of standing ovations. The audience had no idea of the real life tragedy that was taking place; they knew only that they loved their Kath and her mesmerising voice.

Kathleen's skeletal structure had been compromised by the cancer. During the performance a fragment of bone had splintered from her femur, causing excruciating pain. But from her hospital bed she laughingly told the nurses to make her well quickly so that she could get back to work.

Kathleen Ferrier never sang in public again.

Touring with the Company

11

A FTER *Orpheus* Ronnie went into rehearsals for an upcoming tour of the provinces with the Covent Garden Opera Company, yet the memory of Kathleen Ferrier in such agony haunted her. The cast sent messages for a speedy recovery to the hospital, and there was talk of plans to present the final two performances of the opera in April when she had recovered.

Susanna in Mozart's *The Marriage of Figaro* was a new role for Ronnie. She and Joan Sutherland, cast as Countess Almaviva, worked hard on their preparations. Ronnie was also engaged to reprise her roles as Sophie in *Rosenkavalier* and as Mimi. Here she was on sure ground, for the recent production of *La Bohème* had generated unstinted praise. Hugh Reid, erudite critic of opera and ballet writing as H.S.R., presented a well-considered account of the cast and the Company in the January 1953 edition of the influential journal *Musical Opinion*:

It is seldom indeed that we have a performance of *La Bohème* in which the part of Mimi is so ideally cast as it is in this season's production at Covent Garden. In Veronica Dunne, from Dublin, the character is personified. It is a shy, yet curiously authoritative reliving of the fragile role and it was a commentary on Miss Dunne's complete identification of herself with Mimi that the other members of the cast adopted an unusually protective attitude towards her. Their initial interest became a concerned regard for her well-being. The anxiety and grief in the final act seemed not at all simulated. Indeed I do not recollect this scene ever having a sharper poignancy. On the break in the score, at the point of Mimi's death, the whole audience seemed to be involved, so utter was the few moments' silence. There were other instances throughout the course of the opera where the sincerity of the performance steadied the tendency there always is in *La Bohème* for a situation or passing incident to tremble on the brink of bathos. But the final scene, coming at the climax of the opera as it does, and so being the most precarious, was made real and dramatic to a degree that is seldom our lot to experience.

Sir John Barbirolli, who conducted, had much to do with this sensitivity. He scaled the orchestral volume to the intimacy of the performance on the stage. The voices were never submerged. They came across unforced and clearly articulated. Even Miss Dunne's tendency to reduce her tone amount at times to the merest whisper was respected as heightening the dramatic tension.

Just ten days after *Orpheus*, Ronnie was in Cardiff at the start of a nine-week tour that took in the cities of Edinburgh, Glasgow, Liverpool and Manchester. She had been invited to join the Company on a tour to Bulawayo, Rhodesia in July, but she declined; she had other plans for that month.

Mounting a tour required meticulous planning with all the disparate pieces slotted together like a giant jigsaw. An initial itinerary was sketched out, and venues considered for their ability to stage full-scale productions with the necessary scenery docks, wardrobe space and dressing room accommodation for a large company. Availability of the theatres had to be ascertained and dates arranged to fit in with the planned route. Unlike a play or musical which is the same every night, an opera season, if only for a week, changes its programme, sets, cast, costumes and score for each alternating performance. The logistics of loading and unloading scenery and costumes for at least two productions in every city were enormous. A single performance can involve anything up to four changes of scenery, two hundred separate costumes with jewellery and accessories for three different acts, and props and furnishings, all to be transported by rail or trucks. About twenty-four stage staff, including sceneshifters, lighting and sound technicians (and requisite equipment), electricians and wardrobe assistants travelled with the principals and chorus. The orchestra alone could have sixty members. A couple of hundred people might be on the move from one city to the next, and train or bus journeys had to be booked. At each destination individuals had to sort out and pay for their own digs, which invariably turned out to be less than salubrious, and in some instances no more than dives.

A suitable selection of operas needed to be agreed. As soon as a production ended in one city, everything had to be loaded up and sent out to the next city on its particular itinerary. Several productions could be touring the country at the same time. In addition to *La Bohème*, *The Marriage of Figaro* and *Der Rosenkavalier*, the Covent Garden Spring tour featured *Tristan and Isolde*, *Fidelio*, *Aida*, *A Masked Ball* and *Il Trovatore* – all huge, popular operas with massive sets. Six conductors shared the musical direction: Sir John Barbirolli, Emanuel Young,

Peter Gellhorn, Vilém Tauský, Reginald Goodall and James Gibson. At the Palace Theatre, Manchester, Ronnie's performance came under the spotlight in the *Daily Telegraph* on 25 March 1953:

> Veronica Dunne, as Mimi, and John Lanigan, Rudolph, shared the triumph of the evening, catching all the high lyricism as well as the tragedy of the romance – and not only in the famous love duets. Jess Walters, Inia Te Wiata, and Geraint Evans sang and acted all the shades of characters which can so easily be just types. What a splendid voice has Inia Te Wiata. Hella Toros sang with rare mischief in the street café scene, which was all life and movement.

It may have been all life and movement on stage, but it was a gruelling schedule for the cast. On performance days a good meal at lunchtime had to sustain them until after the show, when they might meet for supper, but they were all financially hard up and often exhausted. Ronnie, however, ran on pure adrenalin and was always ready for a get-together and her co-star, John Lanigan, tried valiantly to keep up with her.

In the middle of April, Ronnie joined Sir John Barbirolli and the Hallé Orchestra on a tour of Cork, Limerick, Waterford and Dublin with *Messiah*. Her co-soloists were contralto Kathleen Joyce and tenor William Herbert. The bass was Marian Nowakowski, famed for singing 'The strumpet shall sound' until he was quietly informed of his error. Sir John had high praise for the singers and Our Lady's Choral Society, whom he held in great regard. After the final performance in the Theatre Royal, Dublin on 25 April, Ronnie had some time to attend to a pressing matter – her wedding plans.

Peter's parents were dubious about their son's choice for a wife – it did not seem proper for a girl to be on the stage. The McCarthys owned O'Dea & Co. Ltd., famous for Odearest Mattresses. They had given each of their children a house upon their marriage and Peter was to be no exception. In the absence of Ronnie (another black mark) mother and son inspected many homes suitable for a family before settling on 37 Bushy Park Road in the Dublin suburb of Rathgar. It was a Victorian, red brick, four-bedroomed house in an excellent location, with a large and sunny rear garden. Over the years it had been neglected and was in poor condition, but when Ronnie was brought to see it she was thrilled. She asked her father to have a look. William cast his expert eye over the property and deemed it solid and well built – it would make a fine home for his Ronnie. As his wedding present, he undertook to refurbish and redecorate the house from top to bottom. It was all very exciting.

But there was trouble at home. Josephine refused to discuss any arrangements with Ronnie; in fact, she stopped talking to her altogether, such was her disapproval. She felt Ronnie was throwing away the career in which they had all invested so much time, effort and money because it would not be possible for her to continue working and have a happy marriage. But she knew the iron will of her daughter; there was no point trying to get her to see reason.

Peter was concerned that if the press got to hear about the wedding of their favourite opera star, it would rapidly turn into a circus. They approached the priest in the local parish church with a strange request – could they arrive for the ceremony the moment the church doors opened? Ronnie went shopping on her own for her wedding dress and trousseau before her return to Covent Garden. The day she flew to London she was in F.X. Buckley's, on Moore Street, buying rashers and sausages, black puddings and thick steaks.

Kathleen Ferrier, with her friend and carer, Bernie, had recently moved to a ground floor flat in St John's Wood. One afternoon in May, Ronnie stood outside the flat with two laden bags, packed with food guaranteed to build someone up after illness. She rang the bell and Bernie came to the door. She was glad to see her, but said Kathleen had had a very bad night and was not up to visitors. As Ronnie handed over Buckley's finest fare, she heard a voice float down the hall. 'Is that Euridice? Please send in my little Euridice.' But Bernie sadly shook her head. It was with a heavy heart that Ronnie turned away. A few days later she received a note from Kathleen thanking her for her thoughtfulness.

Kathleen Ferrier died on 8 October 1953.

Honeymoon

12

Veronica Dunne married Peter McCarthy in her local parish church, the Church of St. Vincent de Paul, Marino, Fairview on 1 July 1953 at 7.30 in the morning. She wore an elegant white suit with a pillbox hat and a single strand of pearls at her neck. Her simple bouquet was far removed from the elaborate arrangements delivered to her dressing room.

Peter and Ronnie after their wedding in July 1953

Ronnie off on her
honeymoon. At the airport
with her father and mother

After the ceremony, Ronnie and her new husband Peter were driven to the Shelbourne Hotel, Dublin, where they enjoyed their wedding breakfast (literally) with fifty guests in the Adam's Suite. Disgruntled journalists were not allowed upstairs to take photographs, and the couple slipped out of the hotel early to catch a midday flight on the new de Havilland Comet aircraft to fly to London and on to Rome.

Ronnie had married into a family whose name was synonymous with a good night's sleep. In 1893 Peter's great-grandfather, Michael O'Dea, established an Irish bed-making factory in Limerick, aptly named Odearest (O'Dea Rest). The company quickly expanded and by 1904 set up a new factory on Stafford Street (now Wolfe Tone Street) in Dublin. Michael O'Dea's daughter, Margaret, married Peter McCarthy (Peter's grandfather) whose family had a successful furniture shop in Limerick. In time, Peter became Managing Director of the firm and brought his two sons, Denis and Peter, on board. Denis took over the furniture and mattress department and Peter was responsible for floor coverings.

During the 1940s and 1950s the company raised its profile by launching a series of witty cartoons in the press, many of which featured on the back of the Gaiety Theatre programmes in which Ronnie appeared. One of the most famous of these portrays the mythical emblem of Odearest, Mrs O'Dea, using a trusty Odearest mattress to conceal her life savings. The slogan reads: 'Odearest, put your money in a good mattress'.

The mattress on the wedding night almost caused a rift before the marriage had even begun. Monsignor O'Flaherty met them at the airport, and teased Ronnie about her four suitcases to Peter's two. He left the couple at the Flora Hotel on Via Veneto where Ronnie had made a booking. The bellboy struggled with the four heavy suitcases Ronnie simply could not travel without, and a further two belonging to Peter, then he showed them up to a room with two single beds on opposite walls. Peter looked at Ronnie and exclaimed, 'What in the name of Jesus have they done?' She was so angry she phoned down to the desk demanding, 'Where is the matrimonial bed?' 'Madam,' replied the receptionist, 'why don't you position the two beds together?' They took themselves off to dinner in a huff, but by the time they got back a more congenial arrangement had been put in place and all was forgotten.

Their days in Italy were filled with love and feasting, sparring and

sightseeing and getting to know each other. In Rome, Ronnie delighted in displaying her new husband to old friends, and in showing off her fluent Italian and ease with foreign ways to Peter. They dined with the Monsignor, who arranged for them to have an audience with the Pope, and on one beautiful day he took them out to Villa d'Este on Lake Como in his old truck.

Then it was off to Capri for two weeks – a very different Capri from the one that Ronnie and Molly had experienced in 1948. No warships in the harbour, the water was drinkable, and the Grand Hotel Quisisana now fully lived up to its opulent name. In glorious sunshine the couple strolled through the town, and hired a canoe for a leisurely trip round the bay, but with Peter in the back paddling manfully and Ronnie in the front acting like a girl they went around in circles getting more and more furious until finally putting the oars to good use by splashing each other. Neither realised that the boat was filling with water, and as they neared Canzone del Mare it started to sink. Only then did Ronnie discover that Peter couldn't swim. She grabbed hold of him and was pulled under momentarily, but they eventually scrambled onto dry land, exhausted.

Peter had been warned about sunburn, but not for him the hat or the cream and his head turned red as a ripe tomato. Ronnie slathered him in Calamine Lotion, and then laughed uproariously because he looked like a ghost! From Capri there were excursions up the coast to Pompeii and Herculaneum and to the pretty town of Amalfi on the Gulf of Salerno. They got chatting with two men who were travelling around Europe and Peter, always a man's man, was glad to share a few pints and a smoke with them.

The four got on so well they journeyed back to Rome together and went out on the town with the Monsignor and his friend, Monsignor Ryan. The couple were due to return to Dublin, but decided at the last minute that Venice was a must-see. They cancelled their flight from Ciampino, and arranged to catch up later with their new acquaintances, who were going on to Munich.

Peter alighted from the train in Venice and hailed a gondola to convey them in style to the legendary Hotel Danieli. All six suitcases were loaded up, but as the gondolier pushed away from the moorings, the boat started to list. Off he hopped quick as a flash, pulled the boat to the side, threw the cases on the boardwalk and left them, stranded. Nothing for it but to walk all the way to the Danieli. Grumbling about thieves and Italy and women and luggage and Ronnie, Peter seized two of the heavy cases and walked about fifty yards while she stayed behind. He left them to go back for the others, passing Ronnie as she traipsed by carrying two of the lighter ones.

She minded the cases while he returned with the last two and struggled on a further fifty yards before leaving them to go back for the first two, again passing Ronnie, who ignored his choice and expressive comments with her nose in the air. This merry dance lasted all the way to the hotel and Peter was fit to be tied. He was finding out that his wife had the spirit of a lion and the stubbornness of a mule and there was more to this marriage lark than he could ever have imagined. So that was Venice.

The train journey through the German countryside was sobering, with so much devastation, so many destitute people. Munich itself had been virtually flattened; the only statue of note left standing was the Virgin Mary in Marienplatz. They met their friends and went out to see one of the few remaining tourist attractions in the area – the *Hofbräuhaus* brewery where Adolf Hitler had declared National Socialist policies and held functions in its famous beer hall.

With five weeks of exhilarating honeymoon behind them, it was back to Dublin and all the excitement of the new shiny house and the start of their life together. Although it had never been discussed, Ronnie and Peter assumed that their separate lives would continue in much the same way as before they were married. Both were in for a shock.

13 Marriage and beyond

Do you ever feel warmly towards someone you have never met? You see their picture, perhaps, in a paper, and you hope that they will live happily ever after. That was the feeling I had today when I read that Veronica Dunne was to be an Easter bride, though it would mean giving up her career.

Immediately, my mind went back to an evening last autumn at Covent Garden, when a young and attractive Irish singer received an ovation for her rendering of the rôle of Mimi.

Covent Garden at last! What wouldn't the future hold in store? Yet she is prepared to give it all up, the tremendous sacrifices, in money, time and concentrated effort, to settle down, instead, like any other housewife.

Do I make it sound dull? How stupid of me. I meant it to sound glorious, for that is what I think it is ... a glorious gesture on the part of this girl with the wide-set eyes, the gentle expression, who had the world of opera at her feet.

And although we have never met, Veronica Dunne, may I, as one of your cheering audience that night at Covent Garden, congratulate you even more warmly now on the rôle you have chosen to play in the future.

I am sure you will never regret it. Good Luck. You have earned it.

GODFREY WINN, *Woman's Illustrated Magazine, March 1953*

 EACH MORNING, Ronnie drove Peter to work. She returned home to direct the maid on tidying the house. After lunch she went down to the shops to buy food for dinner. She prepared the meal and went to collect Peter at five. They dined at seven. Both enjoyed having company in and they often entertained. Peter resumed his social life with his pals. During the day, Ronnie tried to make herself busy, but she caught herself watching the clock as it ticked down the hours. When she found she was pregnant, the McCarthys were delighted.

Caterina Mancini was singing Leonora in Verdi's *Force of Destiny* with the DGOS in December. After the wonderful performance, Ronnie, heavily pregnant, went backstage to greet her old friend from Rome. She bumped into Margaret Burke Sheridan, who looked her up and down. 'So that's what you've been doing with yourself,' she sniffed. 'Well, that's the end of your career!'

Peter Bernard McCarthy was born in Gaffney's Nursing Home, Earlsfort Terrace, Dublin on 10 April 1954. Ronnie had very much wanted to call the baby Hugh after Monsignor Hugh O'Flaherty, but the McCarthys wished to continue the tradition of naming the first-born son Peter. The baby had to be christened within four days of birth. Ronnie was bitterly disappointed when the matron would not allow her to leave the nursing home for the occasion. She watched from the window as Peter and the family left for the church with little Peter. Her first question on their return was, 'Did he cry?'

Champagne and flowers, a layer from the wedding cake sliced and diced, her beaming husband, sister May and satisfied grandparents grouped around the bed, talking, laughing. Ronnie was momentarily outside the chatter, with a tiny, vulnerable infant in her arms. But she was not alone, not yet. As was the custom, her maternity nurse, Nurse Yates, would accompany herself and the child back to Bushy Park for a two-week settling-in period before resuming her duties at the nursing home. As in all moments of anxiety, Ronnie told herself to breathe, and she looked up at her father and smiled.

In September, it was with amusement tinged with irony that Ronnie read that she was one of nine people recognised by the *Irish Press* as 'Women who put Ireland on the map!' Novelist Kate O'Brien, dress designer Sybil Connolly, stained-glass artist Evie Hone, film star Maureen O'Sullivan, BBC announcer Noelle Middleton, model Anne Gunning, actress Siobhan McKenna and ballet director Ninette de Valois all shared this distinction with Ronnie, who was cited as having shot to international status as an opera singer. Meanwhile, she was desperately trying to find work.

She could not approach Covent Garden where her copybook had been well and truly blotted, but she picked up some radio broadcasts. She had performed just once on stage since her marriage, at a Sunday concert in the Gaiety Theatre, but it wasn't until October 1954 that the work started to roll in with a couple of Radio Éireann Prom Concerts in the Gaiety with conductor Milan Horvat. In November and December she was delighted to appear with the DGOS again in a well-produced *La Bohème* by Harry Powell-Lloyd where she was partnered by English tenor Walter Midgley. The *Evening Herald* commented that 'As Mimi she sang with exquisite ease, and inflected the part with much feeling'. She alternated these four performances

with four as Micaëla in *Carmen* with Marianna Radev and Jess Walters – just the sort of work she craved. She was back! And when she was invited to join The Irish Festival Singers on a tour of Canada and the United States she leapt at it.

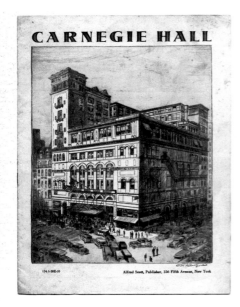

Peter was shocked – how could she leave him and her nine-month-old son at home for a whole three months while she went gadding about the United States? He did all in his powers to dissuade her, but Ronnie was adamant. She had already approached Nurse Yates about taking up a permanent position as nanny and there was a housekeeper who could cook. No one would go hungry or neglected; all would be cared for. Peter could come out to join her for a holiday and bring the baby with him. She pointed at the itinerary. Two words leapt off the page: Carnegie Hall. It was the chance of a lifetime.

January 1955. The tour got off to a shaky start in St. John's, Newfoundland – the very extremity of Canada, reputed to be the foggiest, windiest, cloudiest city in the country. The reputation is well earned and a howling gale kept many theatre-goers away, but, according to a local newspaper, *The Journal,* those who braved the storm were well rewarded with Irish folksongs, ballads and melodies and 'heartily enjoyed every minute of the excellent concert'.

Director and accompanist, Kitty O'Callaghan, chose the programme. She wanted to avoid the hackneyed old songs like 'Mother Machree' and 'Macushla', which belong in the English music hall. Instead, she wished to showcase the rich heritage of Irish music penned by such composers as Charles Villiers Stanford, Thomas Moore, John F. Larchet, Hamilton Harty and Arnold Bax. Kitty arranged much of the music herself with a sure touch, making use of the virtuosity of Terry O'Connor on both violin and harp. A long-playing record with fifteen of the most popular songs was produced by Angel Records of New York to accompany the tour.

Great attention was paid to the presentation of the singers on stage. This was to be no motley crew of choristers, but a fully trained, professional ensemble of the finest talent Ireland had to offer. One of Ireland's foremost dress designers, Irene Gilbert, was commissioned to create gowns for the ladies. It was decided to have identical dresses accented by green, with Kitty's and Ronnie's distinguished by a slightly different treatment. For the second act the ladies wore different identical dresses, with Ronnie wearing a specially designed green gown to reflect her status as soloist. The men's wardrobe was easier – smart black evening suits, bow ties, and a kerchief tucked just so into the breast pocket.

The Irish Festival Singers with Ronnie in dark silk gown and Kitty O'Callaghan in white.

From Newfoundland the company travelled through major cities in Canada before catching a train to Illinois. The *Peoria Star* gave a flavour of the show in their town:

> Five women, six men, the accompanist-director and the violinist who doubles at the Irish harp make up the little company, one that is rich in talent, full of spirit, nicely polished as to style, modest and pleasingly gracious in manner. Such small but effective details as the portrait-like composure in which the women sat while not singing added greatly to the whole memorable picture on the stage. In the generous programme of 31 numbers, there was plenty for everyone to enjoy, from the most familiar Irish whimsy to rollicking songs not heard here before, from traditional ballads sung in Gaelic to others whose every word the audience knew, from wondrous art songs by Ireland's contemporary composers to such hardly traceable old ones as 'Danny Boy' and 'The Palatine's Daughter'.... Dramatic soprano Veronica Dunne, featured throughout, was at her best in Sir Hamilton Harty's setting of 'Sea Wrack', in 'Padraic the Fiddler' done with violin obbligato, and in 'The Last Rose of Summer', sung not just as we know it from von Flotow's 'Martha' but as the Irish have it direct from Thomas Moore .... Each soloist was right for his spot – romantic tenor Dermot Troy particularly in 'My Dark Rosaleen', baritone Austin Gaffney in 'The Wake Feast' and (how different!) 'The Garden Where the Praties Grow', James Cuthbert with his fine bass in 'Father O'Flynn', and high tenor Liam Devally in 'Sile ni ghadhra' and 'Ceann dubh dilis' with the harp.

Chicago, Detroit, Wilmington, Baltimore, Pittsburgh, St. Louis, on and on and on they travelled by bus, as much as four hundred miles a day (all that Equity allowed) to cover the vast distances between the major cities of the eastern United States. A flurry of favourable reviews followed them but Ronnie couldn't help thinking that some of the old ex pats were a mite disappointed not to hear a roistering jig and the old songs of Erin. Everywhere the concerts were a sell-out. In St. Louis they sang to an audience of 3,500 and in Pittsburgh the theatre was thronged.

Ronnie, Austin, Dermot, Liam, James, Kitty and Terry were joined by Sylvia O'Brien, Claire Kelleher, Celestine Kelly, Ethna McGrath, Thomas O'Sullivan (Tomás Ó Súilleabháin) and Arthur Agnew, all noted for their fine voices and musical training, and by Dermot Troy and Ethna McGrath, who were actually on their honeymoon.

Each morning at six o'clock the troupe piled on the bus to go to the next venue. A manager, Eric Zuckerman, had been hired by the promoter to ease their way, attend to any glitches and arrange hotel accommodation. He was a good-humoured man, but he would insist on smoking in the bus, which drove them all mad. They often gave six performances a week, two on Sunday if they were overbooked, and in each city the welcoming committee and sponsors were keen to demonstrate their appreciation by arranging dinners and parties after the show. No matter how weary, the singers had to be friendly and obliging – they were ambassadors for the Irish nation. Sometimes they didn't get to bed until the small hours, and then it was up and on the road again at first light.

Homesickness was simply not in Ronnie's vocabulary. She had been coming and going since she was nineteen and she was now a mature woman of twenty-eight, but she found she was lonely for her little son, and guilty at having left him. She was avid for news of him in her phone calls to Peter, and everywhere she went she was always on the lookout for clothes and toys for him and presents for everyone. Before long she had to buy yet another suitcase to take all the stuff she had bought. It was stowed in the hold of the bus with everyone else's purchases. America was so bright and brash and full of fabulous things after the grey austerity of Ireland.

In Washington she went shopping in Macy's and bought a cocktail dress for a reception that night. It was a dashing little number with a cerise bodice, no sleeves and a two-tone silk taffeta skirt. At the party the prim hostess commented that she must be cold and offered the use of a jacket, perhaps, or a cardigan? A cardigan! Ronnie politely declined. Men kept coming over to chat and the hostess approached again: was she sure she didn't want that cardigan? Ronnie was quite sure.

Carnegie Hall is renowned as the most prestigious concert venue not only in New York but in the entire United States. It is a monumental structure that dominates Seventh Avenue. Inside, the Main Hall is enormously high and seats 2,800 on five levels served by elevators. Ronnie wandered through the lobbies and corridors gazing on the photographs of some of the composers and musicians who had performed there: Pyotr Ilyich Tchaikovsky; Nellie Melba; Pablo Casals; Richard Strauss; Arthur Rubinstein; John McCormack; Jascha Heifetz; Enrico Caruso; George Gershwin; Igor Stravinsky; Marian Anderson; Paul Robeson; Arturo Toscanini; Benny Goodman; Duke Ellington; Leonard Bernstein; Andrés Segovia; Ella Fitzgerald; Louis Armstrong; Billie Holiday. It was a daunting roll call.

On 28 January 1955, the Benefit Concert for the New York Foundling Hospital sponsored by His Eminence Francis Cardinal Spellman and featuring The Irish Festival Singers, was a huge success. In the audience with the Cardinal were: Robert F. Wagner,

Mayor of the City of New York; John J. Hearne, Irish Ambassador; Paul Keating, Irish Consul-General; and a very special guest – Countess Lily McCormack, widow of the Irish tenor. The *Irish Times* account of the event was glowing:

> Veronica Dunne filled the Carnegie Hall in New York in two senses of the word – there was a packed house, numbers being turned away, and her voice carried through the large building beautifully. The enthusiasm for the singers was, according to the Americans themselves, of an order rarely seen in New York.

For Ronnie, one of the most telling moments of the evening occurred during her rendition of Hamilton Harty's 'Sea Wrack'. Just as she was reaching the haunting and dramatic finale of the piece – '*Him beneath the salt sea, me upon the shore, By sunlight or moonlight we'll lift the wrack no more. The dark wrack, The sea wrack, The wrack may drift ashore*' – she caught the eye of a real Irish farmer type with a jaunty cap in the front row who hollered, 'Would ya ever sing "Killarney"?' It was all she could do not to roar laughing.

She had trouble with laughter in Chicago, too. The Irish Festival Singers were booked for *The Ed Sullivan Show*, broadcast live on CBS television every Sunday night to 14 million viewers. This was a special 'Toast of the Town' show staged on the CBS ice rink in Chicago staring the Ice Capades, a travelling ice-skating spectacular.

Ed Sullivan took one look at Ronnie and declared her hair was too dark for black and white television. A couple of days before the show she was sent off to an exclusive hairdresser, Michel of Paris, who drenched her hair in Peroxide bleach before it was dyed. It blistered her scalp and turned her hair so white she was dubbed Harpo Marx. The next day she returned for the dye, and had to endure the torture of rollers and a scorching hairdryer before emerging as a blonde. The dye had to be continually touched up for the duration of the tour.

On 13 March 1955 the Ice Capades were joined by a trick unicyclist, a skaters' badminton match, 'Peg Leg' Bates the one-legged tap dancer, child acrobats, and Danish entertainer Victor Borge, for whom a piano was wheeled onto the ice. One of his most popular routines was playing a weird-sounding tune and becoming increasingly confused until he got the bright idea of turning the score around. As familiar classical music emanated from the piano, he flashed a smile of triumph to the audience – he'd been playing it backwards.

Ronnie's sides ached from laughing, which was not good as the Festival Singers were on next. Victor Borge finished to wild applause. Kitty and her troupe shuffled onto the ice trying not to disgrace themselves by falling over. Ed Sullivan had chosen four of the most

'Irishy' songs in their repertoire to appeal to his audience. Dermot Troy and James Cuthbert each did a number, there was an ensemble piece, and Ronnie brought the house down with 'Danny Boy'.

After the show, it was back in the bus and on the road again to the next venue. The Singers were away for twelve weeks, and it was too long. The journeys were punishing, the well-intentioned hospitality exhausting, and any money they had earned had largely been spent on gifts. After all the plaudits and acclaim, it was a relieved and weary bunch who finally arrived in Dublin Airport. Ronnie was touched to see Peter and her father-in-law there to meet her. She tried to attract their attention, but they were scanning the other singers; they hadn't recognised the blonde in their midst.

Home. She gave her son a big hug, then threw open the cases. As toys and presents spilled out onto the floor Peter grinned. 'Well,' he said, 'that's certainly bribery with corruption!' Back with her family in her lovely house, it all felt so good, so right, and with work lined up for concerts and the winter season with the DGOS, she thought yes, this is how it should be; this is my life.

14

The trouble with Hoffmann

*I*N THE TWENTY-TWO DAYS leading up to 17 December 1955, Ronnie performed fourteen times on the Gaiety stage with the DGOS. She was singing the main soprano role in each of their three productions: Leoncavallo's *Pagliacci*, Gounod's *Faust*, and Puccini's *La Bohème*.

The part of Nedda in *Pagliacci* was a new challenge for Ronnie, although she had studied it with her coaches in Rome. As rehearsals progressed, it quickly became one of her favourite roles. Here was a young girl in love with life, a bit of a flirt and full of fun, with an old husband and a young lover. The music was gorgeous and so was Nedda. The plot, based on a true story, is a play within a play about infidelity and jealousy. A small troupe of actors led by Canio, Nedda's husband, arrives in a village. They set up a stage (and therefore a stage upon a stage) to present a play in which Pagliaccio the clown (acted by Canio), is cuckolded by his wife, (acted by Nedda). Canio himself is consumed by the suspicion that his wife is having an affair. As the opera unfolds, the line between fact and fiction blurs. Canio/Pagliaccio demands to know the name of his wife's lover. When she refuses to tell him, he loses all control and, in a blind rage, stabs his wife. Ronnie added her own symbolic touch by collapsing against a table and, instead of dying on the fake stage, she rolled onto the real stage to die – the line between fantasy and fact has been fatally breached. At this point, Nedda's lover rushes on stage and he, too, is killed by Canio. The audience (the chorus) are horrified to realise that they have just witnessed a double murder. Canio turns to them and proclaims the play's now prophetic last line: *La commedia è finita!* – 'The comedy is finished!'

The role of Canio was played brilliantly by the Italian tenor Antonio Annaloro, and Ronnie responded in kind with a stirring performance. 'The pathetic Nedda was sung with touching sincerity by Veronica Dunne,' wrote the *Evening Herald*, 'and she acted with great effect in the closing scenes – a considerable test of the soprano's dramatic powers.'

The *Faust* production was a disappointment, however. The stage sets were dull, the props tired and only the outstanding performance of Michael Langdon as Mephistopheles garnered critical praise. *La Bohème* fared better. English tenor Charles Craig was one of the best Rodolfo's Ronnie ever worked with, and he was on great form. With Peter Glossop as Schaunard and Ronald Lewis as Marcel, the four main singers charmed Gaiety audiences.

Ending on this high note, Ronnie was happy to have a Christmas at home with her two Peters.

Early in 1956, Ronnie received a call from Covent Garden. Would she be available to sing Micaëla in *Carmen* with the Canadian tenor Jon Vickers on tour with the Company in April? Her relief was profound – perhaps her 'great mistake' had been forgiven. Although five months pregnant with her second child, Ronnie was so slight that no one noticed, and she delighted large audiences in Liverpool and Manchester.

Veronica Mary McCarthy was born on 15 August 1956. She didn't remain Veronica for long, however. Annie, the McCarthy's maid, was much taken with the baby and cooed over her cot, 'Ah, you're a little pet; a little judyjudyjudy', and Judy she became, her official names forgotten.

Ronnie welcomed the opportunity to spend more time at home for the next year. Nurse Yates was replaced by Margaret McCann, a wonderful nanny whom both children, especially Judy, adored.

Yet it was impossible to resist the siren call of music. Over the winter Ronnie studied the scores for two new works at the house, and made frequent forays to the apartment of her friend Kitty O'Callaghan on Baggot Street. Not only was Kitty a superb accompanist, she was also an excellent coach. Whenever Ronnie had to tackle something new, it was Kitty she turned to for advice. Together they rehearsed the *Four Last Songs* by Richard Strauss and Mahler's *Symphony No. 4* for soprano and orchestra. Ronnie always remembered Hubert Rooney's injunction to listen to the music, to be prepared and poised to come in on time, and Kitty was especially helpful in playing the orchestral accompaniments that preceded each of her entrances. This preparation paid dividends during the performance of Mahler's symphony on 17 February 1957 at the Gaiety Theatre. In one section, a twelve-bar phrase is repeated before the soprano sings, but conductor Milan Horvat indicated that Ronnie should come in after the first phrase. Ronnie, certain in her knowledge, waited until the repeat. Afterwards, Horvat was most gracious in thanking her for averting a disaster.

That same month, Ronnie received an invitation to tour with Covent Garden for performances of Mimi in *La Bohème*, three in Cardiff, two in Manchester and three in Southampton, during March and April. She gladly accepted, knowing that she would have ample time to prepare for the work by Richard Strauss.

At the age of eighty-three, German-born Richard Strauss, conductor and composer of songs, operas and symphonies, famous for *Der Rosenkavalier* and *Also Sprach Zarathustra*, became fascinated with a poem by Joseph von Eichendorff, 'Im Abendrot' ('At sunset':) *We have through sorrow and joy gone hand in hand; From our wanderings, let's now rest in this quiet land. Around us, the valleys bow as the sun goes down. Two larks soar upwards dreamily into the light air. Come close, and let them fly. Soon it will be time for sleep. Let's not lose our way in this solitude. O vast, tranquil peace, so deep in the evening's glow! How weary we are of wandering — Is this perhaps death?*

The poem so moved Strauss that he composed an orchestral arrangement for solo soprano voice. Within five months he had composed three further songs with lyrics by Hermann Hesse: 'Spring', 'September', and 'Going to sleep'. 'At sunset' forms the final song in the cycle in which death is contemplated with a sense of calm acceptance.

It was Strauss' wish that the Wagnerian soprano Kirsten Flagstad première his *Four Last Songs*. Sadly, he died eight months before its first performance in London in May 1950, with Flagstad and the Philharmonia Orchestra conducted by Wilhelm Furtwängler.

Seven years later on 4 June 1957, the Gaiety Theatre audience may have been unprepared for the beauty that awaited them, but they were soon entranced by the exquisite lyricism of the *Four Last Songs*, finely wrought by Ronnie and the Radio Éireann Symphony Orchestra under the baton of Éimear O'Broin. As the end phrases seeped quietly into the auditorium, there was a hush; no one wanted to break the spell. Initially the reaction was muted, but it developed into a groundswell of appreciative, prolonged applause. Éimear and Ronnie exchanged glances: job well done.

In July, Covent Garden needed a replacement for Antonia in Offenbach's *The Tales of Hoffmann* and they turned to Ronnie. She flew to London for just four appearances. This brief visit, however, led to an important engagement. Joan Sutherland was due to sing the part of Antonia during the winter season, but she was preparing for her début in two major operas, *Lucia di Lammermoor* and *Otello*. When she dropped out after the first few performances, Ronnie was

Ronnie in the 1950s

in an excellent position to step in. During November and December she sang with an old friend in the role of Hoffmann, 'the wee Belfast man' James (Jimmy) Johnston, famous for his salty tenor voice and practical jokes.

Jimmy and Ronnie had made history together in January 1953 by being the first two Irish singers to take the leading roles in Covent Garden in *La Bohème*. The milestone achieved in that season's production had not curtailed his mischievous streak, and at various performances Jimmy had stuffed fried eggs, or a sausage or ice cubes, into the muff that Musetta brings to Mimi on her deathbed. On another occasion during a performance of *Faust* he taped up the lid of a jewellery box, and Ronnie had to continue singing and acting while trying to prise it open – fortunately she had very strong nails. The Irish duo had a good laugh about those times as they took to the stage again with Otakar Kraus, Edgar Evans and Forbes Robinson in the winter season of 1957.

Coincidentally, the DGOS was also staging *Hoffmann,* but they had a major problem: American soprano Anne Bollinger was taken ill with 'flu, and a late replacement had to be found. Bill O'Kelly contacted Ronnie, who said that if the dates fitted in with the English production she'd be happy to oblige. Fortunately, the dates coalesced nicely. O'Kelly told Ronnie that the theatrical agents, Ingpen & Williams, had been engaged by the DGOS to look after the singers and their fees. Later, Joan Ingpen telephoned Ronnie to draw up the contract, and arranged that she be paid the same fee as Anne Bollinger would have earned, about £90 a performance. Irish artists usually commanded a third of that, the ostensible reason being that they had fewer expenses.

Ronnie flew between London and Dublin for both productions. Jimmy was also due to sing Hoffman at both venues, but just before opening night in the Gaiety, he too was struck down with 'flu. Edgar Evans hastened from London to take over the role and arrived at the theatre with a mere fifteen minutes to spare. Despite these upsets, Mary MacGoris in the *Irish Independent* reported that the singing was 'admirable':

> Mr Evans succeeded in evoking some sympathy for the foolish and really excessively gullible Hoffmann ... and our Miss Dunne covered herself with glory – she was completely convincing as the loving but song-struck Antonia: she looked absolutely delightful and she gave us consistently the best singing of the night.

Following these very successful appearances, Ronnie was quite unprepared for what occurred next. After the final night at the Gaiety, Bill O'Kelly was bristling with rage when he arrived in her dressing room with her 'exorbitant' cheque. He accused Ronnie of holding him to ransom over the fee.

'But,' she said, 'it was Joan Ingpen who arranged the fee, and how did you expect me to get back for each performance – swim?'

O'Kelly would brook no argument. He accused her of being disloyal to him and the Society. He swore he would never employ her again as long as he lived.

Stranded

15

ILL O'KELLY'S declaration came as a crushing blow. Ronnie was at the height of her singing powers. At the very time she needed engagements at home so that she could be with her family, she was denied the opportunity of performing with the only opera company in Ireland.

When an offer came from Covent Garden for her to alternate with Elsie Morison as Blanche in the British première of *The Carmelites* (*Les Dialogues des Carmélites*) by Francis Poulenc in January 1958, she was over the moon. The terms of her contract are indicative both of the esteem in which the Company held her, and of the difficulties under which she was trying to pursue her career. In his letter of confirmation, dated 11 January 1958, David Webster wrote:

> It is understood that Miss Veronica Dunne must remain at home until noon on each day of the performance, or if that is not possible to leave a telephone number where she can be contacted, should we require her at short notice to come over and take Elsie Morison's place if she were ill. In this case, of course, we would pay her return flight from Dublin.

Joan Sutherland (Mme Lidoine), Jess Walters (Marquis de la Force), John Lanigan (Chevalier de la Force) and Sylvia Fisher (Mother Marie) were the other main characters in the gripping and emotional three-hour opera based on the true story of the execution by guillotine of sixteen nuns during the French Revolution.

Les Dialogues des Carmélites had premièred the year before at La Scala, Milan. Although Blanche is the central character, the singing is mainly ensemble, with haunting recitatives and no real arias. Intimidated by life and terrified of rioting peasants, Blanche seeks refuge in a convent. Yet the nuns are not immune to the terror: they must deny their faith or face certain execution. It is an opera of big ideas – war, faith, sacrifice, death – and of one woman's journey to the depths of her fear, and her courage in finding redemption.

It was an intensely dramatic role for Ronnie, culminating in the

chilling finale as Blanche observes the nuns move towards the scaffold chanting 'Salve Regina' above the harrowing sound of the falling guillotine. As each nun is executed, her voice is cut off. Finally, only one remains. Blanche steps from the crowd, takes up the chant, and follows her. Czech-born Rafael Kubelik, who later married Elsie Morison, conducted the opera. Ronnie toured with the Company when the production was taken to the provinces.

At home, there were concerts around the country, and in Dublin Ronnie sang with conductor Dermot O'Hara and the Radio Éireann Light Orchestra at the Gaiety. In the past she had made many guest appearances on Radio Éireann. These engagements now assumed even greater importance, and she enjoyed working with the Radio Éireann Singers and their director, Hans Waldemar Rosen.

The Radio Éireann Singers were a professional group of three sopranos, three altos, two tenors, a baritone and a bass. Radio Éireann was the only radio station available to many people and the programmes had to have a broad appeal. Show numbers, opera, Irish songs, classical, baroque, oratorio, new compositions – the group took it all in their stride and expected their guests to do likewise. When Ronnie arrived for an evening's broadcast, score sheets were often just thrust into her hand and she was on! Ronnie had to hone her sight-reading skills and quickly familiarise herself with a repertoire she had never sung before.

During the 1950s and 1960s the Radio Éireann Singers were based on the fourth floor of the General Post Office on O'Connell Street, Dublin, which was also the headquarters of Radio Éireann. On many a winter's evening Ronnie would enter through the heavy side door on Henry Street and take the old lift up to the studios and rehearsal rooms. There, she might bump into actors such as Brendan Cauldwell, Peg Monahan or Eamonn Kelly, members of the Radio Éireann Players.

Hungarian conductor Tibor Paul had his office near the studio. He was principal conductor with the Radio Éireann Symphony Orchestra (1961-67) and Director of Music for Radio Telefís Éireann (1962-67). A supreme musician, Paul could be a difficult and exacting man to work for, and holding these two posts simultaneously also made him feared, because he had the power to hire and fire without recourse to a higher authority. He also had a pronounced Hungarian accent with an idiosyncratic command of the English language. Joe Dalton, a former member of the Radio Éireann Singers, recounts a story about the conductor. Paul was standing outside his office at 8.58 a.m. waiting for someone to open the door for him. Actor Eamon Kelly was passing by and spotted him. 'How are you?' he asked in his sweet Kerry tones. With a thunderous voice, Paul commanded, 'You, come here!' Kelly, pretending innocence, asked, 'Are you one of the new boys? Don't worry, we'll look after you.' This enraged the conductor, who demanded, 'Do you know who I am? I am Paul.' 'Well now, that's very interesting,' said Kelly. 'Did you ever get a reply to that letter you sent to the Ephesians?'

Tibor Paul. Principal conductor of the Radio Éireann Symphony Orchestra (1961-67)

German-born Hans Waldemar Rosen was a very different character from Tibor Paul. He was big, bear-like man who radiated friendliness and enthusiasm for his chosen sphere, the human voice. He trained some fine singers, including Tomás Ó Súilleabháin, Frank Patterson and John McNally. These two men, Paul and Rosen, and the many musical émigrés who arrived in Ireland after the war, made huge contributions to the cultural life of the country, and to those men and women keen to express and develop their innate talents.

Rosen was a passionate exponent of the baroque composer Heinrich Schütz and encouraged performance of his work. He founded the Radio Éireann Singers in 1951.

Before each broadcast, Rosen, Ronnie and the Singers assembled in the studio with the orchestra and one microphone. They had to get the performance right for the first and only time. In those early years, broadcasts were almost all live – wire recorder devices could get in a terrible mess and tape recorders, spool to spool, were fiddly. On Mondays and Tuesdays there were musical programmes from 7.30pm to 8.00pm. On Thursdays they moved to the Phoenix Hall, Dublin for an hour-long programme with organist Tommy Dando, and on Saturdays they again performed there, this time with the Light Orchestra and Dermot O'Hara for a concert before an audience, all live on air. Among the performers, Ronnie became known for her warmth and great sense of fun.

Gerald Duffy was the bass with the Singers until they were disbanded in 1985, to be replaced by four new, part-time choirs: the RTÉ Chamber Choir; the RTÉ Chorus; the children's choir, Cór na nÓg; and the RTÉ Philharmonic Choir of some 150 people. Colin Mawby was the Choral Director. Gerald became his assistant, and an enthusiastic promoter of all choral singing.

One evening in the 1960s Gerald answered a knock on his door. A swarthy-looking character announced that he was Jim Tate, in charge of security at the American Embassy. Somewhat taken aback by this, Gerald remarked that that was interesting. 'I'm very much involved in an organisation called The SPEBSQA,' said Jim Tate. 'The what?' enquired Gerald. 'The Society for the Preservation and Encouragement of Barber Shop Quartets in America,' said Jim Tate. 'I'm staying just down the road and I heard you're a professional singer.'

Before long, the two were in Gerald's front room engaged in deep discussions about all things choral. Jim admitted that he would love to sit in on a broadcast, so Gerald brought him along to the studios where Ronnie was performing with the Radio Éireann Singers. After the show, six or seven of them decided to go for a drink. They adjourned to The Brazen Head on the quays of the Liffey, the oldest pub in Ireland. They had a few drinks, but Jim Tate, who seemed a nice enough fellow, never put his hand in his pocket when it came to his round. At closing time, Ronnie suggested they all go back to her house for a nightcap. Jim Tate readily agreed, but said he wanted to swing by his place first. They piled into the back of his enormous American charabanc and drove to his house. He went in and came out with laden with crates of every drink imaginable. These were transported to Ronnie's for what turned out to be a very long and hilarious night. During the course of the evening, it transpired that the buying of rounds was not an American custom. If you invite someone out, you pay for everything; when they invite you, they pay for everything. Jim knew he was being transferred back to America and that night would be his only chance to reciprocate, which he did more than adequately.

In April 1958, Ronnie was at Covent Garden singing Mimi in *La Bohème* with the Maltese tenor Oreste Kirkop as Rudolph. Oreste had recently returned from Hollywood, where he starred in the Paramount Pictures version of *The Vagabond King*, and he cut a very fine figure as Rudolph. In the deathbed scene, Ronnie decided to add a little more romance and she stroked her fingers through his hair. It came off in her hand! She mumbled a shocked apology and hurriedly rearranged his toupée. Neither mentioned it again.

At Covent Garden singing Mimi in *La Bohème* with the Maltese tenor Oreste Kirkop as Rudolph, April 1958

The year 1958 was an auspicious one for the Company. The location of the premises on Bow Street had been the site of two previous theatres.

Section of page from the centenary Royal Opera House Covent Garden brochure, featuring Maria Callas and Ebe Stignani in *Norma* (1952) alongside Kathleen Ferrier and Veronica Dunne in *Orpheus* (1953)

The first opened in 1732, the second in 1809; both were destroyed by fire. The third theatre still forms the nucleus of the Royal Opera House. It opened in May 1858 with a performance of Meyerbeer's *Les Huguenots*. The centenary was marked with a sumptuously illustrated souvenir brochure: *The Royal Opera House Covent Garden, 1858-1958*. In his introduction, David Webster stated: 'These pages recall the famous names of the past and the illustrious names of today.' Among cartoons of Mahler and Mascagni and pictures of Nellie Melba and Margot Fonteyn there is a photograph of the famous tenor Jean de Reszke as Roméo in Gounod's *Roméo et Juliette* in the 1890s. Hubert Rooney was a student of de Reszke; how proud he would have been to see his student Ronnie featured in a photograph with Kathleen Ferrier in Gluck's opera *Orpheus* of 1953 next to a photograph of Maria Callas and Ebe Stignani in Bellini's *Norma* from 1952.

Five years on, married and with two children, Ronnie was very far from that young Irish singer Veronica Dunne, who once had seemed destined for every kind of greatness. Now, performing *La Bohème* in London, she was under great stress, torn between professional and personal commitments. After each of her eight appearances, she felt duty-bound to return home, hoping that on the next day of performance there would be no travel delays. But one morning she arrived at Dublin airport to find that London airport was fogbound. In desperation she caught a flight to Birmingham and took a taxi from that airport into the city to catch the train for London. She was in time for the performance, just, but luck had played too great a part. She stepped on stage with a sense of foreboding. Covent Garden could not risk a late no-show for one of its leads. She felt it spelt the end of her association with the Company and, bar two performances when she filled in for the chosen soprano in *Carmen*, she was right. Her career in the operatic world that she loved so much, at home and abroad, lay in tatters. It was difficult to hide her despair.

The Three Choirs Festival, billed as the oldest and greatest music festival in the world, celebrated its 231st meeting at the medieval cathedral in Hereford in 1958. Choirs from Hereford, Gloucester and Worcester cathedrals take turns in hosting the annual event. That September their guest artists included Benjamin Britten, Peter Pears, Elsie Morison and Norma Procter. Under the cathedral's high fan-vaulted roof supported by massive limestone columns, the soloists, the City of Birmingham Symphony Orchestra conducted by Dr Melville Cook and two full choirs, performed Verdi's *Requiem* in a setting as majestic and solemn as the music that resonated through the ancient building. The reviewer in the *Hereford Times* on 12 September was impressed:

> The Verdi gave the festival chorus their best chance to shine so far. They took the opportunity and the result was very fine indeed. In fact, with four principals of the ranking of Veronica Dunne, Valerie Heath-Davies, Charles Craig and Owen Brannigan, it was hardly surprising that the performance was one of the high spots of the week. Theatrical as the work may be, its sincerity was brought out under the baton of Dr Cook. If any points in such a high level performance can be particularly mentioned, they are the Sanctus and the Agnus Dei.

Sir John Barbirolli had not forgotten Ronnie, and just after Hereford she went on a short tour of Edinburgh, Liverpool and Manchester with the Hallé Orchestra to sing the Verdi *Requiem* with Richard Lewis and Valerie Heath-Davies.

In October 1958 Ronnie's much-loved singing teacher, Hubert Rooney, died. And there was more bad news. William Dunne, her father and greatest supporter, was facing financial ruin. There was every danger that he and her mother would be forced out of their home.

16 *Change of tempo*

MISUNDERSTANDINGS, an intransigent architect and work on a major project falling behind schedule led the building firm of William Dunne and his son Bill to incur a cash flow shortfall of £9,000. Creditors were closing in. An agreement was reached which allowed the project to continue, but upon completion of the work William was declared bankrupt. Skilled workers were laid off and the premises at Spring Garden Street closed down. Bill had to sell his house, and eventually he and his family moved to England.

Josephine took the bankruptcy very hard. She had lived a good and honourable life and had never been in debt to tradesmen or anyone else. Now she was fearful of answering the door, and was too embarrassed to go out in public.

May and her husband Dr Michael Curtin had returned to Ireland to live in Limerick. Over the years the two sisters had become close. They each had children and homes to run, and their childhood squabbles seemed no more than normal sibling rivalry. Worried by the plight of their parents, they telephoned each other frequently, and May travelled to Dublin whenever she could. William had a little group of friends and he got out and about, but their mother's health was deteriorating.

Ronnie bought an old Mini Minor so that she could drive to country venues in the morning and return that night after the performance. Cork, Limerick, Galway, Sligo, Wexford were no bother, but once, when she had to travel the long distance to Derry for a concert, she borrowed Peter's car, a brand new Jaguar. It was late and very dark after the show and a kindly priest offered to guide her out of the town. The Jag stalled on the bridge across the Foyle River and neither Ronnie nor the priest could get it started. Mechanics came to have a look and decided to tow it back to the garage, whereupon the sympathetic priest lent Ronnie his car so she could get home. In the morning Peter walked out of the house for work, but he was back in a trice demanding to know where his car was. When Ronnie told him what had happened, he swore he would never let her borrow his car again. He stormed out and had to take her old Mini to work. Next day, the priest drove Peter's car down from Derry and collected his own. He refused all offers of petrol or expenses; he said it had been worth it to hear Ronnie sing.

The Kilrush Operatic Society in County Clare engaged Ronnie to sing Eily in *The Lily of Killarney* by Julius Benedict in May 1959. The opera is based on the drama *The Colleen Bawn* by Irish playwright Dion Boucicault. The Kilrush Operatic Society was an adventurous and ambitious group who took it upon themselves to present high quality operatic productions to the pretty coastal town of no more than 2,000 people. Their annual capital expenditure was a vast sum of about £3,000 which was used for sets, costumes and lighting, and to engage professional soloists, a professional director and conductor, and a semi-professional orchestra.

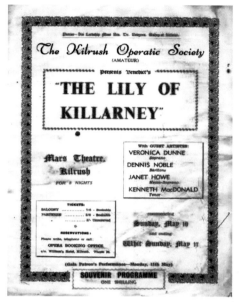

The local people who provided the chorus and small parts gave Ronnie a wonderful welcome. She revelled in playing in a full production again, and in the enthusiastic, pioneering spirit of the company. For that production of *The Lily of Killarney* Ronnie's fellow guest artists were Dennis Noble (whom she had seen on the Olympia stage as a child), Janet Howe and Kenneth MacDonald. George Minne was the musical director and conductor, and the producer was Harold Powell-Lloyd, famed for working with Covent Garden, Welsh National Opera, the Dublin Grand Opera Society and Sadler's Wells, London. Ronnie was in good company and the show, which ran for eight nights, was a sell-out.

Ronnie herself appeared with the Sadler's Wells Opera Company in February 1960 in *La Bohème* when she sang Musetta to Anne Edwards's Mimi and William Aiken's Rudolph. Leslie Ayre in the *London Evening News* had mixed feelings about the production, writing that both Edwards and Aiken were 'monotonously charmless in tone', but conductor Warwick Braithwaite 'brought a sense of purpose to the proceedings', and 'guest artist Veronica Dunne (Musetta) was outstanding in voice and characterisation'.

The following month Ronnie travelled to Neath in South Wales for a performance of Verdi's *Aida*. Aida is a challenging role, with wonderful music and a great dramatic intensity. Ronnie had worked for weeks on the score with Kitty O'Callaghan, and when she arrived on the day of the concert she was ready for anything, or almost anything. The soloists were put up in a house in the town. The hospitable owner showed them to their rooms and then, with a flourish of his hand, indicated an old shed at the bottom of the garden where they might find bathroom facilities! The look on their faces must have been suitably horrified for he burst into delighted laughter. That joke broke the ice for the singers who henceforth set out to have a really good time. In the evening, the Gwyn Hall was packed with an appreciative audience well versed in close harmony and Italian opera. The Morgan Lloyd Orchestra, conducted by Gwilym Roberts, rose to the occasion. All the soloists – Ronnie (Aida), Rowland Jones (Radamés), Valerie Heath-Davies (Amneris), Gerwyn Morgan (King of Egypt) and Redvers Llewellyn (Amonasro) received rousing applause and calls for encores.

In March Ronnie took part in the Belfast Festival for the first of what would become a warm professional collaboration with the eminent composer and conductor Havelock Nelson. For many years, Nelson conducted the BBC Northern Ireland Orchestra, the Studio Symphony Orchestra and the Ulster Singers. Ronnie loved working with him. He and his wife Hazel welcomed many musicians to their home in Belfast, and Ronnie stayed with them whenever she was in Northern Ireland. On that first occasion she sang Mozart's *Exsultate Jubilate* and *A German Requiem* by Brahms in St. James's Church with baritone Eric Hinds, the Ulster Singers and the Studio Symphony Orchestra with Havelock Nelson.

Ronnie received a panicky call from the Kilrush Operatic Society at the beginning of May. They were staging *The Bohemian Girl* by William Balfe, but lead singer Estelle Valéry had lost her voice. Could Ronnie possibly sing the role of Arline? Ronnie got hold of the music, threw her suitcase in the car, and set out on the five-and-a-half hour journey from the east to the west coast of Ireland.

Her appearance had been arranged so hastily that Ronnie barely had time to think before she was at the Mars Theatre, Kilrush, rehearsing with Dennis Nobel as Count Arnheim. Towards the end of Act 2, the Count laments the disappearance of his daughter, Arline. Recalling her fondly, he despairs of ever seeing her again, and sings: *The heart bowed down by weight of woe, To weakest hope will cling.* Ronnie was transported back to a family gathering filled with music and cheer and sweet innocence. Her father's singing, her mother's tears, a home of love and security. How all was changed: Josephine's tears now not of joy, but weighed down with woe.

There was cause for anxiety at home as well. For some time, Ronnie had noticed that six-year-old Peter did not always respond when spoken to. She took him along to the doctor who recommended an ear, nose and throat consultant. After a number of tests, the consultant said Peter was totally deaf in his left ear and had limited

Judy and Peter

hearing in his right, and that nothing could be done for him. He suggested teaching the child to lip read. Ronnie would not let the little boy see her distress. She brought him home and made him a nice tea and life continued as normal. Peter did not learn to lip read, and his partial hearing had no effect on his friends up and down Bushy Park Road. It was only at school that he had a problem when he was accused of not paying attention.

During the next year, Ronnie went around the country in her red Mini singing popular operatic arias and appearing in many charity concerts. She performed some memorable works, including Hindemith's *Das Marienleben* and Elizabeth's aria from the second act of Wagner's *Tannhäuser* with Hans Waldemar Rosen. She also was a soloist in Beethoven's Ninth Symphony at the Olympia Theatre, Dublin with Tibor Paul.

For their tenth anniversary in May 1961 the Kilrush Operatic Society had decided to stage a lavish production of Gounod's *Faust* with an international cast from Ireland, England, Wales, Poland and Australia. Ronnie was engaged to sing Marguerite on alternate nights with Josephine Scanlon. John Carolan and Tano Ferendinos alternated as Faust, with Stanislav Pieczora as Mephistopheles. Russell Cooper and Patricia Lawlor completed the line-up. A series of magical stage-effects was devised, with angels and devils, fire and surprising apparitions.

Ronnie arrived on the Friday to find a chaotic assortment of volunteers, exotic props and scaffolding in the venue that was a theatre for one week only once a year; for the remaining fifty-one weeks it was a cinema. Stage manager Laurence Rush and his crew had gained access to the place only the previous night following the screening of a film, and were working flat-out to get everything ready for the dress rehearsal on the Saturday night. Director Harry Powell Lloyd hurried from place to place, answering questions, issuing instructions. Several members of the orchestra were rehearsing with conductor Captain R.B. Kealy, and the lighting man was shouting for more cable. Ronnie decided to leave them to it and seek out the other singers at Williams' Hotel. A legal exemption to the alcohol licensing law had been granted which allowed the hotel bar and restaurant to remain open until 2 a.m. on the eight nights of performance, owing to the special circumstances of having six resident operatic artistes who would require sustenance after their exertions on stage. It was deemed impractical to prevent locals from also availing of this privilege, so opera week was a happy one indeed. On 14 May the capacity audience, drawn from all corners of the western seaboard, were treated to a marvellous spectacle, as the *Clare Champion* noted:

> Sunday night's opening performance was one of the smoothest in grand opera. No nerves were noticeable nor were any of the usual hitches associated with opening nights. With such a show as *Faust* this was fabulous entertainment in a small town. In particular, the singing of the Flower Song by Patricia Lawlor; All Hail Thou Dwelling, Pure and Holy by John Carolan; and the famous Jewel Song by Veronica Dunne, all of which were in the garden scene, were delightfully rendered .... This opera is a credit to Harry Powell Lloyd, London, who describes it as a stupendous achievement which deserves great support and is a credit to Kilrush.

Far from the fun of Kilrush, back in Dublin changes were underway. For five years, Margaret McCann had been a much-loved nanny for Judy and Peter. When Judy started primary school, there was no need for a full-time carer. Margaret became a restaurant manageress, although she found that leaving her Judy was a terrible wrench. The little girl was inconsolable – the one, immutable core of her existence had disappeared in a stroke. Like her mother before her, she felt she was on her own, striving to cope in a bewildering world of strange teachers and boisterous children. At home there was now just a daily housekeeper, Eileen, who could stay overnight if necessary.

In Clontarf, Josephine's health was a major concern. Ronnie longed to do more for her parents. Her father mentioned that Michael O'Higgins, a singing teacher in Dublin's Municipal School of Music, was emigrating to Australia. Would she consider teaching? There had been just one occasion when she had, fleetingly, considered that possibility – sitting in Sarsfield Hogan's office looking for money to study in Rome. Well, now she needed money again. But she had no training, no teaching experience. She did have years of learning behind her, hundreds of professional performances and extensive musical knowledge. And yet, teaching was supposed to come at the end of a career when no other avenue was open. Ronnie was thirty-four, an age when many singers were reaching their prime. Was she now to admit defeat, and teach?

17 A reluctant teacher

RONNIE WOULD ADMIT TO NOTHING, certainly not defeat. If she had to earn money by teaching, so be it. Lessons would take up only a day or two a week; there was no reason why that should interfere with her singing.

Saturday morning, September 1961. Staff Room, Municipal School of Music, Chatham Row, Dublin. Veronica McSwiney, a young part-time piano teacher, was sipping her coffee and chatting with other teachers during their break. Michael McNamara, School Principal, ushered through the door a woman with wavy auburn hair, a royal blue suit and high heels. He introduced Miss Veronica Dunne as a new member of staff and a ripple of surprised whispers ran around the room.

Veronica McSwiney stood back in awe. Ronnie's reputation as an opera singer was legendary among her contemporaries, and here she was in the flesh! She seemed quiet and pleasant and signed the teaching hours book – like everyone else, she was to be paid by the hour. Then she was gone, off to her first class.

Those initial lessons were nerve-racking for Ronnie. She knew she could sing, but could she teach? She was a performer; it was her lifeblood, her *raison d'être*, her glorious existence, but here she was in a small room with an upright piano and a trembling twelve-year-old child in a gymslip. How to begin? The gentle voice of Hubert Rooney slipped into her mind: start simply with scales and breathing exercises; think about the little bird landing. She struck a chord on the piano and the room filled with sound.

The Municipal School of Music was established by Dublin Corporation in 1890 to provide 'musical instruction at moderate charges for the children of artisans', and to improve training for bandsmen. In the 1930s it was absorbed into the Dublin Vocational Educational Committee. The school was granted college status in 1963 and became known as the College of Music. At that time, four distinct departments were created: Keyboard Studies; Orchestral

Studies; Musicianship Studies; and Vocal, Opera and Drama Studies. This restructuring did not detract from the institution's primary goal, which was to teach music in a practical way and on a part-time basis to students ranging from primary to third level. Typically, lessons might last for half an hour once a week, which could become an hour a week as the student progressed.

Nancy Calthorpe, a notable singing and harp coach in the school, had a wonderful young pupil in Ann Murray. Michael McNamara thought that Ronnie should take over the training of the twelve-year-old, but she did not want to be the cause of bad feeling among her new colleagues. The predicament was resolved when Ann went to boarding school, and the two teachers established a cordial working relationship.

It wasn't long before Ronnie hit her stride and she was taking children and adults for half-hour lessons three days a week. One of her first students was Joe Lane, an accomplished tenor in his thirties who had already sung major roles with the Rathmines and Rathgar Musical Society. Ronnie was delighted with Joe's voice but she knew she could improve his technique and stamina. She explained that what the voice needs is support. 'Build up the strength in the diaphragm' she told him, 'and you will be able to control your breath so that you sing in phrases.' During lessons, she would give him the odd poke and prod to demonstrate her point, and when he got home he had bruises that were difficult to explain to his wife.

Another of Ronnie's adult students was Edwin (Eddie) FitzGibbon, noted for appearing in DGOS productions. When Ronnie heard he wanted to develop his voice to sing Italian opera, she said, 'Come on, lovey, I'll give you a few lessons.' Three times a week for almost a year, she collected Eddie from his office in town and drove him out to Rathgar for one-hour sessions in her front room, thus setting a precedent for what would become the norm during her five decades of teaching – that of welcoming students into her home. Edwin was in transition from baritone to tenor and Ronnie realised he needed a teacher who was more experienced with the male voice. In Manchester to do a broadcast of *La Bohème* with Richard Lewis for Granada Television, she heard two student tenors who had the sort of technique that would suit Eddie. She sought out their teacher, Frederic Cox, Principal of the Royal Manchester College of Music. She arranged for the two men to meet, and this led to a long and fruitful association between Frederic and Eddie. The episode set up another precedent, that of Ronnie being fearless in pursuit of her students' best interests, even to her own detriment.

Talented soprano Anne Makower had been a pupil of Brian

Anne Makower

Boydell's before she went to England to work for the BBC as a production assistant. She was tempted back to Ireland by the prospect of joining the brand new television service, Telefís Éireann. This was pioneering work in which few people in Ireland had any expertise, and soon the lowly production assistant was being called upon to direct a variety of programmes from current affairs, with *Broadsheet*, to a cookery slot with the finger-licking Monica Sheridan, from children's afternoon entertainment to a discussion conducted entirely in Welsh! All these items were presented from one small studio originally designed as the News Studio, and as the programmes changed during the ad breaks, there was a shuffle of people out to let others in. It was quite hair-raising at times, but very exhilarating.

Anne wished to resume her singing with Brian Boydell but he had given up coaching to concentrate on composing. She was told of Ronnie, and from the first lesson she knew she had found her teacher. Ronnie listened to her voice and devised a series of exercises that would bring out its very best. Ronnie's keyboard skills at that time were lamentable, and when she wanted to rehearse a specific aria with Anne, she would chase after a piano student to help out – an arrangement that was beneficial to all three.

On the afternoon of 22 February 1962 Ronnie was at the Municipal School when she received an urgent phone call from a friend of her mother's who said she should come home immediately. Ronnie rushed to Clontarf to find that her mother had suffered a severe stroke. An ambulance brought Josephine to Jervis Street Hospital and Ronnie followed in her car in the belief that her father was to travel there with the friend. At the hospital William failed to appear. Having ensured that Josephine was being looked after, Ronnie flew back to the house and discovered her father waiting on the doorstep. It was all so chaotic that nobody thought to tell May or Billo about Josephine's medical emergency. Back at the hospital Ronnie held on to her mother's hand and cried.

A while later, Josephine came out of a coma and gazed at Ronnie sadly. 'Ah darling,' she said, 'all the world's going to come to you, and who's going to look after Daddy?'

Josephine Dunne died that evening. May was distraught at not having been by her mother's side and, Ronnie thought wistfully, she was right. It should have been May that Josephine's eyes rested upon;

May who heard her last words; May that she carried in her heart to the hereafter. But it was she, the other daughter, who said, 'Come and live with me, Daddy. I'll look after you.' The house in Clontarf was sold to pay off outstanding debts and William Dunne moved into Bushy Park. Ronnie went back to work.

And how she worked. Students were keen to be taught by the famous Veronica Dunne and soon she was teaching two, then three, days a week. That did not mean that her stage days were over – far from it. The opera world suddenly started coming to Ronnie again, just as her mother had predicted. Yet as Ronnie worked more and more, the strains on her marriage were beginning to show. Her husband Peter continued to live his own life and had expected the stay-at-home housewife envisaged by Godfrey Winn, which was the social norm, but Ronnie could no more deny her singing than she could deny her life.

After a performance of Mendelssohn's *Elijah* with Tibor Paul in September of 1962 Ronnie was off to the Wexford Festival Opera to sing Suzel in Mascagni's *L'amico Fritz* with Nicola Monti as Fritz

As Suzel in *L'amico Fritz* with Nicola Monti (Fritz). Wexford Festival Opera, 1962

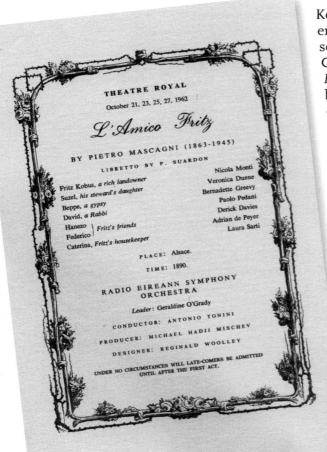

THEATRE ROYAL

October 21, 23, 25, 27, 1962

L'Amico Fritz

BY PIETRO MASCAGNI (1863-1945)

LIBRETTO BY P. SUARDON

Fritz Kobus, *a rich landowner*   Nicola Monti
Suzel, *his steward's daughter*   Veronica Dunne
Beppe, *a gypsy*   Bernadette Greevy
David, *a Rabbi*   Paolo Pedani
Hanezo } *Fritz's friends*   Derick Davies
Federico }   Adrian de Peyer
Caterina, *Fritz's housekeeper*   Laura Sarti

PLACE: Alsace.

TIME: 1890.

RADIO EIREANN SYMPHONY ORCHESTRA

Leader: Geraldine O'Grady

CONDUCTOR: ANTONIO TONINI

PRODUCER: MICHAEL HADJI MISCHEV

DESIGNER: REGINALD WOOLLEY

UNDER NO CIRCUMSTANCES WILL LATE-COMERS BE ADMITTED UNTIL AFTER THE FIRST ACT.

Kobus. It was her first professional encounter with an aspiring young mezzo-soprano, twenty-two-year-old Bernadette Greevy. The music critic of the *Evening Herald* was impressed by the singing of both women, and hailed the Wexford debut of Bernadette Greevy as Beppe as especially memorable.

The accompanying opera, *I Puritani* by Bellini, featured Italian baritone Lino Puglisi. Ronnie had last met Lino ten years previously in Milan. He had been one of the other nervous contestants in the Concorso Lirico competition, chosen to sing Marcello for the *La Bohème* production in which Ronnie sang Mimi. They had both fully vindicated the judges' decisions by making opera their lives. During an afternoon of talk and laughter, they discovered they had much more in common. Lino was very proud of his young son and was amazed that Ronnie had an eight-year-old son and a daughter of six. Ronnie attended his performance as Sir Richard in *I Puritani* and delighted again in the grand and expressive voice that had excelled in the role of Marcello.

Was it only ten years since those heady days in Milan? Ronnie looked back on all that had happened – Covent Garden, marriage, children, performances, teaching – all culminating in the death of her mother. What would the next decade bring, she wondered.

The comeback 18

TIBOR PAUL had a heated discussion with Colonel Bill O'Kelly of the Dublin Grand Opera Society. In his heavily accented English he demanded, 'Vhy do you search de vorld for soprano vhen you 'ave the vooman here?'

Bill O'Kelly capitulated and Ronnie was engaged for the 1962 winter season at the Gaiety Theatre, much to the joy of her many admirers. She was to sing the title role in an outstanding opera – *Manon* by Jules Massenet, which is set during the reign of Louis XV of France. Between 28 November and 7 December she performed with the Radio Éireann Symphony Orchestra under guest conductor Charles Mackerras. Her fellow soloists were Edward Byles (Le Chevalier des Grieux), the New Zealand bass Noël Mangin (Comte des Grieux), Bryan Drake (De Brétigny), and her former student Eddie FitzGibbon (Guillot de Morfontaine). Eddie remembered the rehearsals for the opera as being 'dreadful':

> We were never given enough time for DGOS pro-
> ductions. For the winter seasons singers were hired from
> here, there and everywhere. We all came knowing our
> roles, but not knowing how we would fit in together. We never had
> enough time to prepare, let alone bond. There might have been
> three piano rehearsals and one orchestral run-through. Ronnie was
> expected to perform under the most difficult circumstances, and
> Manon is a difficult role. But she did a very good Manon. She had
> an extraordinary way of making herself look more beautiful. I
> remember she had a big beauty spot that was very fetching. Four
> performances are not enough to develop a role, but the audiences
> came and they enjoyed it.

Ronnie revelled in the role of the flirty and vivacious Manon – a woman who is not as bad, or as good, as she might seem – and in all the emotions expressed through wonderful tunes and duets. Robert Johnston of the *Irish Press* declared that Manon was 'Veronica Dunne's greatest role':

Since the opera was first performed in 1884 this is a part which has been sought after by the greatest sopranos of each intervening decade and Miss Dunne's 'Manon' will not lose by comparison. She carried her portrayal into her singing, preserving beautifully the portrayal of a wilful, wanton girl. Her outstanding aria, apart from the duets, was the clever and delightful 'gavotte' in the opening of the third act – a magnificent piece of singing.

But it was the famous seduction scene that made a deep impression on certain members of the chorus. Twenty-year-old Paddy Brennan and several other young buckos scrambled up to the flies high above the stage each night in time for a bird's eye view of the moment when Ronnie cast aside her cloak to reveal her daringly low-cut gown. And yes, it was modelled almost directly on that worn by Magda Olivero all those years ago in Rome. Paddy, whose parents had attended Ronnie's Covent Garden début, joined the chorus in 1960 and during the next thirty-three years he appeared on the Gaiety stage at least six hundred times. Such is his love of opera in general, and the DGOS in particular, that he has become the archivist for the society's grand seventy-year history.

Ronnie returned to Kilrush in May and June to sing Carmen for the Kilrush Operatic Society's production of the Bizet opera. During that summer, she had more time to prepare for her new role as singing teacher at the College of Music. When she entered the doors of Chatham Row in September, she was confident that she was capable of doing the job adequately, but whether or not she would ever actually come to love it was another matter. Her heart was still on the stage.

On 30 October 1963 Monsignor Hugh O'Flaherty, the 'Pimpernel of the Vatican', died in Caherciveen, County Kerry. Ronnie was deeply saddened by the news. She later wrote:

> I have always considered Monsignor O'Flaherty my hero. Whenever I am asked to define the qualities of heroism I simply revisit the very real image forever buried in my mind of the tall priest standing beside me in the caves with tears streaming down his face. I remember how obvious it was that he was tortured by the idea of human suffering and that he would go to any length to stop it. It was this powerful motivation that made all those incredible stories credible. It was this source of strength that provided him with an endless reservoir of goodness, which he used to alleviate the suffering of any person no matter what their race or religion. Since my time in Rome good people doing good things always remind me of the Monsignor. My measuring tape for heroism has always been and will always remain a good priest from Kerry who during extraordinary times was, quite simply, an extraordinary man.

As Countess Almaviva in *Le nozze di Figaro*. DGOS, 1963

The winter season of the DGOS beckoned again, and this time Ronnie was cast in the role of Countess Almaviva in Mozart's *Le nozzi di Figaro*. Her costume was 'resplendent', according to Mary MacGoris in the *Irish Independent*, who added that, although the singing in general was disappointing, Veronica Dunne was 'outstanding .... She sang "Porgi, amor" and "Dove sono" not alone with technical skill and style, but with a moving poignancy and incidentally, looking superb, acted with an affecting dignity and restraint.'

Christmas. Surrounded by her family, with her career back on track and secure in her teaching position, Ronnie felt that she had made it through a very difficult period and emerged fighting. Her one sadness was that her father, William, had moved down to

Limerick to be with May, but he was quite content there and for that she was grateful.

The lack of a dedicated concert hall in Dublin was a glaring omission in the city's cultural life. Concerts took place in churches, cinemas and halls. Major events had to be performed at the National Stadium, a boxing arena with a seating capacity for 2,000 people grouped around the centre ring. The cold draughty space fell far short of being an ideal venue, but such was the appetite for good music that audiences put up with the discomfort. It was there that Our Lady's Choral Society and the Radio Éireann Symphony Orchestra under the direction of Tibor Paul presented Rossini's *Stabat Mater* in March 1964.

The *Stabat Mater* text dwells on the suffering of Mary, the mother of Jesus, during his crucifixion, and has been set to music by many composers. Rossini divided the poem's twenty three-line verses into ten movements for performance by four soloists. The critic that Irish musicians were most keen to impress was Charles Acton of the *Irish Times*. He was full-hearted in his praise of the singers at the Stadium:

> It should be a matter of real pride that a small country can produce so fine a quartet of solo performances as we heard from Veronica Dunne, Bernadette Greevy, Edwin FitzGibbon, and Harold Gray. The two women were particularly fine. Veronica Dunne is in splendid voice. Her style and phrasing were ideal for the music and the utter conviction she brought to *inflammatus* in particular added to the best performance I have ever heard from her. Her duet (*Quis est homo*) with Bernadette Greevy was lovely .... Edwin FitzGibbon sang *Cujus animam* with nicer quality than I have heard before .... Harold Gray had less sense of Italian style than the others, but what a fine voice he has, how well managed and how musical!

In May 1964 Ronnie was once again in Kilrush to sing one of the greatest roles for soprano, that of Tosca in Puccini's huge, sweeping opera. This production was a colossal undertaking for the small society, and also for Ronnie, who had spent many hours learning the role with Kitty O'Callaghan. She arrived in Kilrush to find a dashing new English conductor in town, Nicholas Braithwaite, whose father, Warwick, had conducted Ronnie at the Sadler's Wells Opera Company in 1960.

Tosca was a baptism of fire for Nicholas, and how he enjoyed it. The orchestra under his tentative command consisted of about twenty-four semi-professionals (instead of the seventy or so normally required), made up in equal measure of musicians from the army and the accomplished Healy family from Dublin. There was only one full rehearsal in the cinema-cum-theatre, and Nicholas had to stand on a crate for each performance so he could be seen from the stage. But he

recalls that 'Veronica Dunne was superb, as were the whole cast, all of whom were unfailingly supportive of me, the rank beginner':

> I remember one night in Act III at the end of the duet Tosca and Cavaradossi are in a clinch and the music pauses. The gaoler comes in and announces 'Time now' when it is time for Cavaradossi to be shot. At the third performance the gaoler missed his cue and the singers, orchestra and I were stuck on the pause so I sang 'Time now'. The gaoler heard me, came running out, and sang 'Time now' much to the amusement of the audience. The story went round the town and every night thereafter he was greeted with gales of laughter. By the end of the week he was singing 'Now is the hour' but was still greeted with hilarity by the audience.

One of the most exciting young opera companies in Great Britain, Welsh National Opera, engaged Ronnie to sing the role she had made her own – Mimi in *La Bohème*. She made her début at the New Theatre, Cardiff on 7 October 1964 with the French-Canadian baritone Robert Savoie, tenor Stuart Burrows, David Gwynne, Australian soprano Jenifer Eddy and conductor

Bryan Balkwill. Under the headline: 'No frozen mitts for this *Bohème*', the *South Wales Echo* reported that 'One of opera's biggest tearjerkers had the audience wild with delight at the end of the performance.' Veronica Dunne 'gave a warm-hearted performance' and 'perfectly brought out the character of the ailing seamstress.'

Ronnie had been singing Mimi for over ten years, and she had approached several producers about the lighting in the final scene. At the beginning of Act Two, Mimi and Rodolfo are carefree and in love. Rodolfo buys Mimi a *cuffietta* (little bonnet) from a street vendor. When the lovers separate in Act Three, Rodolfo keeps the bonnet, which he treasures. In Act 4 Mimi is on her deathbed, but is momentarily revived when he gives it back to her. She presses it to her heart and remembers all the happy times they shared. When she dies, Rodolfo is inconsolable and the opera ends. That bonnet represented the few happy days in Mimi's tragic life. As life ebbed, Ronnie allowed the bonnet to trail on the floor, still clutched in her fingers, and she thought it would be very effective theatrically for all the lights to be dimmed save for a single spotlight focused on the bonnet; then that, too, should fade out. Unfortunately, this idea was never taken up.

After the performance in Cardiff, Ronnie did not see the glowing review in the *South Wales Echo* the next morning. She was already at home in Dublin having caught the 3 a.m. sailing from Fishguard, collected her car from the pier in Rosslare and driven back in time to oversee breakfast and become a housewife again. The following evening she undertook the journey again, driving to Rosslare, catching the ferry and taking a train to Cardiff where she hung around the theatre all day and tried to catch a few hours sleep in her dressing room. She was aware that she was placing a huge amount of stress on her voice, but she returned home after that performance, too, and the next.

While Ronnie was gaining a reputation as an effective teacher at the College of Music, she was always preparing for the next big engagement. December 1964 proved to be one of her busiest months ever with the DGOS at the Gaiety Theatre when she sang in two operas – as Sophie in Richard Strauss's *Der Rosenkavalier* and as the priestess Leila in Bizet's *Les Pêcheurs de Perles*. All her vocal technique and stamina were put to the test in singing such demanding roles on consecutive nights, but her performances were highly praised. Exhausted but relieved, she was glad to take a well-earned Christmas break.

Dual roles 19

FOLLOWING HER SUCCESS with Welsh National Opera the previous year, Ronnie was elated when the company asked her to appear as Tosca in Puccini's opera, with the famous Czech baritone Otakar Kraus as Scarpia and Welsh tenor Rowland Jones as Cavaradossi.

For sheer dramatic impact *Tosca* has it all – jealousy, love, lust, torture, murder, betrayal, suicide – all heightened by the intensity of Puccini's music. During rehearsals Kraus shared his experience of the opera with Ronnie, and the two worked on moves together, especially for their emotionally charged scenes in Act 2. Kraus stressed that Tosca would be rigid with fear in the presence of the all-powerful Chief of Police. The opera is set in 1800, a tumultuous period in the history of the city of Rome which had been occupied by the French Republic, then by the Kingdom of Naples and was about to be overrun by the French again. Ronnie had walked those streets after the devastation of war. She admired the courage and resilience displayed by the Roman people in the grip of tyranny. Having stabbed the hated Scarpia, Tosca watches him die. She takes the safe conduct paper from his hand and stands over him, exultant. Through clenched teeth and in a harsh, guttural voice, she exclaims: '*E avanti a lui tremava tutta Roma!*' ('And before him all Rome trembled!'). Ronnie recalled a typical Roman gesture of defiance, and she spat on his prostate body. She had never seen this gesture enacted, but it felt right. The music critic from the *South Wales Evening Post* was captivated by the performance of 17 March 1965, calling it 'a masterpiece of musical tension':

> Last night's Welsh National production at the Grand Theatre, Swansea, was distinguished by a truly superb Scarpia and a Tosca whose imaginative response to the challenge of this most exacting role was matched by her quite remarkable vocal power .... Veronica Dunne, prima donna from Ireland ... has a richness and a range of tone colour which made her performance as effective in sotto voce passages as in the impassioned climaxes. There have been proud Toscas and agonised Toscas. Last night we saw a very human Tosca whom tragedy dignified. This was particularly noticeable in

Veronica Dunne's singing of 'Vissi d'arte', the achingly lovely aria in act two in which Tosca laments the unjustness of her fate. Miss Dunne started to sing it almost lying on the settee. (Jeritza, Puccini's favourite Tosca, used to sing it lying on the floor.) Unlike many Toscas, she realised that this was an aria for poignant rather than powerful singing. It was a beautiful performance.

Ronnie was again travelling back and forth between Ireland and Wales, but on stage all travails were forgotten in the commanding presence of Otakar Kraus who brought such authority to the role of Scarpia, with a voice that was clear and strong.

The production dates clashed with an important occasion for Ronnie's daughter Judy, who had been due to make her First Holy Communion with the rest of her class. Ronnie arranged for Judy to have a private ceremony a few days later with her friend from Rome, Father Henry Nolan. Determined to make the event special, Ronnie held a feast for family and friends after the church service. Madeleine Kestro, whom she had befriended while singing in Brussels, travelled from Belgium for the occasion with a magnificent heart-shaped cake baked in her parents' patisserie. At the time, there was an outbreak of foot-and-mouth disease in Britain that the Irish government were trying to keep out of Ireland. When Customs officials at Dublin Airport asked what was in her box, Madeleine replied in faltering English that it was a heart. The officials panicked, thinking it was an animal's heart, and doused her in disinfectant from top to bottom. 'You Irish – you are crazy!' she protested. But the cake was mercifully unblemished and later admired and devoured at the party.

The next day nine-year-old Peter got a scare when Madeleine fastened her eyes on his pet rabbits in the garden and said, in all seriousness, that they looked ready for the pot! For Judy, the whole episode emphasised just how different she was from her classmates:

> In the beginning of my childhood no other mother worked, no other mother had a career, a sense of notoriety. I often wondered why is my mother not like X's mother, cooking dinner and doing laundry? When I made my Holy Communion, I couldn't do it with my friends because my mother was singing in Wales. I had to do it on my own and learn all the prayers, so the nuns used to take me out of class for extra tuition and I was livid with her. She made it the most magnificent day possible, with all the family, but still I was pissed off. That was the first time I realised that I was different, that the schedule of things in my life did not revolve around me, but around her career.

Ronnie was not always around for her children on a day-in, day-out basis, but when she sensed trouble all her antennae were alerted. Some years later, she received a message from the Reverend Mother at Judy's secondary school informing her of misconduct. Ronnie experienced a plummeting sense of *déjà vu*. She marched down to the convent, all guns blazing, to do battle for her daughter; she would not behave as her mother had done and meekly accept the authority of a nun. Judy's great sin was that she had been caught smoking a Carroll's cigarette in the bathroom. True to family tradition, she was expelled! There were no recriminations at home; on the contrary, Judy felt Ronnie was her champion, but she was no pussycat. If she had been on the tear with her friends, Ronnie was on to her like a lioness: where were you? who were you with? what were you doing? It was not a *laissez-faire* childhood. There were structures and boundaries and, even if the children did not come first in Ronnie's artistic life, they were cherished and protected.

In April 1965 Radio Telefís Éireann commissioned one of Ireland's finest young composers, Seóirse Bodley, to commemorate the birth of the poet W.B. Yeats on 13 June 1865. Bodley was an admirer of Yeats's poetry and he set to with enthusiasm. He selected quotations from five poems in the collections *The Green Helmet and Other Poems* (1910), *Responsibilities* (1914) and *The Tower* (1928) with which to form his song cycle for soprano and orchestra. These poems trace the passage of life from childhood through to adulthood, love and disappointment and on to inevitable death. This gloomy progression is echoed by Bodley's title *Never to have Lived is best*, taken from Yeats's poem 'A Man Young and Old: XI. From Oedipus at Colonus': '*Never to have lived is best, ancient writers say; Never to have drawn the breath of life, never to have looked into the eye of day; The second best's a gay goodnight and quickly turn away.*'

The singer has to perform both the male and the female roles, so she had to have a wide range, and as the score is complex and non-traditional she is sometimes required to pluck the notes out of nowhere. Bodley turned to the one soprano he knew could do justice to the work – Veronica Dunne. She was flattered to be asked but dismayed by the short time they had to prepare – about two weeks. Seóirse arrived at Ronnie's house for rehearsals and laid his score on the piano:

> I asked Ronnie what sounds she could make with different parts of her voice. In 'No. 3: The Mask', for example, there is a dialogue between the man and the woman, and I found Ronnie could raise her chest voice up to about G. She is a heavy dramatic soprano and I tailored the piece to suit her voice. Rehearsals were interspersed

by drinks, which were invariably dark and light Vermouth mixed with ice. These were ingested liberally and with great good humour, and in the end we had a piece that worked.

Ronnie sought assistance from her new friend, pianist Veronica McSwiney, and together they practised the music time and again, to be ready for the world première on Friday, 11 June 1965. It opened Dublin's 20th Century Music Festival in the Saint Francis Xavier Hall, Dublin, with Tibor Paul and the Radio Éireann Symphony Orchestra. Mary MacGoris in the *Irish Independent* noted that 'the work is certainly dramatic and effective in the modern idiom. Veronica Dunne surmounted the vocal difficulties with glowing colour and impressive agility.'

September 1965 was the start of a new year at the College of Music. Ronnie now had her own permanent music room, No. 20, Chatham Row. The students quickly dubbed it The Labour Ward, where embryonic talents had to endure hours, months, years of intensive training before emerging as fully formed singers. When that happened, Ronnie had no hesitation in pushing them to seek new opportunities, new training, wherever their careers took them.

Ronnie was teaching three days a week and lamented the lack of piano skills and all those times she had absconded through the sitting room window as a child when she was supposed to be practising. Her plight was recognised, and sympathetic piano teachers would send along pupils to play for her students.

One day Dr J.J. O'Reilly knocked on the door to her practise room and said, 'This is a talented young guy I've got whose sight-reading is terrible. See what you can make of him.'

'Darling,' said Ronnie, 'come in.' Before he could utter a word, seventeen-year-old John O'Conor was sitting at the piano fretting through an aria from Rossini's *The Barber of Seville.*

Dr O'Reilly nurtured some outstanding Irish pianists at the college. Veronica McSwiney and John O'Conor both began their studies with him in the 1940s and 1950s respectively. They each started in a class of fourteen children seated before dummy keyboards of four octaves with properly spaced printed notes. Dr O'Reilly was seated at his piano at the top of the room; they would listen and try to copy what he did. One by one they would get up and play that week's piece for him. After a year, the children progressed on to various teachers, Dr O'Reilly choosing to teach the one or two that he considered displayed the most promise. John had been with him for more than ten years. Dr O'Reilly knew that working with Ronnie's students would broaden the lad's knowledge and sharpen his playing.

Ronnie's teaching methods and her exceptionally fine ear intrigued John. She strove always for excellence and would persist until it was achieved. She talked about the 'colour' of music and when someone was singing a phrase, she could get him or her to change the colour of it to suit the particular words. Dr O'Reilly was insistent on producing beautiful sounds, and Chopin and Mozart had written about trying to imitate the human voice on the piano. In a very practical way, John was now learning how a singer modulates the sound. He started searching for different tonal qualities on the keyboard, and yet, how wonderful to be able to sing. He plucked up the courage to ask Ronnie if it would be possible. 'Stand up,' she said, and struck a chord on the piano. 'Sing me that scale.' He sang and she laughed: 'I think you'd better stick to playing, lovey.'

Occasionally John had his knowledge broadened in ways Dr O'Reilly could not have envisaged. One Saturday Joe Lane came in for his usual lesson. As the class proceeded, Ronnie became more and more disgruntled. Eventually she hurled the music at him and told him to get out. 'And the next time you come in for a morning lesson,' she shouted, 'do not have sex with your wife the night before!' Joe went beetroot and shuffled from the room. His wife Lucy produced child number four shortly thereafter.

Despite such distractions, Joe and Lucy became firm friends with Ronnie and her husband Peter. The two men shared a passion for sport and horses with another friend, Ned Thornton. They were all past pupils of Belvedere College, Dublin, and members of Old Belvedere Rugby Club, and they followed the games avidly. Ronnie came to refer to the three of them as the Traveling Wilburys because they palled around everywhere together. Peter even tolerated Joe's singing lessons in the house because, he said, his voice was lyrical and didn't overpower him.

In his home in Terenure, young John O'Conor was fighting for his future as a pianist. His mother was adamant that there was no money in it and wanted him to become an accountant with a permanent, pensionable job. A compromise was reached when he agreed to take a music degree at University College Dublin so that he could at least teach when the piano-playing scheme collapsed. The trouble was that the degree course was almost entirely academic, painfully reinforced by the comment of a professor during John's Second Year who asked, 'When are you going to stop practising the piano and start studying your music?' His one respite was playing for Ronnie's students. 'Come along to the College on Thursday and Saturday,' she would say. 'And come up to the house on Sunday – I've someone entering the Feis Ceoil that you can play for.' As the day became evening she would thrust a glass of wine in John's hand, slap a thick steak on the pan and persuade him to stay for dinner.

Ronnie was juggling teaching, performing and holding a home together with the help of her housekeeper Eileen. She rose at six in the morning, spent an hour practising, breakfasted with Peter and Judy and saw them off to school, drove to the College of Music, taught all day, ate a banana for lunch, came home, prepared dinner if she was not performing, and retired late at night. She bought food for the table and ensured that her children were looked after. When on her own, she limited herself to a gin and tonic before dinner and one afterwards, but with visitors she had a very generous hand. Both she and Peter were gregarious and loved entertaining friends from theatrical and racing circles to dinner parties with huge roasts and free-flowing wine and conversation, and their wild, bohemian parties were legendary.

One of their guests was Harry Christmas, director of EMI Records in Ireland. He realised that there would be a resurgence of interest in Irish music coming up to the fiftieth anniversary of the Easter Rising, and he engaged Ronnie to make an album with her friend Havelock Nelson. She stayed with Havelock for a couple of days in Belfast while they recorded *Celtic Songs*. He accompanied her on piano as she sang a selection of Irish favourites, including 'The Lark in the Clear Air', 'Róisín Dubh', 'I Will Walk with My Love', and 'Faithful Johnny'. The *Irish Times* rejoiced that the new LP had been issued: 'It is a record of lasting importance ... there is always a market for traditional songs of this sort.'

For the 1965 autumn season of Welsh National Opera, Ronnie appeared as Marenka in a production of Smetana's *The Bartered Bride* at the New Theatre, Cardiff. There she made the acquaintance of Philippe Perrottet, heralded as a brilliant up-and-coming producer and choreographer. This, his first full-length production for WNO, was lauded for its lively feeling for movement and colour, particularly in the circus scene. It was back to a circus of a different kind for two productions with the DGOS.

The role of Marenka in Smetana's *The Bartered Bride* at the New Theatre, Cardiff, 1965

Anne Makower had recently directed the first screening of an opera on Telefís Éireann. A.J. Potter had written *Patrick* especially for television. The three acts with multiple sets were staged in the new Studio One at Radio Telefís Éireann's headquarters in Donnybrook. The space was too small to contain the orchestra and conductor, however, and these were miles away in the Saint Francis Xavier Hall. There were links between the two venues and monitors were hung over the studio floor so that the conductor's top half was seen by the singers and he had a monitor to see them! The entire production had to be recorded in one take – the least slip could mean that they would have to start all over again – but it worked. On the strength of this, the DGOS asked Anne to direct *La Bohème* at the Gaiety Theatre in December 1965. 'It was scarifying,' she says, for not only was her singing teacher, Ronnie, in the title role, but the DGOS seemed stuck in its ways:

> There was just a week of rehearsals, so I realised I couldn't put my mark on it. All I could be was a traffic cop – just make sure they didn't fall over the furniture. I couldn't begin to think about interpretation or the balance of singers or anything. It was very frustrating. I wanted to have a good set without being extravagant – a room for the attic with the skylight effect. That was

Preparing to be Mimi. Gaiety Theatre dressing room, 1965

a battle. I told Colonel Bill O'Kelly I wanted a designer and he said what do you want a designer for; it's only an attic. Which said it all. I ended up designing it myself and I'm not a designer, but I was determined to break the habit somehow. I got a friend to help me do the drawings, and it was built and painted. It was OK, not wonderful, but at least it got away from the ubiquitous flats with painted shadows.

Charles Acton's review in the *Irish Times* reveals the results of Anne's work as seen from the other side of the proscenium arch. He urged his readers to go along to the Gaiety for a thoroughly enjoyable evening:

> Anne Makower designed admirable sets that were consistent with the opera and that imparted into the garret the necessary bit of colour with sunset and coverlet, and who succeeded in actually putting some production into a DGOS opera. If she did it all in two days (as I understand) what a really good opera we would have had with four! Veronica Dunne looked the part, acted the part and (of course) sang the part really well. Two highlights were 'Donde lieta' in Act III and her beautiful singing in Act IV. The music, the phrasing, the nostalgia were all there at the end and the tragic reality of Mimi's death.

Charles Craig, Ronnie's favourite Rodolfo, was praised, as was James Pease's Colline, with John Hauxwell and John Rhys Evans completing the quartet and Harold Gray conducting.

Ronnie was also appearing in the accompanying opera at the Gaiety, Mozart's *Don Giovanni*, in a new role for her – Donna Elvira. Between 3 and 18 December 1965 she sang four performances of each opera, and not only Charles Acton but all the newspaper critics were lavish in their praise of her magnificent voice, the pathos, grace and fervour she brought to both roles, and her supreme command of the stage each time she stepped onto it. Notwithstanding this, it seemed that she had, after all, been on borrowed time with Bill O'Kelly, and Ronnie was never again invited to sing with the Dublin Grand Opera Society.

Premières, recordings and disasters

20

At her home in Bushy Park Road ... Veronica Dunne, a talented artist with a charming sense of humour ... leans back comfortably, legs stretched, feet crossed, her head resting on the back of the large settee in the lovely drawing room.

*J*AMES H. REIDY interviewed Ronnie for the *Irish Independent* in June 1966. The article paints a picture of a busy and contented woman, whose work helped her to maintain a 'balanced, healthy approach to the day-to-day problems of bringing up children .... I have never found it a disadvantage,' she said.

'As she talks, you note her happy, cheerful manner, dark-auburn hair, good looks and neat casual dress (I like casual wear, and love all colours, perhaps blues particularly). The many pictures on the walls are interspersed in a framed selection from a Flemish book-of-hours series ... Near the piano is a cover of her recently made LP of Celtic songs, and on the music rest is the score of Gerard Victory's new work from poems by Rimbaud.'

Veronica Dunne

It was to be a time of firsts. *Voyelles*, the Gerard Victory piece, was a modern composition for soprano, flute, vibraphone and strings, lasting about thirteen minutes. Colman Pearce conducted its world première in the Saint Francis Xavier Hall, Dublin on 27 July 1966. 'Ronnie was always game for anything,' he said. 'Rehearsals with her were hilarious – she would make a joke at any time and if a note didn't spin for her she wouldn't be slow in using an expletive! For a new work, the singer has to get the music into themselves; as conductor, I can make a few suggestions but Ronnie was always right on the ball.'

Ronnie had rehearsed in the Saint Francis Xavier Hall with Tibor Paul for the Irish première of *Orchesterlieder* by the Swiss composer Wladimir Vogel. It was an unfamiliar piece for the orchestra and they were growing restive and resentful under Paul's dictatorial direction. The great conductor sensed rebellion and he turned on them, shouting, 'You think I know nothing? I tell you I know fuck all!' Members of the orchestra smirked into their scores. The piece opens with a blast of music and Ronnie had to pick an F sharp out of nowhere to start. She came in, pitch perfect. Tibor Paul stopped in amazement and asked her where she had got the note. 'Maestro,' she replied, 'I've a tuning fork up my ass!' This time the orchestra roared with laughter. The performance took place on 29 January 1966; the tuning fork was in perfect working order.

In March Ronnie was with Welsh National Opera for two productions – Mozart's *Don Giovanni* at the New Theatre, Cardiff and Smetana's *The Bartered Bride* at the Grand Theatre, Swansea. Music critic Peter James greeted her portrayal of Donna Elvira in *Don Giovanni* as 'technically assured and appropriately dignified'. Her performance as Marenka in *The Bartered Bride* provoked more enthusiasm. She was singing with an old friend, Stuart Burrows, as Jenik. 'Company captures freshness of an exuberant opera' trumpeted Frank Gold of the *South Wales Evening Post*. Burrows was praised for the 'Puccinian flavour about his singing' and Ronnie was equally impressive, 'especially during the last act where, for a while, all the gaiety is forgotten when she [Marenka] mistakenly believes Jenik has abandoned her for money. The aria in which she sings of her despair was tenderly moving, the score rising to the greatest music of the opera with true tragic fervour.'

Back in Dublin Ronnie prepared for a unique occasion. The fiftieth anniversary commemoration of the 1916 Rising was given enormous importance by the Irish government, which promoted political debates, cultural events, Roman Catholic religious services and social gatherings throughout the country, with an emphasis on eulogising those men who had fought and died in the Easter Rebellion. Brian Boydell, Professor of Music at Trinity College Dublin, composer of modern music, Anglo-Irish Protestant and avowed pacifist, was therefore both surprised and honoured when the state broadcaster, Radio Telefís Éireann, invited him to write a work for the anniversary.

Brian Boydell collaborated with his great friend Tomás Ó Súilleabháin. (Tomás had sung as Thomas O'Sullivan on the Irish Festival Singers' tour of the United States in 1955.) Tomás wrote the libretto by incorporating Yeats's poem 'Easter 1916' ('MacDonagh and

MacBride / And Connolly and Pearse / Now and in time to be, / Wherever green is worn, / Are changed, changed utterly: / A terrible beauty is born') with poems from nationalists killed in the Great War, including Francis Ledwidge's lament for Thomas MacDonagh ('He shall not hear the bittern cry') and Tom Kettle's 'Reason in Rhyme'. Words and music complement each other in a composition that is, in turn, sombre, haunting and fiery.

A Terrible Beauty is Born is a cantata for three soloists, a narrator, choir and orchestra. The world première was at the Gaiety Theatre, Dublin on 11 April 1966 and featured Our Lady's Choral Society, narrator Conor Farrington and the Radio Éireann Symphony Orchestra conducted by Tibor Paul. Following the performance, the headline in the *Irish Independent* was: 'Boydell work makes powerful impact':

> The writing is complex and difficult but at all times musical. The orchestration is richly imaginative and colourful and the vocal lines make demands on the singers but the tessitura [general pitch level] is always within their range .... Of the soloists, William Young (baritone) was the most impressive .... Bernadette Greevy (contralto) was in splendid voice ....Veronica Dunne, an accomplished and sensitive artist, sang magnificently.

EMI Records produced a special recording to commemorate the Jubilee: *From 1916: The Best of Ireland's Music* with Veronica Dunne and the Irish National Orchestra and Choir. Some of Ronnie's favourite songs were included: 'Padraic the Fiddler', 'My Singing Bird', 'Shaun O'Neill', 'Sea Wrack' and 'The Mother'. Leading British critics chose this and the *Celtic Songs* LP as being among their Ten Best Records of 1966. In 1968 and 1970, baritone Eric Hinds joined Ronnie and Havelock on two recordings: *She Moved Thro' The Fair* and *Around The Ring of Kerry* which were successful at home and in the United States. Irish tenor Uel Deane joined Ronnie, Eric and Havelock in 1968 on a recording of *Irish Love Songs* from Balfe, Wallace and Benedict.

Driving to venues up and down the country with Ronnie at the helm could be an interesting experience. In April she borrowed her father's car, a huge Jaguar, for the three-hour trip to Limerick for a performance of Verdi's *Requiem* at St Mary's Cathedral. Fellow soloists Eddie FitzGibbon and Joe Dalton were in the back on plush leather seats when Ronnie, ever the hostess, called over her shoulder that they should pull up the centre section and help themselves to brandy or champagne. As they hit the open road, Joe noticed the dial on the speedometer in rapid ascent from 70 to 80 to 90 miles per hour. Eddie was getting more and more nervous and his leg started to quiver. 'R-R-Ronnie,' he stammered, 'where's the jacks in this thing?' Joe suggested she slow down or she would be caught for speeding through the towns. 'Oh no,' she said. 'This car is one-and-a-half lengths longer than a normal car, so it'll take the same time for this one doing ninety as it would be for the other one doing sixty!'

Eddie and Joe were more than greatly relieved to spy the spire of the cathedral. Ronnie swerved to a halt outside and they hurried in to give thanks for a safe delivery. Tibor Paul and Bernadette Greevy were already there and, during a break in rehearsals, Ronnie and Eddie strolled around the twelfth-century building. Ronnie paused before a statue and giggled. The inscription read something like: *This is a memorial to Bishop so-and-so who managed to establish cordial relations with all with whom he had intercourse.* She pointed it out to Tibor Paul who couldn't for the life of him see what was so funny.

Laughter was never a problem with the Kilrush Operatic Society. Ronnie sang Norina in Donizetti's *Don Pasquale* with them in May and Charles Acton reported in the *Irish Times* that she was 'delightful'. Although he commented on her articulation – 'I did wish that I could have heard her words' – he declared that she had 'a lightness of touch' and was, in fact, 'the best part of the whole production'. He commended the Society for managing to continue 'this remarkable venture'. Sadly, that 1966 season was the last for the small hard-working group who for fifteen years had proudly presented the rich world of opera to so many people who otherwise might never have seen such performances.

One freezing Saturday afternoon, 19 November, 1966 Ronnie received a phone call from Covent Garden. Joan Carlyle, their soprano in Mozart's *Le nozze di Figaro,* had become ill. The performance was on Wednesday – could Ronnie possibly fill in for the part of the Countess? It was a fantastic opportunity to take to the stage again at Covent Garden, but Ronnie reluctantly explained that the last time she had performed the role was with the DGOS in 1963 and she doubted whether she could get up to speed in such a short time. Her fears were brushed aside. 'We have no one else,' she was told. 'Europe is snowbound and we can't get anyone into London. You'll manage; you always do. Come on over.'

By sheer bad luck, Ronnie had lent her score to a student whom she could not contact, and the shops were closed on Sunday, so she spent most of the next day and night playing a recording of *Figaro* over and over. Sleepless and filled with apprehension, she caught the flight out to London on Monday. She went into hastily arranged rehearsals on

Tuesday morning, only to be confronted by the news that it was effectively a first night with all the critics invited. It was an entirely new production to Ronnie, and it contained additional recitatives. With the score at last in hand, Ronnie worked until she was literally in tears before coming to the difficult conclusion that she could not master the work well enough to give a creditable performance. To be fair to the rest of the cast, Ronnie pulled out with abject apologies. The opera was cancelled, and Ronnie flew back to Dublin, devastated. There is a twist to the saga. John Copley of Covent Garden delighted in recounting the witty tale of the Irish stand-in who declared in her 'leprechaun voice' that she 'only did the numbers, not the recitatives'. This anecdote was repeated by the baritone Thomas Allen in his book *Foreign Parts: A Singer's Journal* (1993). It had evidently come as a surprise to everyone, including Ronnie herself, that she was not, after all, superhuman! The opera went ahead on Saturday, 26 November with the Spanish soprano Pilar Lorengar as the Countess.

Ronnie in 1965

There were more firsts for Ronnie that year, including excerpts from Hugo Wolf's *Mignon Cycle* conducted by Seóirse Bodley and Kodály's *Te Deum* with Colman Pearce. In January 1967 she sang the role of Marietta in Victor Herbert's *Naughty Marietta* at the Cork Opera House, and in April Tibor Paul was the conductor for Britten's *War Requiem* at St Patrick's Cathedral, Dublin. He insisted that Ronnie sing from the pulpit, which was definitely a first!

It was twelve years since she had sung on the stage of Carnegie Hall and in 1967 she was on another legendary stage – the Royal Albert Hall. The Saint Patrick's Day Concert on 16 March was billed as an annual celebration of Irish song, music and humour. Ronnie appeared with ten other popular Irish artists, including Kathleen Watkins, Butch Moore, Joe Lynch, Dermot O'Brien and Louis Browne, and bands, pipers and dancers.

That summer, Ronnie took young Peter and Judy to Italy. She rented a house in Rome for a month and brought them to all the sites of her youth and entertained them with tales of her honeymoon. The children were impressed by her fluent Italian as they travelled farther afield to Capri and Naples. When Peter came out to join them for a week, they spent a carefree family time together that was over all too soon.

In September and October it was back to familiar material, and boat journeys, when Ronnie sang Donna Elvira in Mozart's *Don Giovanni* with Welsh National Opera at the Grand Theatre, Swansea, and then at the New Theatre, Cardiff. The opera was a revival of the previous year's production by Michael Geliot and with almost the same cast – Forbes Robinson, Patricia Reakes, Stuart Burrows, David Rhys Edwards and John Gibbs. Andrew Porter, editor of *The Musical Times*, wrote that Geliot brought out the comic aspects of the drama:

> But it is a 'human comedy' which does not obscure the serious emotions. Elvira, brilliantly and quite deliberately played by Veronica Dunne as a lady past her first youth, desperately clinging to the one romantic experience she has known, can cut a ridiculous figure, but she is not the less tragic for that .... There were several passages of vocal delicacy; Miss Reakes and Miss Dunne were both specially eloquent in accompanied recitative.

In April 1968 Ronnie was on stage at the Savoy Cinema, Dublin for another first, that of performing Janáček's *Glagolitic Mass*, with a text in Old Church Slavonic and a Slovakian conductor, L'udovít Rajter. In November of that year, Ronnie teamed up with Hans Waldemar Rosen for the Irish première of Anthony Milner's oratorio *The Water and the Fire* at the Saint Francis Xavier Hall. To learn, practise and perfect all these new works was an extraordinary feat, especially as Ronnie was teaching at the College and at home, and fulfilling concert engagements.

One of Ronnie's greatest challenges came when she and Havelock Nelson tackled Olivier Messiaen's *Harawi*. *Harawi* is a song cycle for soprano and piano written by the French composer, organist and ornithologist in 1945. The surrealist poems of Harawi (written by Messiaen himself) describe the love-death of Tristan and Isolde, using symbols derived mainly from Peruvian folklore. The text is in French, although Messiaen uses South American words, not for their meaning, but for their onomatopoeic qualities, as in the fourth movement when 'Doundou Tchil' suggests the ankle bells worn by Peruvian-Indian dancers. Writing of the work's Hindu rhythms, ape sounds and birdsong, Charles Acton called it a 'strange, unique, evocative, wonderful masterpiece'.

Ronnie and Havelock worked tirelessly on the score for five months, and Ronnie had countless sessions with Veronica McSwiney and other pianists before the piece was ready in time for the Belfast Festival. On 26 November 1969 *Harawi* was performed in the Harty Room at Queen's University and recorded for BBC Radio 3. Charles Acton declared it a triumph then, and also one year later, when

Ronnie and Havelock again performed it for the Dublin Arts Festival in Trinity College:

With Havelock Nelson

> Even among Messiaen's works, this 'Chant d'amour et de mort' (the piece's subtitle) is unique in its atmosphere, in its continuing 50-minute intensity. It is written for a 'grand soprano dramatique', and we are fortunate in having one in Veronica Dunne, who has now surely reached her prime. This was a performance of total authority, understanding and innermost feeling. She and it were as though one. Two sidelights on the performance were her unfailingly taut rhythmic standards and the great range of emotional and interpretative colouring she put into her voice. All that may sound as though it were a solo and not a duet, whereas Dr Nelson's playing matched Miss Dunne's singing all through. The one would be

nothing without the other, and yet I think that her absorption and intensity inspired him .... Yesterday's performance was a real privilege.

Not everyone shared Acton's enthusiasm. The performance in Belfast began at ten o'clock at night. Many people walked out halfway through, perhaps favouring a pint in the pub instead. The fifty or so who remained were treated to a *tour de force*, despite the fact that Havelock was running a temperature of 102 with influenza and Ronnie was recovering from laryngitis.

The following morning, Ronnie was again in the Harty Room with more modern music, this time by the English composer Humphrey Searle, who had been a pupil of Webern. Having expended so much effort on *Harawi*, Ronnie had given less attention to Searle's *Songs* and knew she would have to improvise here and there. Just before the recital, she was dismayed when the composer handed out music sheets to everyone in the audience. 'Holy Moses,' she said to Havelock at the piano, 'what they're reading and what I'm singing are going to be completely different!' Afterwards, Searle approached her with tears in his eyes, clasped both her hands in his, and exclaimed, 'Wonderful, wonderful!' Ronnie looked over at Havelock, who turned away to hide his laughter.

Ronnie was looking forward to Christmas, but on 23 December 1969 William Dunne died. *Oh My Beloved Father.*

Room 20, Chatham Row

21

JOHN O'CONOR had such fun with Ronnie and her students at the College of Music that his academic work took a very back seat. On one occasion Fionnuala Hough, a lovely young soprano, was rehearsing Norina's aria from Donizetti's *Don Pasquale* in Ronnie's Room 20 at the College. It's a laid back, flirty aria during which Fionnuala had to pop a marshmallow in her mouth. With her mouth full, Fionnuala couldn't actually sing. Ronnie suggested cutting the marshmallow in half. They eventually cut it into eight pieces, which was just about manageable.

He may have been learning pragmatism, but John was not hitting the books with any enthusiasm. He was in University College Dublin one day when a professor walked by and pointed to the noticeboard. 'You needn't bother looking at that in September,' he said. 'Your name won't be there when you finish your final exams.'

John fled to Ronnie in Chatham Row. 'What am I going to do?' he wailed. 'I'll fail my exams.'

'That's nonsense,' said Ronnie. 'Tell you what: I'm taking the children off for a holiday on the Spanish Riviera. Come along and lie on the beach for a week and then go home and study like crazy.'

Her son Peter had discovered a love of horses and he decided to stay home for the summer and ride. His life was about to take a turn for the better. He had just left Belvedere College (his father's alma mater) to become a boarder at Mungret College, Limerick – a school at which he would shine in athletics and leadership.

Judy was about thirteen when she, John and Ronnie stayed in an apartment at Tossa de Mar on the Costa Brava. They chatted, laughed and lazed by the sea. Ronnie cooked, they drank wine and had long soporific evenings. One afternoon they were leaving the beach when Ronnie spotted an unusual sight – a car from Ireland. A couple of bedraggled lads in dark glasses were heading towards it and Ronnie hailed them. It turned out they were driving around France and Spain and sleeping in the car because money was tight. Ronnie immediately invited them back to the apartment for a shower and a good meal. When they had tidied up, Ronnie was on the terrace. She held out large gin and tonics with her customary toast: 'Here's to your bright eyes. May they never meet.' One of the lads blushed, and it was only then that Ronnie had a look at him without his sunglasses – he was totally cross-eyed. She was mortified, and more circumspect with her toasts thereafter.

When John got home he studied for twelve hours a day, took his finals and graduated with honours, much to everyone's surprise except Ronnie's. Just before one of her recitals with Havelock Nelson, John ran through the repertoire with her. At the end of Brahms' poignant song, 'Alte Liebe', for singer and piano, Ronnie looked up and said, 'That was incredible!'

'Yes,' said John fervently. 'You were great.'

'No,' said Ronnie. '*You* were incredible. We'll have to do a recital together.'

John could not believe it. More than anything he wanted to be an accompanist – he just loved working with singers. Ronnie arranged everything. John was a young proud man of twenty-three when he performed with Ronnie at the Royal Hibernian Hotel, Dublin and before an appreciative audience he knew he had found his life's calling.

Unable to fund studying abroad, John began teaching full-time at the College of Music. On 4 March 1971 he accompanied Ronnie in two works at the Goethe Institute, Dublin: Messiaen's *Harawi* and the world première of James Wilson's *Irish Songs*. James Wilson was an English-born composer who had come to live in Ireland in the late 1940s. Wishing to express his gratitude to the country that had been his home for over twenty years, he dedicated his *Irish Songs* to two of its most celebrated musicians, Veronica Dunne and Havelock Nelson. His use of seven texts from Swift, Moore, Lever, de Vere, Darley, Dowden and Stephens portrayed his views of the Irish character in songs that ranged from raucous humour to deep tragedy. Charles Acton commented that the cycle was

> ... well made, varied, fitting to the words without arbitrariness and convincing. Edward Dowden's 'Swallows' was particularly effectively caught. The piano part throughout sounded idiomatic and authentic. Mr O'Conor brought out its qualities very well and Miss Dunne captured the full spirit of all the songs, the soft and slow as well as the immensely lively. And what astonishing power and musical sound this soprano [sic] can show on the G below the stave!

With such experience and reviews, John's future as an accompanist seemed assured. However, later that year he was awarded an Austrian

Government scholarship that enabled him to move to Vienna to study, and in 1973 he was awarded First Prize at the International Beethoven Piano Competition. His career as an international pianist spun into orbit and he has achieved phenomenal success with his performances and as a celebrated teacher. He sometimes harkens back, however, to a piano piece by Franz Schubert. Playing the Impromptu in G flat, op. 90, No. 3, he says, is the closest he has come to singing like Veronica Dunne.

Emboldened by the success of his song cycle, James Wilson was receptive to Ronnie's suggestion that he should compose another work that she could pair with Messiaen's *Harawi* in concert. For the libretto he turned to Ian Fox, who selected poems and prose from an English translation of 'Táin Bó Cúailnge' ('The Cattle Raid of Cooley'), taken from the twelfth-century *Book of Leinster*. It is a bloody tale of greed and jealousy over the capture and possession of an incredibly fertile bull. Battles for the bull resulted in many men being slain. Legendary Irish hero Cúchulainn was forced to kill his stepbrother and best friend, Ferdia, before himself being mortally wounded.

The Táin, dedicated to Veronica Dunne, premièred on 29 June 1972 in the Examination Hall at Trinity College Dublin during the Dublin Festival of 20th Century Music. Wilson described it as a 'monodrama' for singer, piano and percussion. With pianist Courtney Kenny and percussionist Jeffrey Cosser in position, Ronnie made a majestic entrance from the back of the hall in an impressive chieftainess gown with a gold band on her head. Charles Acton wrote that she 'gave a magnificent performance, exploiting to the full the resources of speech, declamation, and pure song that James Wilson provided for her. She has such a splendidly dramatic speaking voice that the soft transition to song made me wish for more speech.' He marvelled again at the range of Ronnie's voice, for it was rare that a soprano could sing so splendidly in the middle of the bass clef. Although uncomfortable with the ferocity of both the story and the music, Acton was moved by 'the beautifully lyrical setting of 'Cúchulainn's Lament for Ferdia', considering it one of Wilson's finest compositions.

It was Christmas 1972 and Harry Christmas hosted a dinner party for his major stars and business associates in EMI Records. Entertainment was provided by the 'class act' of Ronnie, with Havelock Nelson on piano, and the 'trendy act' of the folk group We4, led by Larry Hogan with Suzanne Murphy on vocals and tambourine. Harry Christmas had always maintained that Suzanne should have her voice properly trained, preferably by Veronica Dunne, but

Suzanne Murphy and the folk group We4

Suzanne didn't want her folk singing ruined by heavy operatic techniques. At the party, all the members of the group were surprised by how friendly and relaxed Ronnie was, not at all the 'grand dame' they had expected, and when she invited them for an informal lesson at her house they readily agreed.

A few days later after drinks at Bushy Park and a practice around the piano, Ronnie drew Suzanne aside. 'You should leave that group,' she said. 'Your voice is too good. Come to me, darling, and you will wear diamonds!'

It was the first, but certainly not the last-time that Ronnie would utter this immortal phrase to those whom she knew had 'it'. And she was usually right, in every respect! But at that time Suzanne thought that Ronnie was quite simply mad, and dismissed the suggestion.

Some months later We4 broke up. Suzanne was invited to sing on Radio Éireann and BBC television on her own – a prospect that she found unnerving. She picked up the phone and asked Ronnie for a few preparatory lessons. Ronnie agreed, on condition that Suzanne didn't run away again. After the programmes Suzanne thought the job was done, but Ronnie had other ideas. 'You have to give up your job,' she said. 'You need to study full-time and then join an opera company.'

Suzanne gaped at her. The woman was definitely bonkers! 'Ah,' she said, playing for time, 'could I use your loo?' As she bolted the door behind her, she thought, 'Help! This person sees something in me that I don't have at all. What's she up to? Is she trying to relive her life through me? Does she want to take over my life? How am I going to get out of this?' When she felt sufficiently calm, she returned to face Ronnie, and agreed to at least continue studying.

Work at the College now occupied more and more of Ronnie's time and energy. Early on she had realised that an hour a week with promising singers was just not enough. She would often tell students to sign up and pay for their allotted time, and then teach them during any breaks she had at no extra charge. If someone had to cancel their lesson, Ronnie would phone Suzanne or another student to see if they wanted to take it up, and they invariably did.

Ronnie filled every minute of her day, and would then give extra lessons at home. She was also encouraging piano students like Paul Dorgan to play for her pupils and consider careers as accompanists.

Paul remembers that Ronnie seemed to be the first person to arrive at the College and the last to leave. 'It was dangerous to knock on her door to say "Good morning" because invariably she'd ask you when you'd be free to work with so-and-so, or could you play for someone's lesson.'

When Ronnie had an accompanist, she could be scathing to a singer who had not worked on her assignment: 'As a teacher I can cope with a lazy student, but don't waste the accompanist's time by singing wrong notes, wrong rhythms, wrong words.' Summarily dismissed, the student would depart, to be replaced by the next person waiting outside her room for just such a chance.

It was a time of change at the College of Music. The principal, Michael McNamara, retired in 1969 and Dr O'Reilly temporarily held that position. Frank Heneghan was appointed in 1973. He gave up his job as a design engineer in Manchester and returned to Dublin. At the College he combined teaching the piano with the work of administering a venerable institution. Heneghan appreciated the number of enthusiastic students Ronnie attracted to the College, although he wasn't always in tune with her methods. One thing they were in agreement over was the importance of choral work; the new principal was very keen that the College should be represented by first-rate choirs.

At home in Bushy Park, seventeen-year-old Judy was ready to stretch her wings and asked Ronnie if she could go to Aix-en-Provence for the summer to stay with a family and learn French. Ronnie was all in favour and they booked the flights and made the travel arrangements together: Dublin-London, London-Marseilles and a bus to Aix. Ronnie drove her out to the airport and they nearly missed the flight. As Judy was about to rush off, Ronnie held her arm. 'I'm going to say one thing to you, dear,' she said. 'A stiff cock has no conscience – that's all I'm going to say.' Armed with this shot across the bow, Judy sallied forth and soon discovered she had inherited her mother's sense of adventure. She loved travel and was never fazed by difficulties in a foreign country.

Joe Lane persuaded his wife Lucy to study with Ronnie. The couple first met when performing in a musical, and their singing both separately and together in a semi-

Joe and Lucy Lane

professional way formed the backdrop to a long and very happy marriage. Lucy was accustomed to appearing with the Rathgar and Rathmines Musical Society and particularly loved Gilbert and Sullivan operarettas, but Joe felt Ronnie's training would strengthen her voice. Although she knew Ronnie socially, Lucy was terrified going into her first lesson at the house, but it was a very professional encounter with no chitchat, no quarter given for friendship, just concentrated breathing exercises and repertoire. Lucy worked hard there and in Room 20, and she noticed her standards rising. Despite having four young children she practised diligently and gained Ronnie's respect. One dreaded afternoon, however, she had to turn up for her lesson and confess that she was pregnant with number five! The next time Ronnie saw Joe, she berated him saying, 'No sooner have I got her voice right but you go and make her pregnant again!' Childbirth, however, was a doddle compared to the test which Lucy had yet to face.

Feis Ceoil! Two words that can strike dread, anticipation and hope into the fluttering hearts of aspiring classical musicians. The competition, held annually in Dublin, is the main showcase and proving ground for students and, by extension, their teachers. Ronnie's students had always performed well at the Feis but in 1974 she knew she had the material for something truly ambitious in the 'Operatic Ensemble' section. She would present the trio from Strauss' *Der Rosenkavalier* with Lucy Lane as The Marschallin, Suzanne Murphy as her lover Octavian and Fionnuala Hough as the girl Sophie.

The trio in the final act is gloriously musical and fiendishly difficult for the singers as the voices weave in and around each other. Octavian is torn between his older mistress and his young fiancée, and in the emotional climax of the opera The Marschallin gracefully releases Octavian to follow his heart, and leaves the stage to the young lovers.

Ronnie chose Paul Dorgan as accompanist because she knew he could cope with Strauss' intricate orchestrations. They rehearsed for weeks at Ronnie's house but couldn't make it come together. They were using an English libretto, but to get the nuance and rhythm of the piece it has to be sung in German, a language that none of the girls knew. Suzanne and Fionnuala said they would give it a go but Lucy said that even if she could learn it she'd never pronounce it properly. But she gave in, listened to the recording, read the words over and over, and despaired.

One evening the rehearsal was going badly and Ronnie was furious. 'I don't care if we stay here all night,' she said, 'this has to be improved!' By that time they were hungry and frustrated. They fought and worked and worked and fought until eventually it started to fall into place. Ronnie realised they were all exhausted, and now that there was a glimmer of hope she was ready to be friends again. 'Come on,' she said, 'let's have a drink.' When she fetched the gin they drank it like water. Joe Lane arrived an hour later to find Ronnie at least upright, but Paul had collapsed under the piano, Suzanne was stretched full-length in front of the fireplace, Fionnuala was sobbing quietly in a corner and in the kitchen his wife Lucy was pleading for 'a heel of bread' to soak up the alcohol. 'You're all a total disgrace,' he said, 'and I don't care who knows it!'

Never one to do anything by halves, Ronnie asked Philippe Perrottet, who was in Dublin to work on three productions for the DGOS, to advise the girls on movement, emotion and acting. She hired beautiful costumes, dressed the piano with cloth and candelabra, found children to be extras and staged the entire trio as close as possible to an operatic production. It was a triumph! The Metropolitan Hall in Abbey Street, Dublin had never seen anything like it before and they scooped First Prize.

Ronnie was ecstatic, but it wasn't her only entry at the Feis that night. Joe Lane was competing in the 'Operatic Trio' section. Unfortunately, that very day he had to entertain important associates in the wine business and, when he turned up for the competition, Lucy suspected he wasn't one-hundred-per-cent. She accompanied him to the dressing room and waited outside by the four-rung ladder used to access the stage. She knew Joe had not had an opportunity to try on his costume beforehand and when he emerged from the dressing room she was dismayed to see that his white tights were far too small with the gusset ending just above his knees! They could hear Paul Dorgan playing their introduction but it was physically impossible for Joe to step onto the ladder. Lucy and the two other singers supported him as he leaned back, shuffled up and scrambled onto the stage. He used his coat to shield the wardrobe malfunction from the audience, but it was not his finest performance. The baritone lost all confidence and the soprano was, quite rightly, livid. Observing this from the gods, Ronnie didn't know whether to go down and kill Joe or cry with laughter. She ended up laughing. And when it was all over the three girls could round on Joe saying, 'Now who's the disgrace!'

Suzanne Murphy won the prestigious Dramatic Cup at that Feis and she began to think that maybe Ronnie was not so mad after all. Her parents were impressed, too, and they asked Ronnie's advice. 'She's got it,' she told them, 'and if she studies full-time she will go international.' That clinched it. They agreed to fund her studies with

Ronnie and Suzanne gave up her job. Her days now took on a very different hue. Every morning at six she got a phone call from Ronnie to make sure she would be at the College at eight for her first lesson. Then she worked on repertoire with an accompanist or on her own until mid-afternoon, when she went home for a rest to prepare for more work or rehearsals in the evening. Although swept up in Ronnie's enthusiasm, she found the training tough:

> It's hard because you can understand the idea of getting the voice to do what you want but the muscles don't always respond. Also, it's a question of finding the space in your mouth, your throat, how to manage the spin of breath to get an evenness of sound, and not to interrupt the various vowels of a word or make clunky consonants. The thought process and the muscles used are so amazing and so minuscule at the same time, but it is the whole body that's involved. Ronnie would say 'Show me your hands, lovey.' She put my hands around her ribcage and it was like a barrel – strong. I was only a slip of a thing and I'd say, 'I can't do that'. But with singing and exercise the intercostal muscles gradually strengthen and open up the ribcage a bit more. The more space you have in the ribcage the more the lungs can grow into that space, giving you more breath to work with. The tongue, the jaw – it all comes into it. There were days in Ronnie's room when I would cry in frustration and fear that I would never be able to make everything work together, let alone remember it all. But Ronnie kept me at it. 'Drop your jaw,' she'd say, because the jaw needs to be loose (but not collapsed!) to manage the breath. Everything takes hours and hours of practice. Sometimes you just have to let go, and suddenly it's there, and you're singing.

A couple of months later Suzanne got one of those breaks that are lucky only if you have the wit and ability to act on them. Veronica McSwiney was the pianist for Irish National Opera, an innovative touring company which brought productions all over Ireland with the aid of a truck and a cleverly designed flexible set which could be erected in a couple of hours. Tony Ó Dálaigh and his great friend Gerald Duffy from the Radio Éireann Singers had founded the company in 1964. Veronica heard Suzanne sing at the Feis, and since the company was casting Rossini's *La Cenerentol*, she arranged for her to have an audition. Tony and Gerald were awestruck by Suzanne's voice and immediately offered her a role as one of the sisters. Then fate took a hand, as Tony recalls:

> Before we got into rehearsals Cinderella had vocal problems and I rang Suzanne and asked if she would play the lead. 'Certainly,' she

Suzanne Murphy as Angelina (Cenerentola) in *La Cenerentola*. Irish National Opera, 1974.

replied with great confidence. She worked with accompanist Courtney Kenny and she was sensational. We opened in Dublin and she got rave reviews. The tenor was Paddy Ring from Limerick and, of course, so is Suzanne, so when we were going to Limerick we made a big thing of the advance publicity. We played in the Jesuit Hall but the audiences were not great. As we were dismantling the set, Suzanne looked around the empty house and said, 'In ten years time they won't be able to afford me.'

Ronnie was helping Suzanne to develop her voice from mezzo to soprano and there were hours of practice at the College and at Bushy Park. Other students, too, spent more and more time in her house. 'We singers just took over,' said Suzanne. 'We felt we were part of Ronnie's music family and we were entitled. Anyone who interrupted simply wasn't tolerated, and that included her real family!'

There was consternation at the house when Cliff, the pet poodle, broke his back and had the use of only his front legs. The vet wanted to put him down but Ronnie said, 'Certainly not, I'll get him better.' She brought him to work every day where he sat on her lap wrapped in towelling nappies and blankets. Every hour or so a student would have to turn him so he would not get bedsores. Suzanne was singing Mozart's *Queen of the Night* aria; as she hit high F, Cliff suddenly pooped all over Ronnie. 'Hey Suzanne', laughed Ronnie, 'that's the worst critique you're ever going to get!' They threw open the windows but the place stank for days afterwards. Ronnie made a sling with a knot on the top so that she could bring Cliff for walks while suspending his hindquarters. He eventually got the hang of walking on his own, but one leg was weaker than the other so he went round in circles. Like a ballerina he had to focus on where he wanted to go and pirouette around to it. One day at the house students teased him by calling 'Cliff, Cliff, Ronnie's coming.' He eagerly began his shuffling pirouette towards the door, but when he reached, it they said, 'Ah, poor Cliff, she's not there!'

For a few weeks during the summer of 1975 Suzanne stayed at the house when Ronnie and Peter were on holidays. Judy and young Peter called her Big Bird because she was so tall with blonde hair and long eyelashes. Suzanne was learning more repertoire and rehearsing for *The Secret Marriage* by Domenico Cimarosa with Irish National Opera where she was to play the lead soprano, Carolina. Judy was still at school and Peter was an undergraduate at University College Dublin. He had become a successful amateur jockey, and spent most of his free time at the stables of legendary horse trainer Paddy Mullins in Goresbridge, Co. Kilkenny. The main attraction at Goresbridge was Paddy Mullins's daughter, Sandra, and Peter was more than happy to be gradually accepted into the large and close-knit Mullins family.

Ronnie returned in August in time for the Kilkenny Arts Week which attracted great artists and large crowds. John O'Conor enchanted a capacity audience in St Canice's Cathedral with his recital of works by Brahms and Beethoven. Later in the week James Wilson's new monodrama *Fand* was premièred with Ronnie, pianist Veronica McSwiney, percussionist John Fennessy and flautist Doris Keogh. The piece was composed to precede *The Táin* in performance. James adapted the text from the 'Ulster Cycle' myths to describe Fand, the otherworldly woman who appears as a sea bird to the hero Cúchulainn. On 26 August 1975 the clash and cries of ancient Irish goddesses and warriors resounded around the medieval cathedral, separated by a contemplative interval as Veronica McSwiney played Field's *Nocturnes*. In the *Irish Times* Charles Acton wrote of Ronnie's 'tremendous dramatic ability, the great range of her expressive voice created most vivid experiences .... The evening did make very clear what a wonderful asset Veronica Dunne would make for the straight

Irish stage .... The Theatre Festival and our professional theatre should take note of a great actress.' Little did he know that Ronnie had been trying to tell anyone who would listen that she was a great actress since appearing in her own productions at the age of eight!

A new year beckoned at the College of Music and, with it, new challenges. Angela Feeney from Belfast was one of many students who benefited from Ronnie's generous hospitality. She lived as a member of the family in Bushy Park for four years while attending classes in the College and receiving extra tuition from Ronnie. In 1978 Ronnie was thrilled to be able to place Angela with Munich State Opera – the first of her fledglings to fly to the Continent.

In 1976 Ronnie was not only training Angela, she had fourteen other students at the College, but something was missing in Room 20 – a mirror. Unknown to themselves, singers can get into the habit of producing strange facial expressions, so they need to be able to see what they are doing while singing. It was against College rules to hang anything on the wall, but one girl said she would get the mirror and a lad said he had a drill. On the appointed day the students gathered, mirror and drill at the ready. As the boy started to drill, Ronnie thumped on the piano, Suzanne hit top doh and the mirror was secured to mad applause. It was grand practice for Suzanne's appearance in *The Secret Marriage*, which was hailed by all the critics as a triumph.

With that performance Suzanne stepped from the Irish stage and went international, just as Ronnie had foretold. Her début with Welsh National Opera on 8 September 1976 was a momentous affair for Suzanne, her family and for Ronnie, who greeted her portrayal of Constanza in Mozart's *Il Seraglio* with tears of pride and elation. Amid the hugs and champagne after the performance, Ronnie reminded Suzanne of all the work, sweat and moments of despair up in Room 20. 'But wasn't it worth it, lovey?' It certainly was. Suzanne had found her spiritual and professional home with Welsh National Opera. She would sing there and on the world stage for more than thirty years until herself becoming a fine teacher and promoter of young singing talent.

22 *The opera world is a stage*

RONNIE WAS WORKING at least thirty-six hours a week but getting paid for sixteen, and she was still part-time. To become full-time, she needed to have a music degree and pass a state examination in spoken Irish and she didn't know which was harder. Peter Sweeney, an organist and teacher at the College, helped with her academic studies, as did Nancy Calthorpe. Every morning she rose at five to write music notation and theory, using the white Formica table in the kitchen as a blackboard. She also took lessons to improve her piano skills. The Irish was another matter – she could not utter a word of it. But if she could master Italian, German and French, surely, she told herself, she could learn a modicum of her native language. Ronnie was informed that one of the questions that invariably came up in the exam was '*Cad a dhéanann tú?*' ('What do you do?'). She wrote out a five-minute spiel in English that one of her students, Nicola Sharkey, translated into Irish, and learned it off by heart.

The dreaded morning arrived. Ronnie was ushered into a drab room at the Department of Education and a bespectacled civil servant, looking exactly like Éamon de Valera, regarded her sternly across the desk. He questioned her closely *as Gaeilge*, and as she had not the foggiest idea what he was saying she replied '*Is ea*' or '*Ni hea*' ('Yes' or 'No') as seemed appropriate from his intonation. At last she got her cue: '*Cad a dhéanann tú?*' and she launched into her speech. He listened patiently until she ran out of steam, shuffled his papers, crossed his hands on the desk, cracked half a smile and said in English, 'You got it!'

She had to travel to Belfast for her external music examination, the Licentiate of Trinity College London, and she got that too. In later years she became a Fellow of Trinity College London, following an examination in Belfast during which she was accompanied by Havelock Nelson.

In 1976 Ronnie, armed with her new degree, became a full-time teacher at the College of Music, and soon afterwards was promoted to head of Vocal, Operatic and Drama Studies. Her new position sounded grand but it entailed onerous administrative duties in addition to a demanding teaching schedule. But she was not daunted; in fact, she had plans for the clutch of bright, enthusiastic young singers all ready and eager to perform. 'We have the voices,' she said. 'Let's put on an opera!'

The College had not staged an opera for a quarter of a century and there was no budget for such a venture, but Ronnie insisted that she would find whatever funds were required and they could hold the event in Chatham Row.

Five of Ronnie's students, from back, left to right: Anna Caleb, Deirdre Grier-Delaney, Nicola Sharkey, Marie-Claire O'Reirdan, Meryn Nance

Auditions were held among all the singing students at the College for not one but two of Mozart's operas – *Don Giovanni* and *The Magic Flute*. The allocation of roles was the duty of the casting director, a process in which Ronnie played no part. But she did arrange that her friend Gerald Duffy, an experienced choral coach, would train the chorus and conduct the singers, and that Gertrude (Trudi) Carberry, a fine accompanist at the College, would play the orchestral parts on the piano.

Rehearsals generated a wave of bubbly excitement. Invitations were issued, parents were primed, and on the chosen night the audience crowded into the small assembly hall for *Don Giovanni*. Ronnie rose to say a few words and, although she had sung before thousands in some of the largest concert halls in the world, she felt apprehensive. Many of the students about to appear were hers; much of the work involved was her work. It was another test, but she thrived on tests. Having welcomed everyone, she announced that the assembly hall was to be renamed the John McCann Hall in recognition of all the politician had done to raise the status of the College. Then, in a moment laden with symbolism, she withdrew, leaving the stage to the students. Terry O'Sullivan, who wrote 'Dubliner's Diary' in the *Irish Press*, picked up the story on 18 January 1977:

> A school of opera in Dublin? We were present at the illustration of the idea in the College of Music in Chatham Row last evening. Produced and directed by Veronica Dunne, about a week ago a talented group of young and happy singers presented a concert version of *Don Giovanni*. It was so reverberantly good that it had to be repeated. In the tiny John McCann Hall you get some of the bathroom effect. Everybody has a huge voice, resonant and full of hidden resources of power. The singers not merely sang. They enjoyed every absurdity of the score, as when one sings 'No' and another sings 'Yes'. Veronica Dunne has assembled a grand young team: Pat Sheridan, Nora Ring, Frank O'Brien, Joseph Browne, Frank Dunne, Colette McGahon, Fionnuala Hough and George Vaughan. Visitors last night included Colonel Bill O'Kelly of the DGOS and Mr Charles Haughey, TD.

O'Sullivan's comment about a school of opera was prescient (perhaps it had been whispered in his ear) for Ronnie was highly motivated to initiate just such an undertaking. She also felt it was a scandal that Ireland's capital city had no dedicated concert hall, a concern she raised with her many friends, including the newly elected President of Ireland, Patrick Hillery. But on that night in 1977 her role was one of welcome, and her greeting for Bill O'Kelly was as warm as for everyone else. Whatever personal feelings might linger, she knew that her students needed every advantage in the cut-throat world they were entering, and Bill O'Kelly was a very important contact.

A few days later, Ronnie presented *The Magic Flute* at the same venue. She produced it as a semi-action performance which Charles Acton deemed 'a splendid and magnificent occasion – exciting, most commendable and well done'. The cast was large but he felt the students were so superb that each one should be mentioned: Frank Dunne, Anna Caleb, Angela Feeney, Sheila Roche, Barbara Graham, John Brady, Fionnuala Hough, Nicola Sharkey, Marie-Claire O'Reirdan, Deirdre Cooling, Frank O'Brien, Randal Courtney and Peter Granwell. He singled out Seán Mitten, Patrick Sheridan and Deirdre Grier-Delaney for their verve and sheer professionalism.

Deirdre Grier-Delaney had recently returned from Brussels with her husband and four children. Deirdre was an accomplished and successful singer who felt she had got into the habit of doing something a little wrong, but could not put her finger on it. Ronnie heard her sing, noted the niggle, and together in Room 20 they tried to correct it. Ronnie brought Deirdre literally back down to earth with her breathing technique. 'Lie on the ground,' she said. 'Put your hands on your chest and think like a baby. A baby breathes with the tummy going up and down, never the chest. As we grow older we start to breathe higher, so the breath doesn't go right down to the bottom of our lungs. Relax the tummy down to get out it of the way for the lungs to fill with air.'

Over the next year or two Deirdre was poked and prodded by her enthusiastic tutor. 'Push out there,' she'd say, thrusting her fist into Deirdre's stomach or diaphragm. 'Support the sound.' But try as she might the instruction had come too late for Deirdre. She had had a wonderful career and sung in world-class venues, all with the encouragement of her husband Michael, who once memorably declared: 'If you ever tell me you didn't do your practice because you had to iron my shirts, I'll be disgusted!' With the help of her husband, mother-in-law and several au pairs, Deirdre had fulfilled all her ambitions. It was time for a new challenge.

'You will be a teacher,' Ronnie stated. When Deirdre began to protest, she waved her objections aside. 'You will carry on what I am doing. You will be very good. It's all arranged. You start on Saturday morning. Go to Frank Heneghan and tell him that Ronnie says you're to be a teacher.'

Deirdre had a music degree, a 'Premier Prix' from the Opera Studio, Brussels, and she had fluent French and vast singing experience. Like her mentor, Deirdre started with youngsters and gradually built her reputation as an inspiring teacher.

Ronnie, who was normally a patient teacher, ever ready with praise for the slightest improvement, lost her rag one day with a student who had not learnt his music. 'Out! Out! Out!' she shouted and he left, half-laughing because she was being so dramatic. A child of about twelve was waiting, petrified by the sight of this angry woman who suddenly caught sight of her and sweetly intoned, 'Are you here for an audition? Come in, lovey. Come and sing for Ronnie.' On another occasion the man who was next in the queue entered the room and before he could utter a word she clamped her hand on his jaw and pulled it down. 'Now,' she said, 'sing this.' The man was going ahhhh ahhhh because his jaw was clamped. 'You're so tense,' said Ronnie. 'Loosen your jaw, darling.' When she finally released him he cried, 'Jaysus, missus! I'm here to fix your bleedin' phone!'

The annual Feis Ceoil competitions were uppermost in every music teacher's mind throughout the year, but the spring term at the College of Music was manic! Ronnie prepared so many contestants for each category that she never stopped working, and every year these students were dubbed the Ronnettes. One spring Paul Dorgan was brought on board to rehearse the singers. Two weeks before the competition Ronnie sent him off to find an empty room with a piano so that she could send singers down to him. Purcell's 'Hark! the Echoing Air' was the required piece for sopranos, and one by one twelve students trooped into his room to give it their all. What had started as a pleasant ditty for Paul became, around number six, torture, and sheer hell by the end of it.

As the competitions loomed, the house at Bushy Park was turned into a music studio, counselling centre, feeding station, costume department, hair and make-up salon, transport hub – Ronnie loved it. If a student needed a suitable dress for performance, it was begged or borrowed and, when all else failed, Ronnie would reach into her own pocket to pay for it. On Saturday morning rehearsals would begin at nine o'clock for singers and their accompanists, and in the kitchen there was enough food and drink to lubricate the Russian army. During one session word came through that a student of Ronnie's had given birth. Jubilant, they composed a telegram and phoned it through: *Congratulations on the birth of your baby. Love from all of us at the V.D. clinic.* Within five minutes a supervisor rang to check on the propriety of the wording. When all was explained, the telegram was sent. Ronnie's creativity and imagination knew no bounds when it came to the Feis. Bits of furniture in the house would be earmarked to become props on the Metropolitan Hall stage, and Judy once got home from school to find her bed gone.

Dublin, 1977: The Feis Ceoil that year was an extraordinary achievement for Ronnie and her students. Anna Caleb, Nicola Sharkey, Marie-Claire O'Reirdan and Colette McGahon scooped no less than twelve cups between them! It was unheard of for one teacher to present students of such a high calibre that they would effectively sweep the board in their vocal categories. But Ronnie knew what it took to be a singer; she had found out the hard way.

Ireland, 1946: Becoming an opera singer was tantamount to running away and joining the circus. Performing on the stage had connotations of louche characters and sleazy back streets. It was no place for an impressionable young girl who would fall into wicked ways. And to study abroad, on your own, was a foolhardy venture that would end badly. If, by some miracle, you escaped with your reputation and everything else intact, the proper thing was to marry, have a family and settle for being a housewife for the rest of your life.

Imagine then, nineteen-year-old Veronica Dunne setting forth alone on a journey into the unknown. An innocent abroad in a war-torn land, with few connections and no recourse to home, confronted with nauseating food and contaminated water but refusing to give in, determined to find her teacher, make her mark. Imagine the intelligence to sack that teacher, acquire another and then realise it was not enough merely to sing. There must be language, there must be movement, there must be deep appreciation and expression of music, word, story, character. Imagine that girl sourcing the coaches to teach her repertoire, choreography, stagecraft, foreign languages; attending performances of classical music, ballet, opera, folk; singing at every possible venue; learning the tools of her trade. Then, you do not have to imagine David Webster, managing director of the Royal Opera House, Covent Garden declaring that in Veronica Dunne he had the whole package – the complete opera singer.

The whole package is what Ronnie wished to impart to her students. But few facilities existed at the College. Ronnie had to fight for ensemble work, recitative classes, language classes, sight-reading classes, body-strengthening sessions, acting skills, and as for three hours a week of singing lessons and three hours of vocal coaching, that was never going to happen. So she did it on her own. Many of her students got three hours plus a week, for which Ronnie was unpaid. She arranged foreign language tuition for those students who had imminent concert engagements or exams, and for pianists like John O'Conor and Paul Dorgan to act as répétiteurs and accompanists. At eight in the morning two or three times a week, she held hour-long classes for singing students who, with their teachers' permission, wished to improve their breathing technique, upper body control and stamina. She encouraged everyone to go to musical events in the city, and she sent her male students to audition for Ite O'Donovan and the Palestrina Choir at the Pro Cathedral in Dublin, to improve their ensemble work and sight-reading. When external performance opportunities came up, Ronnie would invariably suggest a suitable student. If any of her colleagues from the opera world were in town, she inveigled them into giving master classes at the College to broaden the singers' horizons and, perhaps, establish worthwhile contacts.

Almost without realising it, Ronnie was developing a full-time, third-level degree course for singers on a part-time, shoestring budget. It was little wonder that students were clamouring to be taught by her, cluttering up the corridors of the College morning, noon and evening, and annoying Frank Heneghan, who wanted an orderly, regulated institution. The two were often at loggerheads – one with a flamboyant, can-do attitude, the other with a cautious, what-if mentality. But Ronnie was grateful to Frank, for in many ways he let her do her own thing, despite his misgivings.

The 1977 Feis Ceoil yielded more benefits to the College than silverware. During the competitions Ronnie heard the pianist Alison Young accompany singers and she suddenly thought it would be wonderful to have a professional on hand every day for her own students. There and then she asked Alison to join her at the College. At the time, Alison was busy teaching, conducting choirs and bringing up a family, but she seized the opportunity to work with Ronnie, whom she knew through her husband, baritone William (Bill) Young. Bill and Ronnie had sung together many times, most notably on Brian Boydell's cantata *A Terrible Beauty is Born*.

Alison and William Young

Alison was brought in initially as répétiteur to work with three students. It had not been squared with Frank Heneghan, of course, and eventually she got the call from the principal's office to say that she must be formally interviewed before becoming a member of staff. When all was correctly processed, Alison's workload increased and soon she had twelve students for one hour each a week. She coached style, language and music, corrected notes or phrasing errors and repeated passages patiently until both singer and coach were satisfied. The student had separate classes with the teacher, but if something important were coming up, all three would work together.

An important family event took place on 5 April 1978 when young Peter McCarthy married Sandra Mullins. The wedding took place in the village of Paulstown, five miles from the Mullins family home in Goresbridge, County Kilkenny. The occasion was given a full page spread in *The Irish Tatler & Sketch* magazine, with many of racing's most famous names present. The couple worked in England for some years before returning home where Peter briefly joined his father's firm, but their hearts were in the country. Peter and Sandra settled in Gowran, County Kilkenny, and together established the Dungarvan Stud, specialising in the breeding and training of racehorses.

Wedding of Peter to Sandra Mullins, with his parents

Hailing from another picturesque area in County Kilkenny, every Saturday George Vaughan and his wife Nora Ring travelled from Thomastown to Dublin for lessons with Ronnie. George was a founding member of the Kilkenny Arts Festival in 1974 and was vitally interested in the cultural life of his county. He mentioned that there was a great interest in singing in his area, and to his surprise Ronnie, who was already so busy, agreed to give lessons in Thomastown. George persuaded the Kilkenny Vocational Education Committee to sponsor the venture, and arranged that Ronnie could use the school at which he taught art as a venue. Every Monday at nine o'clock she commenced her classes with students lining up in the corridor. George was the last to have a lesson after he finished work at four o'clock, but Ronnie felt he was too tired by then to benefit. 'I'll teach you at your house before school starts, lovey, but I expect you to be fully warmed up by the time I get here.' To reach Thomastown by eight, Ronnie had to leave Dublin at five in the morning and pray she wasn't stuck behind a tractor on the narrow winding roads. George was supposed to be up and practising at six and he was, the first few times, but gradually it came down to the sight of Ronnie pulling into the lane when he would hastily dress and pretend to have been working very hard. After her classes, Ronnie had to set out on the road back to Dublin in the dark, blinded by the lights of huge trucks thundering towards her, and not reach home until well after 9 pm.

Early in 1978 Ronnie declared that, with all the talented singers around, they should put on an opera. With little money for the enterprise, they settled on Donizetti's *Don Pasquale* because it can be performed without a chorus, and George approached the Clarkes from Atlanta, Georgia who owned historic Kilfane House near Thomastown. The Clarkes were a theatrical couple who enjoyed staging dramas in their Regency drawing room. They were delighted at the prospect of opera during the balmy July evenings. Pupils in the school fashioned and erected sets, a local dressmaker made costumes, students from Dublin came to lend a hand, and Ronnie produced. The performers included John Brady, Claire Skerritt, Dan Farrelly and George Vaughan, with Trudi Carberry as accompanist. The 'stage' was an alcove at the side of the house. Although small, the space became enchanted with the backdrop of the beautiful garden beyond, and through the French doors the audience could see the swinging lanterns of Dr Malateseta (played by George) and Don Pasquale approach through the gloom. The only difficulty was the resident peacocks which were liable to screech at inopportune moments! Despite that, all three performances were so successful, the production made a tour of the provinces.

But things were not going well for Ronnie and her husband Peter who, over the years, had drifted further and further apart. After twenty-five years of marriage, they finally agreed to separate, a decision that was distressing for them both. During these difficult times, Ronnie placed great faith in Saint Charbel Makhluf of Lebanon, and renamed her house in his honour.

Ronnie's spirits were at a low ebb, but she still had to teach, and to perform. At the end of August she was in the Saint Francis Xavier Hall in Dublin with the first orchestral version of James Wilson's *The Táin*, and at the Kilkenny Arts Week with Schoenberg's song cycle *Pierrot Lunaire*, a complex work for solo singer and an ensemble of five versatile musicians. The instrumentalists were John O'Conor (piano), Deirdre Brady (flute and piccolo), James Daley (clarinet and bass clarinet), Thérèse Timoney (violin and viola) and Betty O'Sullivan (cello). Ground-breaking in its day (1912), Schoenberg used the *Sprechstimme* vocal technique which is a cross between speaking and singing. Charles Acton commended conductor Seóirse Bodley for communicating through his colleagues 'a deep understanding of the work'. Ronnie's rendering of the *Sprechstimme* technique left him puzzled, but Acton praised her 'superlative acting with her voice, her total bringing out of the spirit and mood of the poems and the meaning and colour of the words ... this great musico-dramatic occasion deserved recording.'

Work was Ronnie's solace, yet the days back at work in September felt long and tedious. Kevin Hough, baritone, pianist and all-round entertainer, was a member of the very musical Hough family, all of whom attended the College of Music. Ronnie trained both Kevin and his sister Fionnuala, and Kevin appeared in many shows at the Gaiety and the Olympia theatres. When he decided to branch into concert management, he knew the very people with whom he wished to commence his new career. His first venture on 8 December 1978 at the Royal Dublin Society was a sell-out.

Kevin Hough

The billing was simple: Veronica Dunne, soprano; Geraldine O'Grady, violin; Havelock Nelson, piano; Valerie McGovern, compère. The fare on offer was light classical, and it went down a storm! Writing in the *Irish Times*, Charles Acton reported that O'Grady's interpretation of Beethoven's Romance in F, op. 50 would have 'melted the stoniest heart with the most exquisitely beautiful tone'. In the first half, Ronnie sang three lieder and three French songs, but Acton felt it was in the second half that she fully triumphed with 'Mi chiamano Mimì', Musetta's waltz song and Mimi's farewell, all from *La Bohème*. 'What a superb Puccini stylist she is,' he wrote, 'and how good to hear again just how Mimi should be sung! Here was authority and, much more, really moving artistry.' Ronnie regained some of her buoyancy, and Kevin Hough Productions was launched into many years of successful shows on stage, radio and television.

Judy, who had trained as a nurse in Dublin's Jervis Street Hospital, left home to work in Dallas, Texas. Ronnie's house was eerily quiet. She filled it with students and friends, and suddenly it was 1979.

Ronnie had been performing regularly for more than thirty years. Although she could not know it at the time, one of her last concerts was in the Edmund Burke Hall at Trinity College Dublin. On a cold night in January, Ronnie, John O'Conor and Seóirse Bodley took to the stage together. There were many old friends in the audience, including Aloys Fleischmann, Brian Boydell, John Kinsella, Jane Carty and James Wilson, as well as Seóirse's wife Olive, John's wife

Seóirse Bodley, Ronnie and John O'Conor

Mary and Ronnie's sister May. Following a rousing performance to a packed gathering, one of audience was heard remarking, 'I must say I thought Ronnie was smashing!'

Ronnie teamed up with John again in July when they spearheaded an international music workshop at the Gorey Arts Festival, Wexford, which was opened by the Minister for Health, Charles Haughey. It was a week of hard work and high jinks, Ronnie always on the lookout for that rough grain of sand that she could turn into a lustrous singing pearl.

Back at the College, the pearl came to her. Ronnie happened to be down in the office when Edwina, the secretary, received a telephone call enquiring about teachers. Edwina passed the phone to Ronnie. The lady tentatively explained that her daughter's choirmaster thought she had quite a good voice and they should be doing something about it. 'Bring her along,' said Ronnie, 'and I'll listen to her.' Alison Young was in on that audition. She remembers the lovely young girl with a long tie-dyed gypsy skirt and beautiful fair hair entering Room 20 like a gleam of sunlight. It was Patricia Bardon.

The first time Patricia saw Ronnie, she thought Wow! 'She had a mass of auburn hair and wore a silver grey crocheted suit with watch chains and fobs hanging over her ample bosom and on her feet were killer-high stiletto heels. She was so dramatic, so magnetic.'

Ronnie's reaction to Patricia was equally enthusiastic, for no sooner had the girl sung a few phrases than Ronnie was jumping up and down. 'When can you start?' she asked. 'Tomorrow after school? One day you will be a famous opera singer!'

Opera singers were old and fat and that wasn't what Patricia had in mind for herself at all. She wanted to be smooth and sexy like Aretha Franklin singing the blues, but she was bowled along by the whirlwind of Ronnie's energy. As soon as she was learning simple arias the blues went out the window and she discovered the sheer joy of singing. She left school a year later to study full-time and threw herself into Ronnie's extraordinary world. But Patricia was no pushover as a pupil:

> I used to get on the wrong side of Ronnie for not producing enough work. When you're a youngster, there are a number of things you want to do, besides sitting down and memorising. I would be on the receiving end, and there would be tears. I think she thought I was a bit lazy, but I was getting my priorities right. In order to make sure I covered the work, she would bring me into the College at 8am, just to teach me discipline. It was murder! She sprayed herself liberally with Opium perfume and first thing in the morning the air would be thick with its strong, heavy smell. Those lessons lasted a couple of hours, then she'd bring me back later as well – she was incredibly generous.

Patricia Bardon

During the 1980s the inner city area of Dublin was quite depressed. Ronnie saw that there was a need for a project to harness people's natural creativity, and she started a programme of performing arts in the Gleeson Hall at the Kevin Street College of Technology. Every Saturday from nine in the morning until six at night she organised ballet classes, modern dance, mime, singing and Shakespeare. Classes were divided between children and mothers. They set up a choir and held performances. For a year and a half it was hugely popular, with about three hundred people participating, but then there was a problem with peeping toms who hovered around outside and leered in at the ballet dancers. Principal Frank Brennan felt he had no alternative but to end the project. Ronnie tried to set up a similar programme in Ballyfermot but there was never the same degree of interest and the venture fizzled out.

In 1981 the event that all music lovers in Ireland had been waiting for finally arrived – the opening of the National Concert Hall in Earlsfort Terrace near Saint Stephen's Green, Dublin. The Victorian building with its impressive façade had originally been constructed for the Dublin International Exhibition of 1885. It became the central location for the newly founded University College Dublin in 1908, but when the university began its move to a new campus in the early 1960s the building was left neglected and the Great Hall within started to deteriorate. It took three years and £3,500,000 to renovate and convert into a modern concert hall with a seating capacity of 1,262. Special attention was paid to acoustics, lighting, comfort, the preservation of the original pillars and plasterwork and the addition of all the latest facilities, putting it on a par with the best in Europe, and making it a fit home for the RTÉ Symphony Orchestra.

The programme for the opening concert featured the première of Seóirse Bodley's *Ceol: Symphony No. 3*, commissioned by RTÉ, and a performance of Beethoven's *Symphony No. 9*, conducted by Colman Pearce with the RTÉ Symphony Orchestra, Our Lady's Choral Society, the RTÉ Singers and Chorus, and the Choristers of Saint Patrick's Cathedral, Dublin.

A special preview was held for the men and women who had toiled long and hard to ensure that Ireland's National Concert Hall was a building the nation could be proud of. It was a momentous occasion for all the musicians, particularly the solo singers, Violet Twomey, Bernadette Greevy, Louis Browne and William (Bill) Young. As they took their positions on stage, Bill murmured to Louis: 'Tonight you are going to make history, for yours is the first voice that will be heard in our new concert hall.' After a masterful performance of *Ceol*, a man in the gallery shouted: 'Follee that, Beethoven!'

At the grand state opening on 9 September 1981, President Hillery and his wife Maeve surveyed the beautiful auditorium with pleasure, knowing its future was in good hands. The twelve members of the government-appointed board of directors were already in place and included Ronnie, Bernadette Greevy and Seóirse Bodley, with impresario Fred O'Donovan as chairman. A headline in the *Irish Times* of 11 September captured the relief of concertgoers: 'A proper music centre at last.'

Ronnie was appointed to the board three times, serving from 1981 to 1996. The board had a hands-on role during the early years of the National Concert Hall (NCH). They met once a month and decided

matters of crucial importance, including the engagement of artists and guest orchestras. This led to many heated discussions among the strong-minded participants, which were generally amicably settled.

At the College it was Ronnie's students who were making the headlines. Twenty-two-year-old mezzo-soprano Anna Caleb had been a student of Ronnie's for ten years when she gave an afternoon 'coming-out' recital at the NCH in April 1982. With accompanist Alison Young she delivered a varied programme to a near capacity audience, leaving them in no doubt that here was a singer of exceptional talent.

At the concert Anna was presented with a cheque for £1,000 from the new 'Threshold Award' – a trust that Ronnie initiated to assist young singers entering the professional field. She knew only too well that, while singers appreciate plaudits, what they require is money to pursue their studies and careers. Anna Caleb more than fulfilled everyone's expectations. On 12 September John Honohan of the *Sunday Independent* reported news of a major competition:

> Ireland held a proud position among the nations last week when, at the prestigious S-Hertogenbosch International Singing Competition in Holland, young Dublin opera singer Anna Caleb carried off first prize. Anna, who, in the last couple of years, has sung herself into the hearts of so many people, won the mezzo-soprano and alto section [the Kathleen Ferrier Prize], which

Members of the board of the National Concert Hall, 1981. From left back: Noel Coade, Donald Potter, John Ruddock, Gerard Victory, Col. F. O'Callaghan, Dr. Seóirse Bodley, Richard Stokes.
Front: Moira Pyne, Dr. Bernadette Greevy, Fred O'Donovan (Chairman), Dame Ruth King, Veronica Dunne.

Anna Caleb

required four days' heats to get through the thousand competitors from all over the world.

Anna was back in Dublin within a couple of days to take part in the celebration of the first birthday of the NCH presented by the Young Irish Artists. Many of Ronnie's singers performed. The full strength of the company appeared in the last item, the finale of Mozart's *Marriage of Figaro*: Nicola Sharkey, Joseph Cotton, Virginia Kerr, Anna Caleb, Emer O'Flaherty, Randal Courtney, Marian Finn and Paul Kelly. Writing in the *Irish Times*, Charles Acton was enthralled by the young singers: 'With minimal acting and platform dress, they conveyed the intricacies of the scene delightfully, and especially, Miss Sharkey could not have been anyone but Susanna, and Miss Caleb started perfectly as the damn little nuisance that Cherubino is.' But where, he lamented, were the top brass from the DGOS? 'Do they not care about Irish artists who may be world stars or at least a great deal better than some of the foreigners they bring us in for their principal parts?'

If there was one thing that Ronnie considered a nuisance it was traffic wardens. There were just two dedicated parking spaces outside the College – one for herself and one for Frank Heneghan. Ronnie was always in so early, it was usually not a problem but if someone took her space she either parked at a meter that had to be fed all day by students running in and out with coins, or she took a chance in an unauthorised spot. One summer morning she was with Thérèse Feighan and Patricia Bardon in Room 20 when she glanced from the window and spied a warden below placing a ticket on her car. 'Well, I'm not having that!' she exclaimed, and flung the contents of her coffee cup out the window. A couple of minutes later there were loud footsteps in the corridor and Edwina entered closely followed by the drenched warden making accusations. 'Dear, dear,' said Ronnie. 'Wasn't us, was it girls? Must have come from the room above', and she resumed her lesson.

Patricia Bardon had gained valuable experience in the Feis Ceoils, and in the spring of 1983 Ronnie decided she was ready for serious stage work with the DGOS. Patricia auditioned for a small part in Puccini's *Manon Lescaut* and the major role of Maddalena in Verdi's *Rigoletto*, and in both she was successful. In total she clocked up fourteen performances in Dublin and Cork, and she loved it – the rehearsals, the Italian stars, the atmosphere around the theatre, the excitement of performance, the buzz in the audience. Now she knew what Ronnie was talking about, and she knew she wanted it.

Jane Carty, a senior music producer with Radio Telefís Éireann and a keen promoter of young talent, nominated Patricia to represent Ireland in a new, worldwide competition – the Cardiff Singer of the Year, organised by the BBC. Angela Feeney was nominated to represent Northern Ireland. Both girls reached the finals that were televised live on 24 July 1983. At home in Dublin, Ronnie and Alison Young watched avidly as first Angela and then Patricia performed. The winner was the experienced Finnish soprano Karita Mattila. Much to everyone's surprise, especially her own, eighteen-year-old Patricia was placed second, and Ronnie and Alison hooped and hollered around the sitting room. Interviewed after her extraordinary success, Patricia paid tribute to her teacher, Veronica Dunne, who had trained two of the eighteen singers in the final of the international competition.

Although still a student, offers of engagements poured in for Patricia, and she relied on Ronnie's advice in choosing which she should accept. She was also awarded a two-month Goethe Institute scholarship to study in West Germany. Anna Caleb was heading for Germany on a two-year contract in Karlsruhe, and Angela Feeney was enjoying her career with Munich State Opera. With Suzanne Murphy now a top star at Welsh National Opera and Patricia in demand in Britain, Ronnie's students were making names for themselves on the big stage in Europe.

23 Cabbages and kings

$\mathcal{I}$T WAS 1984 and time for another opera at the College, but why leave it there? 'Let's put on two,' said Ronnie, 'and this time we'll invite everyone!' She was planning a gala affair and the hall in Chatham Row was too small. The College of Music was now affiliated with the other Dublin Institutes of Technology. Ronnie knew the Gleeson Hall at Kevin Street College of Technology was a good size; lads from the Bolton Street School of Engineering could make the scenery and props, and students from the Cathal Brugha Street College of Catering could provide the food.

Despite getting some of the work done 'in house', major funds were required to stage two costumed productions with professional producers, conductors and orchestras and to hire lighting and equipment. Ronnie rolled up her sleeves and got on the phone to suppliers to the colleges and the businesses that had backed her in the past, and to her friends and contacts in the music world. Programme advertisements were sold, sponsorship was promised and bit-by-bit the funding started to come in.

Meanwhile the parts were cast for A.J. Potter's *The Wedding* and Vaughan Williams's one-act opera, *Riders to the Sea*. The lucky few were Liam Brady, Paul Kelly, Randal Courtney, Edel Loftus, Frances Lucey, Miriam Blennerhasset, Rebecca Smith, Terry Lawlor and Des Capliss in *The Wedding*, and Patricia Bardon, Ciaran Rocks, Emer O'Flaherty, Judith O'Brien and Aileen Creed in *Riders to the Sea*. The appearance of Louis Lentin, director of stage and television, created quite a stir at the College. He was there to produce the shows, and excitement increased when the students learned they would perform with the Pro-Arte Orchestra, conducted by Colman Pearce. Répétiteur Clive Shannon and Chorus Master Gerald Duffy rehearsed the band of singers, and the countdown to the big night began. The Gleeson Hall at Kevin Street was prepared, stage sets and lighting organised, and the buffet for the reception after the show was set up.

Ronnie invited everyone, including the President of Ireland, Patrick Hillery, and his wife Maeve, with whom she now had a strong family tie; their son John had married her sister May's daughter, Carolyn, the year before. The heads of the Dublin Institutes of Technology attended, as did Mary Robinson and members of the Dublin City Vocational Education Committee management, government ministers and public representatives, friends of the arts, parents and friends of the students.

Joe Erraught was one of the lecturers at the Cathal Brugha Street College of Catering. He was in charge of the cuisine at the event and he recalls that the guests arrived dressed up to the nines, which added to the great sense of occasion generated by Ronnie:

> Ronnie was the powerhouse – you never said no to Ronnie. She was all about the music, but my attention was focused on my students producing food good enough for the President. It was a real showcase for them. We prepared a buffet of hot and cold savouries, canapés and sandwiches. During performances I was sometimes roped in as bouncer – they were very strict about not letting people through the door of the hall while someone was singing. Ronnie seemed to be everywhere; she was able to watch and manage all the comings and goings. There was one guy who was trying to gain entry and no sooner had I stopped him than Ronnie was down like a shot. 'Let the blighter in,' she hissed; 'he's one of our main sponsors.' We were all in awe of Ronnie – she was so glamorous and dynamic. I never thought the day would come when I'd get to know her personally.

Glamorous and dynamic she may have been, but that never prevented Ronnie from doing the practical stuff. Deirdre Grier-Delaney was on hand for the productions at Kevin Street and while the high and mighty were enjoying posh nosh upstairs, she and Ronnie and a few others made sure the hoi polloi downstairs didn't go hungry:

> We bought cabbages for coleslaw the day before and made buckets of the stuff. And we got ham and salads and, as we prepared enormous platters of food, Ronnie would have us in hysterics with her jokes. We must have catered for two hundred people easily – a fork supper for all the mammies and daddies. After one of the performances, I was in a blue and white evening dress supervising the serving and Ronnie was on the stairs greeting everyone with 'Darling!' and sorting out who was going upstairs and who down to us. Someone said, 'Ronnie, there's too many upstairs' and she started

re-directing. It was mayhem! I remember flitting from one table to the next thinking we're running low and going into the kitchen area to bring out more platters and somebody stopped me and asked, 'Are you the catering manager?' It was such fantastic fun!

The fun intensified in April as the whole College was swept up in a major production of the Rogers and Hammerstein musical *The King and I*, staged at the Gleeson Hall in Kevin Street. Professionals Frank Gormley and William Halpin were brought in as producer and musical director, but otherwise it was students all the way, including the twenty-four-piece orchestra. There were fifty-five singers with a children's chorus, and twelve dancers from the School of the Performing Arts, Ballyfermot. Andrew Murphy and Mary Clarke were cast as the leads, but some of the other students wished to be divas rather than choristers. Ronnie scoured the College for volunteers and then bustled down the road to Peter's Pub, a favourite haunt, took one look at the assembled chancers and said, 'You, you, you and you – if you're not in rehearsal in five minutes you're out of the College!' The place was cleared pronto! Ronnie set about fundraising, tapping all her staunch supporters, including F.X. Buckley, whose famously advertised '*Meat par Excellence*' she had been cooking since her Covent Garden days. A newcomer on the staff was drama coach Miriam O'Meara. Her creativity did much to inject valuable acting technique and stagecraft into all their productions and promoted a vibrant school of drama at the College.

Just two months later, six of Ronnie's students – Frances Lucey, Mary Clarke, Marie Hogan, Paul Kelly, Anne Millea and Ciaran Rocks – sang in the first Dublin performance of Handel's opera *Alcina* at the NCH. Regina Hanley, who sang the role of Bradamante, studied with Anne-Marie O'Sullivan. Anne-Marie had put a great deal of work into getting the opera staged, as usual on a budget of next-to-nothing. Amidst all the enthusiasm, it seemed entirely appropriate that members of the RTÉ Symphony Orchestra should be conducted by a young man on the threshold of his career, David Jones, a past pupil of the College of Music and a music graduate of Trinity College Dublin.

Ronnie and her husband Peter had been separated for some time when he became very seriously ill. She nursed him through that illness in Bushy Park and there he remained as her friend, often accompanying her to social gatherings and concerts when he felt well enough. Every summer, the two of them took off to see Judy in Dallas, where she was working as an ICU nurse. They became friendly with Richard Gaughan, Judy's American boyfriend, and with Louis and Kitty Johnston, who treated Judy as the daughter they never had (although they had six sons!). There were other new friends, including Mrs Lucy Ball Owsley, who had fond memories of Ireland, having lived in the country for some time in the 1930s when her husband had been the American Envoy to the Irish Free State. Ronnie was a favoured guest at afternoon tea in Mrs Owsley's mansion. She also entertained in the sumptuous penthouse of The Orchid Hotel, and one year Ronnie and Peter were invited there for luncheon. As it turned out, Peter was the only man among many beautifully coiffed and chapeau-ed society ladies. Dismayed by the spartan fare on offer – lettuce, iced water and not a trace of alcohol – Peter sneaked off for a quick smoke in the bathroom. All hell broke loose! Alarms sounded, water spurted from sprinklers and security guards materialised out of nowhere to quench the fire. But no fire could be discovered. It was a mystery which Peter did nothing to resolve.

The announcement of Judy's forthcoming wedding to Richard in Dublin sent Ronnie into a flurry of planning. She arranged the University Church on Saint Stephen's Green, followed by a reception at the Shelbourne Hotel. A large contingent of family and friends travelled from Dallas, and Louis Johnston hosted a dinner for fifty guests at the Berkeley Court Hotel in Ballsbridge.

Ronnie's daughter Judy, on her wedding day

On the morning of 20 September 1986 Judy was at home in her wedding gown when the doorbell rang. It was her nanny, Margaret McCann, who said, 'I just wanted to see my baby off.' Judy hugged and hugged her. They cried a little, and then Margaret helped to arrange the veil with the greenery of Ireland entwined among the yellow roses of Texas. As Judy left the house with her father, she felt a circle had been completed; she was ready for her new life. During the marriage ceremony, Suzanne Murphy and Angela Feeney gave a beautiful rendition of Schubert's 'Ave Maria', but Richard got a fright when the priest announced he was to marry Veronica Mary and he did a double-take at Judy!

Aspiring musicians gravitated towards the College of Music or the Royal Irish Academy of Music (RIAM) in the heart of Dublin. Mairéad Hurley was studying piano at the Academy when she heard there were paid teaching hours available at the College. She rambled into Chatham Row one day to offer her services and suddenly she was working with singers as a quasi-répétiteur. The set-up of the vocal department puzzled her. Many of the students had part-time or full-time jobs. They would be in the College before breakfast for their session with Ronnie on the floor in the John McCann Hall and, given all the strange exertions and breathing exercises, some would actually faint. They would spend as long as they could studying with their teachers or practising on their own, squeeze in their jobs, then dash back down to the College in the evening for ensemble work or rehearsals. Then there were the ones like Ciaran Rocks who gave up his work and was trying to cram five grades of music theory into one year so that, as Ronnie said, he could 'get it out of the way'. These singers who seemed so driven, so melodramatic and colourful fascinated Mairéad.

Ever on the scent for pianists who were halfway willing or inclined, Ronnie collared Mairéad one day and asked her what she was doing for the summer. 'The summer?' asked Mairéad. 'Come on in,' said Ronnie. 'There'll be plenty of work.' And work there was. The rest of the College was empty but it was one of Ronnie's busiest times. She could set her own timetable and page after page of her bulging diary was filled with names and times, arrangements and rearrangements. The system usually worked, but there were those occasions when someone required extra coaching and whoever was outside would be told, 'Come back in half an hour, lovey'. This was quite maddening to the waiting student, only assuaged by the thought that some day it could be they who needed more time. As soon as Ronnie was finished with one student, she sent them off to

Mairéad Hurley

Mairéad: 'Ronnie would give her all for someone with a good voice. It didn't matter if they couldn't read music or made loads of mistakes. She'd give them tons of singing lessons and hand them over to me to straighten out the practical bits.'

Mairéad marvelled that Ronnie never seemed to be in a bad mood or let anything faze her for long. She was in Room 20 one evening when they heard that the baritone Jack O'Kelly had got a part at the Wexford Opera Festival. Ronnie tried to phone him with congratulations and offer yet more lessons but she couldn't make contact. She looked up the Golden Pages of all things and found a number in Carlow that she rang and asked to speak to Jack. When told that Jack wasn't there at the moment, Ronnie asked that a message be given to him about coming for a singing lesson. The man enquired who was calling. 'I'm Ronnie Dunne, Jack's singing teacher in Dublin.' 'But Jack doesn't do singing at all!' 'Oh,' said Ronnie. 'Well, tell him to come up and audition for me anyway!'

One day it was Ronnie who was puzzled when some fellow named Bonzo from a pop group called Utah telephoned to inquire about a lesson. The lesson never transpired, but when she met the man on a radio programme and heard him sing, she informed him he was not supporting his voice properly and if he kept on like that he would ruin it, which left Bono rightly miffed!

Over the past twenty-five years the reputation of the College had soared, particularly in the vocal department with its cohort of excellent teachers. Ronnie's endeavours had not gone unnoticed. On 2 April 1987 she was conferred with an honorary degree of Doctor of Music from the National University of Ireland, which cited her as 'a lady who, after a distinguished personal career, now devotes her gifts to furthering those of a succession of gifted young Irish singers'. Having described Ronnie's national and international career, emphasis was placed on her virtuosity as a teacher:

Veronica Dunne brought together her own outstanding musical ability and a total commitment, passing on to her students the benefits of her wide artistic experience and the strict musical discipline which she had practised herself. Whilst clearly, the finished singer, in recital or opera, displays his or her own gifts, the steps leading to these heights must have been guided by dedicated teaching, and it is right that we should honour the teacher as well as the artist .... Today in Music as in most other fields talent alone is not enough. It must be nurtured and guided. Milton spoke of,

The melting voice through mazes running,
Untwisting all the chains that tie
The hidden soul of harmony....
I ask you to admit to our role of honorary graduates a lady who has
laid bare that hidden soul for so many Irish singers.

Deeply honoured by such recognition, Ronnie was delighted to joke
with her friends: 'Doctor Dunne to you, darling!'

The National Concert Hall 24

ONNIE HAD BEEN APPOINTED to a second term on the board of the National Concert Hall (NCH) in 1986 and she resolved to make a difference. She was chatting to fellow board member Gerard Gillen over dinner one evening and said, 'You know, Gerard,' there are plans for an organ in the hall – let's make it happen!'

Gerard was Professor of Music at the National University of Ireland Maynooth and an organist of international repute. He was also a part-time teacher at the College of Music and knew Ronnie casually. In the years to come he would get to know her a great deal better.

Chairman Lewis Clohessy and the other board members of the NCH were very much in favour of promoting the organ, and Ronnie set to work. With little or no state aid for the project, she approached Dr Anthony (Tony) O'Reilly, an alumnus of Belvedere College and an acquaintance of her husband's in the rugby and horseracing world.

National Concert Hall, Dublin

Tony O'Reilly was chairman of the huge H.J. Heinz Company of America. He invited Ronnie and Gerard down to his beautiful house in Castlemartin, County Kildare. After lunch Ronnie declared that she wouldn't leave without a contribution towards the organ. Several lunches and meetings later the Heinz Company agreed to support the project.

In 1988 a dinner was held at the NCH to pitch the idea of the organ to leading lights in Irish business. Among those present was Paddy Dowling, deputy chief executive of the Allied Irish Bank; he knew little about music but was struck by Ronnie's enthusiasm. He asked what the plan of campaign was. When told there was no plan, he offered to take on the project because, he said, "quite frankly none of you has a clue"! He devised a scheme whereby companies would commit to putting up £10,000 each. Since the estimated cost of the organ was about £500,000, that would require a good deal of commitment.

Ronnie believed that the project would interest Mrs Owsley and some of her wealthy connections. A trip to Dallas, therefore, seemed opportune and Gerard, Ronnie and Lewis Clohessy hitched a ride for most of the way with Ben Briscoe, Lord Mayor of Dublin, who was going to Denver with a delegation for Saint Patrick's Day 1989. Two concerts were organised in the United States to interest people in the project. The advance publicity headlined Veronica Dunne accompanied by Gerard Gillen on piano, along with several other Irish musicians. Gerard discovered that travelling with Ronnie was the greatest fun:

> We had rehearsed two or three songs at my house before we left; things like Gershwin's 'Summertime' and some of Moore's Melodies – Ronnie knew not to overexpose herself. Although her voice wasn't what it had been, she had a wonderful way of interpreting a song and delivering it, and she loved performing. Ronnie is a very attractive looker and she wooed and charmed her way over there with such style. She came absolutely to the point and asked people for money in a way that didn't offend. Ronnie was very much the *éminence grise* of our operation.

From Denver the threesome flew on to Dallas where they stayed with friends of Ronnie's. They lunched with Mrs Owsley and her son and received a modest donation, enough to have made the trip worthwhile.

Back home, Ronnie regaled her close friends and neighbours Geraldine and Alec O'Riordan with tales about the trip. Geraldine is a lover of the arts and a wonderful support to Ronnie in all her endeavours. Alec, who had been an outstanding cricketer with 72 Irish caps, was a club player and member of Old Belvedere with an interest in rugby. The O'Riordan children came to regard Ronnie and Peter as their surrogate grandparents, and hardly a week went by when the two couples were not at each other's houses for impromptu dinner parties. 'Ronnie is a marvellous cook,' says Geraldine. 'We'd be in her house having a drink with Peter. Ronnie would arrive at about seven o'clock, her arms laden with two bulging bags of groceries, a big smile on her face and a story about something funny that had happened with one of her students. Within an hour she'd have us all seated at the table with the most delicious food.'

Ronnie had become involved with the Dublin Grand Opera Society again. She liked the direction in which it was heading under its first professional general administrator, David Collopy, who had been appointed in 1985. David had previously managed the Wexford Opera Festival whose committee had embraced the notion of presenting audiences with exciting productions. He wanted to promote an operatic industry in Ireland with indigenous talent, training and opportunities, which was at total variance with the tradition at the DGOS of hiring in a job lot of producers, directors and artists, sticking the singers on stage to do their arias (in their own costumes irrespective of what the Irish designer had in mind) and then packing them back to Italy until the next season. This resulted in no fostering of Irish singers, and no harmonisation between stage and orchestra pit, or sense of the theatrical elements between each piece being brought out. David believed it was no good anymore for the fat lady to sing – modern opera-goers demanded drama and spectacle. He was a little surprised to find a kindred spirit in Ronnie:

David Collopy

> For somebody who had her training in a certain type of opera presentation I would have assumed her focus would have been on the voice and the rest didn't matter. Not so. Ronnie wanted the organisation to be more dynamic. She wanted it to have international reference points, as opposed to catering merely for the stalwarts of Irish opera who could come and close their eyes! Both she and I wanted to be challenged and enchanted by opera. We wanted that 'suspension of disbelief' which had been so lacking in most DGOS productions to date.

However, a huge effort would be required to turn the massive ship of the DGOS midstream. Ronnie already had so many calls on her time and energies that she ended her official connection with the company, but she remained very supportive of David's activities.

David got more than his fair share of challenges in 1989 when, at very short notice, the Gaiety Theatre suddenly withdrew the DGOS contract for the spring season. The artists were booked, the orchestra lined up, the publicity was in place, but there was suddenly no venue. In desperation David contacted the NCH, which had never put on an operatic production, and they did not have flats or wings. Nor did they have consecutive dates available; so any staging would have to be broken down after each of the three performances. It was a nightmare prospect but David and his small team decided to go for it. They created a stage on the stage with wings, a rocky outcrop and an imposing four-column façade. It nearly killed them physically, but the production is still talked about as having the absolute Wow factor. The opera was *Norma* by Vincenzo Bellini and the three stars were all Ronnie's former students: Suzanne Murphy, Angela Feeney and Marie Walshe. Michael Dervan of the *Irish Times* attended the first performance on 28 March. He remarked on the set, which, he wrote, looked a lot better than many he'd seen in the Gaiety. His total admiration, however, was reserved for Suzanne Murphy:

> To call Ms Murphy's Norma a portrayal would not do justice to it. It is more than that. It is an assumption of the character of the doomed priestess in which the singer so thoroughly lives and breathes every phrase and every feeling that she effectively becomes that betrayed mistress and distraught mother.

In the audience, Ronnie was brimming with pride as her girls sang and acted so magnificently.

Ronnie had not forgotten the organ, of course, and the fund received a welcome boost in July 1989 when Tony O'Reilly, on behalf of Heinz, presented a cheque of £70,000 to Gerard Gillen and the board of the NCH. Paddy Dowling's scheme was gaining momentum.

With ever-increasing student numbers at Chatham Row, the College of Music decided to relocate to more grand and spacious premises in Rathmines. In the meantime, the Vocal Department moved to a temporary location on Adelaide Road that was not ideal because there was no sound insulation between the rooms. Ronnie was training a new batch of talented singers, among whom were Finbar Wright, Lynda Lee, Emmanuel Lawlor, Fiona O'Reilly and Martin Higgins. Finbar was an established singer in Cork when he encountered Jane Carty, who urged him to take his career more seriously. He began studying with Ronnie and came to regard her as the musical equivalent of Mr Motivator, behind him every step of the way.

Angela Feeney (Adalgisa) and Suzanne Murphy (Norma)

(Above)
Suzanne Murphy as Norma in *Norma*. DGOS, 1989.

Together they developed a natural warmth in his light tenor voice. Lynda had been performing with the Bunratty Singers for some years and had toured America with them. She knew that being accepted as a student of Ronnie's was the 'golden ticket' to professionalism and she grabbed it. Ronnie teamed her up with Jeannie Reddin, a highly respected répétiteur at the College, and put her through the same tough regime she uses with all her gifted students to prepare them for the life of an opera singer.

Ronnie knows only too well that the demands made on successful singers are very great. Singers need to be well organised. They are constantly travelling, constantly under stress learning new repertoire and technique, attending rehearsals with strangers. Each week, perhaps, a new venue, a new cast, a new set. On stage, they have to think about so much: remembering the music, striving to produce the perfect note, its tone and colour, its strength and power to move; conveying the meaning of the words in Italian, French, German, English or Russian; watching the conductor; interacting with the other cast members; wearing unfamiliar, sometimes uncomfortable clothes and wigs under hot, blinding lights. They require strength of character and self-belief to carry on regardless of what is happening both on and off stage. There is immense pressure and responsibility – the success of a whole production could rest on the shoulders of a top-class soloist. The singer has to stay well, physically and mentally, and look after the instrument that is her or his voice. The work is tough, the rewards uncertain. Yet, for those who are strong enough to deal with these complexities, there is the excitement of a life enhanced by wonderful music.

Ronnie did not train only operatic stars. She received a phone call one day from a soft-spoken young man who requested private lessons. The first time he arrived at her door she was confronted by a bouquet of flowers so large she could not see who was carrying them. Impressed by his pleasant manner, she waved away his proffered music tapes and started teaching straight away. Within a few days his technique had improved and he went back home, delighted. A week later Ronnie was watching television when who should come on but Daniel O'Donnell. 'My God,' she exclaimed. 'That's the guy I was giving lessons to!'

Mairéad Hurley was spending more and more of her time with Ronnie's singers and at the Feis Ceoils and playing for chorus rehearsals at the DGOS. It was stimulating, purposeful work and she loved it. Having obtained her piano degree at the RIAM, she reluctantly began to teach. Her sister had just completed a répétiteur course and was eager to tell her all about it. The professional répétiteur fulfils many roles. She/he is a highly accomplished pianist and works with the singer on repertoire; knows the main operatic languages; and is the person singers turn to when there is a musical problem, and the person most likely to solve it; plays piano during rehearsals, notes the producer's instructions to be practiced with the singer separately, and liaises with conductor and orchestra. The répétiteur is an essential part of the production team and that's exactly what Mairéad wanted to be. She applied for an audition at the Opera Studio in London.

There were changes afoot at the College. For some years it had been an ambition to place the music courses on a full-time degree level, but this proved to be an extraordinarily complex operation, not least in hammering out syllabi and streamlining standards between the four schools – Keyboard, Musicianship, Orchestral and Vocal/Dramatic. Frank Heneghan asked Barra Boydell, who was teaching musicianship at the College, to head a committee and draw up a detailed scheme. The committee included singing teacher Anne-Marie O'Sullivan and they undertook an arduous mission of comparing similar courses overseas and conducting discussions within departments as to which were the most important elements in a three-year course. While Ronnie welcomed the step towards an accredited degree, she was not in favour of the importance attached to academic achievement, which, she felt, could result in someone with a superb voice being excluded from study at the College.

The birth of Judy and Richard's son Kevin in April 1990 brought a special kind of joy to Ronnie. She travelled to Boston in the summer. Judy had to return to work so Ronnie took over the care of the baby. There was no nanny, no intermediary, no engagements to fulfil, and she allowed herself to give full expression to her innate maternal feelings. During the few months she spent in America, she formed a deep bond with Kevin that has been sustained through years of visits back and forth. The arrival of Aidan in 1993 was another wonderful event. Both boys consider Ronnie's house their home in Ireland. When they were teenagers, it was Ronnie who took them to Paris to visit Fouquet's and Montmartre, and Ronnie who brought them to Madame Tussauds and a burlesque show in London, their eyes out on stalks. As young men, they made Bushy Park their base camp while attending university, and when Kevin became engaged, it was Ronnie he brought his fiancée to meet. Judy and Richard and the boys have made exceptional efforts to be present for Ronnie's big occasions; all have shared good times and tough times as a truly united family.

In 1990 Ronnie's sixty-fifth birthday was just two years away; in state-run institutions that means only one thing – retirement. But she was not going to go quietly. There was a terrific burst of activity at the College during 1990/91. The Municipal School of Music (which had become the College of Music) was founded in October 1890. A year of celebrations was planned which overlapped with the two-hundredth anniversary of Mozart's death in 1791. As chairperson of the centenary committee, Ronnie did her utmost to ensure that the profile of the College was raised, with student productions of Handel's *Messiah*, Puccini's *Suor Angelica*, Mozart's *Bastien and Bastienne* and *The Marriage of Figaro*, and a play produced by Miriam O'Meara, *Beaumarchais and Mozart*. For her most ambitious project to date, however, Ronnie had to marshal all her considerable energy and resources in a monumental effort to present two operas back to back – Benjamin Britten's comic opera *Albert Herring* at the Gaiety Theatre and Mozart's *La Clemenza di Tito* at the NCH. Ronnie went into overdrive to raise the necessary funds for both productions, and was cock-a-hoop when the ESB sponsored £11,000 for lighting at the Gaiety.

Albert Herring was scheduled for the end of March 1991 and the

students went into rehearsals months before Christmas. Mairéad had declined Ronnie's invitation to act as répétiteur on the production, feeling she did not have enough experience, and a professional was brought in. However, on New Year's Day she got a phone call. 'You have to come in, lovey,' said Ronnie. 'Vocal coach Ingrid Surgenor is coming over from Wales to work with the singers and the répétiteur has been very bold and pulled out on me.' Mairéad protested that she did not know the opera but Ronnie said, 'You'll be fine, darling. It's not tomorrow but the day after.'

Mairéad struggled through those rehearsals, and every time she looked over she got the thumbs up from Ronnie who said, 'Isn't she marvellous, everybody – isn't she great!' Mairéad survived and ended up doing the whole production, and the one after that! The all-student cast, with John Kearns in the title role, featured Lynda Lee, Assumpta Lawless, Martin Higgins and Eugene Griffin. Producer Ben Barnes directed and David Jones conducted the RTÉ Concert Orchestra.

La Clemenza di Tito was given its first Dublin performance at the NCH on 13 May 1991, and it marked a huge achievement for the College. Ronnie told Arminta Wallace of the *Irish Times* that it was time for the Vocal Department's 200 students to take a bow on their own behalf as well as Mozart's. 'They deserve it,' she said, 'They're ripe, they're ready and they don't get nearly enough exposure in their home city.'

The seven singers involved were all destined for the professional stage. Imelda Drumm, Denise Long and Padraig O'Rourke performed at home and abroad. Of Ronnie's four students, Finbar Wright was off to Spain on a concert tour, Lynda Lee was picked up by RTÉ and Opera Ireland, Fiona O'Reilly had engagements in Cork and Dublin and, out of 400 candidates, Martin Higgins was accepted by the Opera School in London. Mairéad Hurley also received news of her placement on the Opera School's répétiteur degree course. Bryden Thomson conducted the RTÉ Concert Orchestra for the single performance. Ben Barnes, the producer, told Arminta Wallace that he found the energy and verve of the young cast almost as impressive as their singing. 'For me, it's like getting back to the things that got you interested in theatre in the first place. It's not jaded or to do with marketing or budgets or pressure; it's got to do with people starting out on a journey – and it's very refreshing.'

Earlier in the year the NCH had closed down for three weeks and for a very good reason – the installation of the organ. The committee had raised all the money required and incurred no debt. The Irish firm of Kenneth Jones and Associates of Bray had been commissioned to make, install and voice the complex instrument, one of the largest in Ireland, with four manuals and pedals, 52 speaking stops, 4,045 pipes and mechanical key-action. Kenneth Jones designed the organ, including its polychromed and monumental organ-case in renaissance style, complementing the architecture and decorative colour scheme of the Hall. The display contains some of the largest pipes of the organ, of polished tin with gilded mouths and feature pipes embossed and laid with gold leaf all over. The organ was made in the Kenneth Jones workshop and assembled in the NCH. The voicing of the pipes took many months, and continued after the installation, mostly in night-shifts, finishing in the night prior to the inaugural performance.

The pipedream had become a magnificent reality, and the tenth anniversary of the NCH could be celebrated in style. The occasion was marked by two concerts on 28 and 29 September 1991: one for the sponsors and one for the fee-paying public. Distinguished English organist Peter Hurford played works from Purcell, Mozart, Bach and Handel, and Gerard Gillen performed Saint-Saëns' Symphony No.3 (known as the 'Organ' Symphony) with the National Symphony Orchestra conducted by Proinnsías Ó Duinn. The event was televised by RTÉ, with producer Anne Makower at the helm. Speaking to Arminta Wallace of the *Irish Times* before the concert, Gerard Gillen

Drawing by Kenneth Jones
for proposed organ at the
NCH, and his photograph of
the organ in 1991

expressed his pleasure at having a major pipe organ in a concert hall rather than a church so that more people could appreciate its glorious sounds in comfortable surroundings, and he added: 'The organ lobby really began to gather its forces in 1986, when the NCH board – largely prompted by the indefatigable Veronica Dunne – decided that the time had come to pull out all the stops.'

The teaching did not stop, nor the fun. Across the road from Ronnie's music room Ronan Tynan was working as a doctor at the Adelaide Hospital. In his hurry to get to lessons he often appeared in his white coat and she would make a great play about getting him to check her pulse for signs of life. Ronan got a taste of Feis Ceoil madness because her room was submerged in costumes, props and giddy Ronnettes. That year, Ronnie presented a trophy to the Feis, the Veronica Dunne Cup for Operatic Duo, saying she never thought she would see the day when a cup with the initials VD was presented at the Royal Dublin Society.

Ronnie and Desmond Byrne, CEO Irish Life Building Society with her award for 'Outstanding Contribution to Music'

The summer term of 1992 was Ronnie's last at the College. Students and former students got together to organise a grand gala concert in her honour as a mark of deeply felt gratitude, esteem and affection for the woman who had changed their lives, musically and personally. With the help of the Friends of the Vocal Arts they secured sponsorship from Aer Lingus and many other companies eager to be associated with Ireland's great lady of song. The Irish Life Building Society presented Ronnie with its Special Award for Outstanding Contribution to Music in the form of a marble sculpture bearing the outlines of a treble clef and a candle with an everlasting flame.

When Ronnie learnt that she was to be presented with a cheque for £20,000 from the proceeds of the concert for her retirement, her immediate reaction was, 'Right. How can we make that money work?' She mulled over the question with a few friends at home and decided that she would set up the 'Veronica Dunne Bursary' to help talented young singers.

The celebratory concert, 'An Operatic Tribute to Veronica Dunne' was presented at the NCH on Sunday, 28 June 1992. It featured nineteen of Ronnie's students: Patricia Bardon, Anna Caleb, Mary Callan-Clarke, Randal Courtney, Angela Feeney, Thérèse Feighan, Martin Higgins, Paul Kelly, Lynda Lee, Andrew Murphy, Suzanne Murphy, Frank O'Brien, Jack O'Reilly, Marie-Claire O'Reirdan, Ciaran Rocks, Nicola Sharkey, Kathryn Smith, Marie Walshe and Finbar Wright. Ronnie had flown around the world at her own expense to see many of these singers perform, and now they flew back from opera houses in Vienna, Rome, Bayreuth, Munich, Milan, Zürich, Cardiff and London.

Patricia Bardon

Also taking part were many of her old friends. She had sung with compère Liam Devally back in 1955 with the Irish Festival Singers. Anne Makower produced the show and oversaw its recording by RTÉ FM3 radio. There, too, were accompanists Alison Young, Trudi Carberry and Mairéad Hurley. The concert had been a sell-out for months. All Ronnie's family were in the audience, together with a legion of friends, colleagues and admirers from thirty-one years of teaching. She was heralded into the auditorium to a standing ovation, and when she sang 'Danny Boy' with accompanist Ingrid Surgenor, grown men cried.

If people thought that performance was Ronnie's goodbye they were in for a surprise. Ronnie had no intention of retiring. Although it was very difficult to leave behind all that she had built up at the College of Music, Ronnie knew she would have to move on, work with new students. She telephoned Sheila Murphy, director of a revered music school in Dublin, who promptly said, 'Come on over.'

The Leinster School of Music and Drama (LSMD) was established in 1904, and in 1982 had moved to the only surviving residential house on Upper Stephen Street, Dublin. To one side was a car park; to the other was a modern office block. The premises had been converted to provide music rooms and an administrative hub for the supervision of music and drama examinations nationally. One of its most notable piano teachers was the eminent Irish musician Mabel Swainson. On the ground floor were three small music rooms, an office and a big room at the back.

Over a cup of tea, Sheila said she would be only too delighted to have Ronnie on the staff. She led the way up creaky stairs to a small room at the front of the building with a piano that listed sideways on

Suzanne Murphy, Charles
Acton and Angela Feeney after
the tribute concert to Veronica
Dunne, 1992

the sloping floorboards, and Ronnie was appointed director of the newly formed Leinster Opera School.

The quirky nature of the building appealed to the talented group of students who breezed in and out. It felt bohemian and vibrant – a place where creativity could flourish. Several of Ronnie's students moved with her from the College of Music – Ronan Tynan, Róisín Toll, Catherine (Marie) Hegarty and Miriam Murphy.

Sixteen-year-old Miriam Murphy had joined a bunch of her friends from the local choir to attend a master class given by Ronnie at the School of Music in Tralee. When her turn came to sing, Miriam had warbled a few bars of 'The Lord's My Shepherd' when Ronnie jumped up from the piano and uttered the immortal phrase: 'Stick with me, darling, and you will wear diamonds!' After they had both recovered from this excitement, Ronnie took a close look at Miriam and declared, 'You've got absolutely no neck, so you'll have to be a dramatic soprano, but we'll train you as a mezzo first.'

Soon the schoolgirl was travelling to Dublin every weekend for lessons at Bushy Park. After two or three hours of coaching on a Saturday, Miriam stayed overnight with her uncle and went back to Ronnie on the Sunday for another long session before returning home to Tralee on the train. Ronnie would accept no payment for these classes. It was only when Miriam began studying full-time at the

College of Music in 1991 that she had to pay tuition fees, and then only for the basic amount, nothing for the hours of extra work with Ronnie.

Miriam upheld the tradition of the Ronnettes and won several trophies at the Feis. On Ronnie's last year at the College, she and Marie Hegarty competed for the new 'Veronica Dunne Operatic Duo' cup. They sang the duet from *Madama Butterfly*, but Miriam in her wisdom decided to join Marie on the top B at the end and they were marked down, which was devastating, because she had so wanted to win Ronnie's first cup. Miriam moved to the LSMD with Ronnie, and the next year she and Marie did win the trophy which she brandished from the stage shouting 'This is for you, Ronnie!' – a memory that still makes her cringe. In 1993 Miriam won through enough sections to qualify for inclusion in the supreme competition at the Feis – the Gervase Elwes Memorial Cup. Unfortunately she developed a bout of laryngitis coming up to the event. No home remedies had any effect and Ronnie was spitting mad. As a last resort, she phoned Suzanne Murphy in Cardiff, who suggested snake venom! Suzanne couriered the homeopathic pills over to Miriam, who swallowed a few, got as high as a kite, sang brilliantly and won the cup.

Anne-Marie O'Sullivan had taken over from Ronnie as head of the Vocal and Drama Department at the College of Music. Imelda Drumm, who had been her student for ten years, came back to Dublin having sung in the chorus at Glyndebourne. She wished to continue her training and, because Anne-Marie no longer had the time to take her, she phoned Ronnie, who offered her lessons at the house on Saturdays. All went well until one afternoon when Peter opened the front door and said that Ronnie wasn't there. He invited Imelda in and they sat down together to watch a rugby match on television. Imelda's boyfriend was a keen player, so they had a great chat about the game. When Ronnie finally appeared she was full of apologies – she had completely forgotten the appointment! After that, Imelda talked often with Peter. Those eighteen months she spent working with Ronnie were the best:

> Ronnie handed me my career on a plate. She opened up my voice and got the top sorted. 'Keep the voice young' is a favourite expression. 'Keep it clear; don't be darkening it; keep the vowels bright.' She's an amazing support. All she wants is to see you get on and do well. And if things aren't right, she'll tell you, and then she'll fix it – she's a wizard with the voice.

LSMD students were beginning to learn some of Ronnie's eccentricities. They were often called upon to move her car from one space to another because it was cheaper, or to run down to F.X.

Buckley for a sirloin joint. On one occasion, a student was handed five pounds and asked to buy Ronnie a pair of shoes, blue, with really, really high heels, because Ronnie didn't have the time to shop. She was always thinking of her singers and where they could be placed; a student might be told to cycle out to the RTÉ studios in Donnybrook where Jane Carty or Kevin Hough were looking for a singer, or to go along to Opera Ireland who had an opening for a tenor.

The LSMD was thriving, with many talented students. Journalist Marianne Hartigan caught the atmosphere of the place when she interviewed Ronnie for an article that appeared in the Irish magazine, *One to One*. 'Veronica Dunne – Ronnie to her friends – welcomes me into a tiny room in the Leinster School of Music. You know instantly from the surroundings, the "la, la, laa"s coming from other rooms, and her embracing hug that you are in the world of drama, of intense emotion, excitement and hard work.'

When baritone Nyle Wolfe auditioned for Ronnie, he was nineteen and fresh off the train from Cork, hardly prepared for the emphatic response that greeted the first piece he sang. 'Right,' said Ronnie. 'So you won't be studying in Cork anymore and I'm sure John Carolan [his teacher] will be broken-hearted to lose you but you're mine now, lovey. You'll start in September. Go downstairs now and pay your fees and if you want to live with me you can!' Nyle

Nyle Wolfe as Dandini in *La Cenerentola*. Gelsenkirchen, 2005

declined the generous offer of board and lodgings, but Ronnie insisted on fixing him up with somewhere to stay for the night before he caught the train back to Cork the following day. For the next three years Nyle lived in bedsits around the Rathmines area.

At the school he was teamed with répétiteur David Wray, a young English pianist who was Director of Music at the Leinster Opera School. In addition to learning new repertoire and technique, Nyle was also mastering the art of blowing over all pages of the telephone directory using one short puff at a time because, Ronnie said, 'It will put you in control of your breath.' Nyle became busy with professional engagements and was successful at the Feis Ceoil. He observed the competitiveness between teachers like Mary Brennan (whom Ronnie had taught), Bernadette Greevy and Ronnie, yet all were fair to one another and offered opportunities to talented students other than their own. In Bushy Park, Nyle was taught to cook steaks by flashing them on the pan on each side for a few seconds before serving them with large gins and tonic. He found there were always students either living there or just staying for a day or two – people like Anthony Kearns.

Anthony Kearns

'Ronnie would give you the shirt off her back,' says Anthony, 'and if that wasn't enough, she'd feed and water you as well.' Anthony, although untrained, had won many singing competitions back home in County Wexford and around the country. He strayed into Ronnie's orbit in 1993 by singing 'Danny Boy' down a phone line to the Gay Byrne radio show in RTÉ's 'Search for a Tenor' competition, launched to celebrate the issuing of a new ten pound note. A week later, the finalist gathered on Dublin's North Earl Street to sing for radio listeners, a throng of curious shoppers and the adjudicators, who included Veronica Dunne. Anthony won, and after the show Ronnie said, 'If you're serious about this business, come and talk to me.'

Every Saturday Anthony hitched a lift to Dublin for his lesson but Ronnie said it wasn't enough; he had to study full-time with her and at the LSMD. He left his home and his work and moved into Bushy Park. 'Ronnie took me in when I didn't have an arse in my trousers, and then she lifted the phone and got me a job in the NCH. She showed such an interest in me; she'd do whatever it took to get me going.' This included rooting him out of the bed at seven in the morning to practise his breathing exercises and scales before breakfast – 'Get up, Domingo, and do your lilly-lallys!' – or tossing the house keys to him as she dashed out, saying, 'I'll be working until nine tonight, lovey. There's food in the fridge, feed the dog and I'll hear your aria when I get back!'

Anthony got his own digs a few months later, but Ronnie's training continued and the hard work paid off. Over the next couple of years Anthony achieved great results in competitions and was in demand for engagements all over Ireland. He was in Athlone one night when Ronnie phoned him. 'You need to get yourself back to Dublin,' she said. 'You're flying to London tomorrow. You'll be singing on Friday night.' He caught the next train:

> Ronnie drove across Dublin to meet me. It was the day President Clinton was coming to town and the potholes were welded to the road and everything was closed down, but Ronnie had clothes for me, money for me, even my passport. She got me to the airport, put me on a plane and within hours I was singing for Richard Baker of BBC fame who was staging a concert for his mother on her ninetieth birthday.

The tenor for the concert had suddenly become ill and the Irish répétiteur Patrick Healy phoned Ronnie in haste to see if she could suggest a replacement who knew the repertoire. Whether he knew the repertoire or not, Ronnie put Anthony forward for the gig which she realised could be his big break, and how right she was. Among the celebrated singers and musicians at that concert Anthony gave a terrific performance. It was the start of an enduring friendship with Richard Baker and with Patrick Healy, who is now Anthony's accompanist. The two have charmed audiences worldwide and made several recordings together.

Ronnie had become a member of the Friends of the Vocal Arts in Ireland shortly after Leslie Scheps and other singing teachers formed it in 1983. The aim of the members was dear to Ronnie's heart – that of giving financial support to talented students so that they might pursue their singing careers. Considerable subsidies had been presented to many students from contributions made by the FVA and from the sponsorship of business firms.

Ronnie decided that the FVA should administer her retirement fund, the Veronica Dunne Bursary. The question was how to make it stretch and have the greatest impact on the largest number of students. The answer was a competition for Irish singers which would give them a forum to display their talents and offer generous prize money and opportunities.

Early in 1995, two years of committee meetings, planning strategies and intensive fundraising by the FVA came to fruition in the first Veronica Dunne Bursary singing competition. The finals took place in the NCH on 19 January and were televised live on RTÉ Network 2.

Ronnie's husband Peter watched the final on television from his hospital bed. He was gravely ill. Judy came back from America and she and Ronnie took turns in staying with him day and night. On 7 February 1995, Peter McCarthy died.

The huge church in Terenure overflowed as friends from the rugby and sporting world mingled with music impresarios and stars. Ronnie arranged the singing. There were boy sopranos, Ite O'Donovan's Palestrina Choir, and solos from Imelda Drumm and Nyle Wolfe. Ned Thornton gave a humorous homily telling many tall tales of the scrapes he, Joe Lane and Peter had got into over the years, and he recounted the story of Peter answering the phone to people who enquired, 'Is Dr Dunne there?' 'No,' he would reply, 'but this is Nurse McCarthy.' After the service, Ronnie and her family gave everyone chicken and rice back at the house, wine and spirits were liberally imbibed and the stories gathered momentum. Ned and Joe lamented the passing of their comrade, and the end of their adventures as The Traveling Wilburys.

Golden years at the Royal Irish Academy of Music

25

$\mathscr{I}$T WAS THE SUMMER OF 1995. A student knocked on Ronnie's door at the Leinster School of Music to say that John O'Conor was downstairs and wanted to see her.

John had returned from his studies in Vienna in 1976 to become Professor of Piano at the Royal Irish Academy of Music. He had performed worldwide, won many competitions, including the International Beethoven Piano Competition, and had made several recordings. In 1988, he launched the triennial Dublin International Piano Competition, which was immediately recognised as one of the most important piano competitions in the world. John was appointed director of the Academy in 1994. Such was his regard for Ronnie that, as soon as the Academy advertised two positions for singing teachers, he speeded across Dublin to invite her to apply.

John had already initiated an interview procedure whereby prospective teachers were asked to demonstrate their skills. When Ronnie went along, she talked with an interview panel that included Leo Gibney, chairman of the board of governors of the Academy, but what interested John was Ronnie's on the spot lesson:

> A volunteer student was brought in and Ronnie listened to him sing, then she asked if she could touch him. When he agreed, she attacked his diaphragm saying, 'What's happening here?' She started to physically pound him saying, 'This is where the voice

comes from – you're not using this at all. Breathe like this.' She made him realise that the body actually produces the sound; it doesn't just float out on its own. Within five minutes she had changed his voice because he was now singing the right way. After Ronnie left, there were a few other applicants who simply suggested that their student sing a bit louder here or more gently there. Irene Sandford, a wonderful soprano from Belfast, came in and got physical with her student in much the same way as Ronnie had, and with the same beneficial results. We knew we had found our two teachers.

The Royal Irish Academy of Music (RIAM) was founded in 1848 and is Ireland's oldest and most venerable music institution. It is situated in a grand Georgian terrace at Westland Row in the heart of Dublin. From the moment of walking in through the front door, Ronnie felt she had come home:

> Entering the Academy is like going into a real conservatoire. The building itself is olde world and spacious. There are many studios and a teachers' room to meet everybody. All the people there, from the porters on the front desk to the teachers, are so welcoming and friendly.

Ronnie continued teaching at the LSMD for one or two days a week. She added another three days at the Academy. She was allocated Room 38: a light-filled, corner studio in the new, purpose-built building, and the only room to have triple sound insulation – Ronnie's reputation for getting the absolute most from her singers had preceded her!

She was working harder than ever, but she had a good team at home, with her housekeeper Clare and Richard O'Connor the gardener. Richard came to Bushy Park as a lad in 1986 to help out in the garden. When Clare left, he took on extra duties and over the years has become an invaluable support and friend to Ronnie. He comes to the house daily and, in addition to maintaining the garden, he has decorated, repaired equipment, shopped and cooked and cleaned. He looked after Ronnie's old dog Guinness and her last dog, who had turned up on the doorstep one day, stray and bedraggled. Ronnie took one look at her and said, 'Welcome, friend.' Richard and Cara (the Irish for friend) became inseparable and even appeared on television together in 2009 when Ronnie was featured on RTÉ's daily talk show 'Seoige', and Cara was immortalised in Nicola Sharkey's cartoon of Ronnie as Wonder Woman. When Cara died in 2011 both Richard and Ronnie were in tears. With great ceremony, they laid her to rest on the spot in the back garden where she always liked to lie.

At Christmas 1995, Richard erected a tree in the living room and strung up the lights, tinsel and baubles. Ronnie invited Geraldine and Alec O'Riordan and their children, her good friend Kevin Hough, her sister May and her husband Michael, and her brother Billo from England. It was going to be a houseful. Geraldine insisted on doing something to help. 'The turkey,' responded Ronnie immediately. 'You're so good with turkeys – and roast potatoes!'

The festivities were due to kick off at four in the afternoon, but Geraldine and Alec had been running back and forth between the two houses all day and each time there was drink taken. By dinnertime it was a mighty tipsy turkey that was borne unsteadily across the road. After a riotous meal, the assembled company adjourned to the living room. Kevin took his seat at the piano and the singing commenced. And how they sang! Billo, now in his eighties, had continued performing in choirs and acquitted himself admirably, May gave it her best shot, and Ronnie was in fine voice. 'O mio babbino caro', Musetta's Waltz, songs from the musicals – it was like the old days in Clontarf, the three of them together again, singing.

The following year Finbar Wright was on his way back to Cork one night. He dropped in at Bushy Park having just done a show with RTÉ in Donnybrook. He was still in his suit and tie and, when Ronnie opened the door to him, she joined her hands as in prayer and looked

Ronnie with Billo and May, and with Kevin Hough, 1995

up to the heavens saying, 'Thank you, Saint Anthony. Not only do you send me a singer, but one who's already dressed!' She hauled him in, gathered some music, and packed the accompanist Ingrid Surgenor (who was staying with her at the time) and Finbar into the car. Driving through the Phoenix Park she explained that they were on their way to Áras an Uachtaráin. President Mary Robinson was hosting foreign dignitaries and the soprano who was to entertain them at the reception had taken ill. They performed, were given a royal feast, Ronnie returned Finbar to the house, showered him with hugs and kisses and sent him on his way home to his family.

Early in 1998 the LSMD premises on Upper Stephen Street burnt down, and the school moved into temporary quarters in Fitzwilliam Street. This proved unpopular with the street's mainly legal inhabitants, who complained that the level of noise in the school was unbearable, particularly from the sopranos! But they were there only for a few months. In September the school moved to its present location on the seven-acre campus of Griffith College on Dublin's South Circular Road. The Yamaha Company provided new pianos and musical instruments, and the music students were soon integrated into the busy life of the college.

Griffith College Dublin is the largest and longest established private third-level college in Ireland. Ronnie was introduced to its dynamic founder and president, Professor Diarmuid Hegarty, who explained that his passion for opera began with 'Nessun Dorma' in Italia 90 when he had wanted to sing like Luciano Pavarotti but, he said, the next best thing was talking to Dr Veronica Dunne. The two quickly discovered that they shared the same energy, positivity and commitment, the same intense love of opera, and a wicked sense of humour. It was a true meeting of minds, and one that Ronnie would come to appreciate even more in the years to come.

The Dublin Grand Opera Society was reorganised on a professional basis and named Opera Ireland in 1998. Mairéad Hurley was its head of music, and the newly appointed artistic director was Swiss-born Dieter Kaegi. Dieter had worked in opera companies throughout Europe and he brought an innovative approach to productions. With their chairman, Frank O'Rourke, Dieter Kaegi and David Collopy took the risk of presenting operas that were new to Irish audiences, alongside familiar crowd-pleasers, in an effort to invigorate the company – Richard Strauss's *Salomé*, for example, with Verdi's *La Traviata*.

The strategy was paying off with increased attendances, and in the *Irish Times* of 16 December 1999 Michael Dervan commented, 'It's

Ronnie as the Countess in *The Queen of Spades*. DGOS, 2002

really good news that artistic director Dieter Kaegi is managing to make serious headway in broadening the company's outlook.' When Dieter decided to put on Tchaikovsky's *The Queen of Spades* in November 2002 with Ronnie in the role of the Countess, her declaration made headlines: 'I want this performance in *Queen of Spades* to be my swan-song, my goodbye to Dublin audiences.'

Fifty-two years previously the DGOS had given Ronnie her first chance, and it seemed fitting that she should be making her final performance with Opera Ireland, and at the Gaiety Theatre (although, as it turned out, this was not her final appearance). Ronnie told Catherine Murphy of the *Irish Times* that the last time she had seen 70 was on a hall door, but she had lots of energy: 'I drive into the city and work from 10am to 6 or 7pm six days a week. Of course, I haven't been teaching for the last month, I've been rehearsing with Opera Ireland.'

The opera was to be performed in its original language, so Ronnie was not only rehearsing, but also learning Russian! As she says, 'You have to do whatever is required for the role, darling.' Seven of the sixteen-member cast were native Russian speakers.

The Queen of Spades was first performed at the Mariinsky Theatre, Saint Petersburg on 19 December 1890. It tells the story of Herman, a young officer obsessed with gambling and with the idea that the aged Countess holds the secret of the three cards in the game of Faro. He is in love with Liza, granddaughter of the Countess, but she is betrothed to another. Opera Ireland's production ran for four nights from 17 to 23 November 2002. Tenor Peter Svensson from Austria sang the role of Herman, Russian soprano Viktoria Kurbatskaya played Liza, and baritone Sam McElroy from Ireland was Prince Yeletsky. Irish soprano Kathleen Tynan sang the roles of Masha and Chloë. Alexander Anissimov from Belorussia (present-day Belarus) conducted the RTÉ Concert Orchestra in a vigorous and purposeful performance. Harvey O'Brien's article for *Culture Vulture* in November 2002 captured the experience of opening night:

Opera Ireland's current production of *The Queen of Spades* is a sumptuous affair. It is a grandly realized spectacle directed with energy and depth by Dieter Kaegi, lustrously designed by Joe Vanek, and it features an unforgettable performance from Irish opera legend Veronica Dunne as the countess. Though her singing voice is now frail and cracked, Dunne is still a commanding stage presence. Her dramatic characterization far exceeds the expected level of acting in most operas, and is often as frighteningly intense as the best theatrical performances. Her sweet, clear singing is heard only in snippets, but it is fitting that a woman who has now trained two generations of singers should take her place on stage at what must rank among Opera Ireland's triumphs.

Ciara Dwyer of the *Irish Independent* was moved by Ronnie's performance: 'It was a privilege to see her up there, such high-octane energy, such zest for life. In any other country, she would be a dame. This is far from what she called her "swan-song". As the curtain fell she left us with one thought – there's a dance in the old dame yet.'

The old dame was dancing after the show with Judy and Richard

Ronnie makes her final bow to Gaiety audiences – only it wasn't!

Judy, Richard and sons
Kevin and Aidan

who had travelled from Boston with the boys, and with Peter and Sandra, and all the many friends who had gathered to cheer her on. The production at the Gaiety was a sell-out – a feather in the cap for Opera Ireland, and another bow on Ronnie's bonnet.

When all the excitement had died down, the seventy-five-year-old went back to teaching six days a week, scouring Ireland for fresh talent, flying off to European performances of her former students, appearing on television shows such as the Lyrics Board and Theatre Nights, adjudicating for other people's competitions, and preparing for her own. Her competition had established an international reputation and had become a firm fixture on the world's operatic calendar.

The following year Judy, Kevin and Aidan stayed with Ronnie in the summer. They all flew back to Boston in August for a family holiday that included Ronnie's sister May, who was to board

The Irish Tenors; Finbar
Wright, Anthony Kearns and
Ronan Tynan

the plane at Shannon Airport. By coincidence, the three Irish Tenors, all of whom were former students of Ronnie's, were also en route to Boston for a concert on 2 August 2003. Anthony Kearns, Ronan Tynan and Finbar Wright had got together in 1998 and formed the highly successful group.

On the flight out of Dublin Anthony was so delighted to see Ronnie on board that he asked a steward if there was any chance he could use his air miles to bump her up to business class with himself and Ronan. Within minutes she was ensconced in luxury and sipping champagne. Finbar boarded at Shannon, closely followed by May, who was seated at the back of the plane. Judy knew she was going to be in for a long seven hours with her aunt acting the martyr. She asked the steward if May could join Ronnie up front, unaware that Anthony had just made the same request. For the rest of the journey Ronnie, May and the tenors enjoyed a rollicking time and alighted in Boston singing and laughing in rare good form. Anthony gave Ronnie tickets for the show the next night. All three tenors hailed her from the stage of the Fleet Pavilion as the person who had trained each one of them. They presented her with an enormous bouquet of flowers and, with the spotlight upon her, Ronnie took a bow before a crowd of five thousand cheering spectators.

The opera world did not know it yet, but a shining star was about to blaze across its galaxy. Tara Erraught from Dundalk, County Louth, just loved singing. As a child, she was fortunate to have a wonderful teacher in Geraldine McGee. Geraldine entered Tara for her first Feis Ceoil when she was ten. She received a certificate and from then on she was hooked! She wanted to go to every Feis: Newry, Warrenpoint, Portadown, Ballymena, Sligo, Dublin. Tara persuaded Geraldine or her parents to drive her to these places, and would laugh at them for being so nervous while she was in the back seat of the car, half-learning the words to the songs she was about to perform. She did well at all the Feiseanna, supported by her accompanist Jeannie Reddin. In March 2004, Tara was due to take her final school exams in June, but would not miss the Feis in Dublin. For the highly prized Dramatic Cup competition she sang Desdemona's 'Salce' aria from Verdi's *Otello* and she was awarded a certificate.

Tara Erraught

Ronnie made a beeline to her and said, 'Good voice, lovey, but your Italian's shite! Come and see me on Friday.'

When Tara and her mother, Brianain, arrived at the Royal Irish Academy of Music, they were directed along corridors and up stairs to Ronnie's Room 38 at the back of the building. It was full of students; one was at the piano with Ronnie and the others were learning by listening. Ronnie broke off the lesson to tell Tara she could start in September. This threw Brianain into a panic because they hadn't even put the Academy on Tara's college application form. Ronnie made a quick phone call and said, 'OK. Go up the hall and see John O'Conor.'

John had not heard Tara sing, but if Ronnie said she was special and should come to the Academy, he would make it happen, even if he had to bend a few rules. This included fixing it so that Tara could continue working with Jeannie Reddin, who was not on the staff, and in due course the mezzo-soprano was enrolled to study for her BA in Music Performance.

Joe Erraught found it almost incredible that his daughter was to train with the great Veronica Dunne, whom he had last encountered while supervising the catering for her operatic evenings at the College of Music. At first, it was arranged that Tara travel daily from Dundalk for her lessons. When this proved impractical because of evening classes and events, Joe and Brianain decided to buy a house in Whitehall, Dublin which she could share with friends. Tara always tried to get to the Academy early. 'The best thing was to be the first one there for a lesson because if someone didn't turn up later, Ronnie would give me a call. I might be doing counterpoint or ear tests or theory or something, but if Ronnie summoned me, the lecturer would let me go, no questions, so I'd have two lessons instead of one. The more lessons you had with Ronnie, the quicker and further you got on.'

Shortly before Christmas, Tara discovered that the upcoming Feis in March commanded Ronnie's full attention: 'She spent two weeks picking song programmes for her own students and anyone else who asked her – she was brilliant at it. The piece had to suit the singer, be a crowd pleaser, and ensure that the jury could appreciate the singer's particular abilities. Then, when the Feis was on, she'd be there day and night. Even now, she camps out in the RDS and won't eat in case she might miss something.'

In 2005, Tara was aghast when Ronnie told her she could not enter any competitions for a year because she needed more technical work to fully develop and train her voice, and they could not prepare new repertoire. When she saw the girl's distress, Ronnie relented and said that if she studied hard and did really well, she could enter the Veronica Dunne International Singing Competition in January 2007. Over the following year they prepared the eleven arias that would be required should Tara progress as far as the third round.

Tara was working as an usherette at the NCH, revelling in all the wonderful music. Three weeks before the competition, she was up in Room 38 when Ronnie gave her a weird look. 'Don't be working, lovey. You already talk too much; you've got to rest your voice.' Tara agreed to stop.

Two days later, Ronnie spied Tara sitting at the NCH reception desk in her uniform. She marched over, grabbed the twenty-year-old by the arm, bundled her out to the car, drove her to Whitehall, collected a few clothes, and took her back to Bushy Park. The next morning Tara woke up in a panic, thinking, 'Sweet Jesus! I have a harmony counterpoint class.' Quickly she showered, dressed and ran down the stairs to the front door. It was locked. She tried the back door. It was locked. Then she saw the note on the table: *Lovey, there's veal in the fridge for lunch. Richard will be over with your dinner.* She rang Ronnie to say she was locked in, to which Ronnie replied, 'Yes, because I can't trust you out!' Tara phoned Deborah Kelleher, head of musicianship at the Academy, because she thought she would be in big trouble for missing classes. Deborah told her not to worry; her teachers had already been told about the situation. After lunch, Ronnie came home with Alison Young and the three of them worked for the afternoon and had steak for dinner.

This routine continued until just three days before the competition when Tara felt she was getting a cold. 'Acupuncture!' said Ronnie. She brought her for a needle session with a local man in Rathgar before they went on to a rehearsal with Mairéad Hurley at the Conservatory of Music and Drama (formerly the DIT College of Music). Tara fell asleep at the piano. Ronnie got her home, put her to bed and, after a deep sleep, Tara got up the next day feeling refreshed and calm.

The first three rounds of the competition were held at the Freemasons' Hall in Molesworth Street, Dublin. Brianain and Joe and Tara's grandparents travelled from Dundalk each day and initially sat through the singing of all forty-two competitors because they did not know when Tara would be on. Joe was so nervous, he felt sick. Tara made it through round one, and then round two, and on the third day she was in round three, in what she felt was her last chance to shine. She wore her best dress and, for her song in English, she sang the lullaby from *The Consul* by Gian Carlo Menotti, which was inappropriate for her age because it was written for a grandmother, but it was the hit of the day with the audience. After the jury had conferred, Tara was stunned to hear that she was one of the seven finalists. She had no repertoire prepared and there were just two days to the final. She was allowed to repeat one of her arias and she knew Dido's lament by Purcell. Ronnie suggested a French aria from Gounod's *Roméo et Juliette* that Tara had not yet learnt, and then she dropped a bombshell. 'Lovey,' she said, 'I can't help you. It's my competition and I can't be seen to be helping one of the competitors.'

From that moment, Ronnie could not talk to either Tara or Celine Byrne, her other student who had reached the final, nor did she attend rehearsals. A French speaker helped Tara with the text of Gounod's aria and Alison Young went over the music with her. There was a big rehearsal at the RTÉ studios in Donnybrook with the RTÉ Concert Orchestra conducted by French-born Laurent Wagner and, instead of feeling nervous Tara found it 'beyond exciting!' But she had nothing new to wear for the final. Brianain had seen a dress in Dundalk, so the two of them hopped in the car, drove the 80 kilometres to the shop, the dress was tried on and purchased and they hit the motorway back down to Dublin. These four hours should have been spent practising, but Tara was far too euphoric.

On 25 January 2007, the finals of the 5th Veronica Dunne International Singing Competition took place at the NCH. Thirty of Tara's relations and friends bused down from Dundalk and occupied the front row of the auditorium. One by one the seven finalists took to the stage: Mexican tenor Dante Alcalá, Welsh soprano Elizabeth Donovan, Japanese soprano Mari Moriya, British soprano Stephanie Corley, Irish mezzo-soprano Naomi O'Connell, who studied with Mary Brennan, and Ronnie's students Celine and Tara.

After a long interval, the winners were announced. First place: Mari Moriya. Second place: Tara Erraught. The audience went wild, and Joe cried his eyes out! Michael Dervan of the *Irish Times* was impressed with the way Tara 'carried the import of the words and the weight of the vocal line in Purcell's touching "When I am laid in earth"', and by her stylish singing in Mozart's 'Non so più' (from *Le nozze di Figaro*). He continued: 'In Gounod's demonstrative "Que fais-tu, blanche tourterelle?" she revealed an engaging personality and a swagger that brought her cheers from the audience and helped secure her the €5,000 second prize.'

When the excitement had died down, the Dundalkers returned home. Ronnie drove Tara back to Bushy Park and quickly dispelled any notions of instant success by saying, 'It's into fifth gear for you now, lovey. We've got to get down to some serious work!' Tara went to bed and woke up sick as a dog as the flu hit her, and then the phone started to ring with offers of engagements, Ronnie turning down many more than she accepted. After that it was work, work, work. Tara lived with Ronnie for the next year – she was not allowed back to her house in Whitehall until Ronnie felt she could be trusted. She continued in the Academy; technique in the morning and repertoire in the afternoon with Ronnie and vocal coach Dearbhla Collins. In the evening there might be more work with Ronnie and Alison Young, followed by a gin or two. Ronnie got Tara to audition for an operatic summer school near Genoa, Italy which was run by the Italian tenor Ugo Benelli who had been one of the adjudicators at the

2007 competition. Tara spent four summers there working on different roles with the ten other students. It was excellent training, and she learnt to speak Italian like a native.

Tara performed on the Continent and in 2008 won several famous competitions, including the International Hans Gabor Belvedere Singing Competition in Vienna. Arising out of this, she was offered 'Artist in Residence' at La Scala, Milan. She immediately put a call through to Ronnie to ask if she should accept. 'Absolutely not!' said Ronnie. 'You're not ready and it's the wrong repertoire – it's too heavy for you.' But when the Bayerische Staatsoper (Bavarian State Opera) in Munich offered her a place, Ronnie said 'Yes!' Joe was keen that Tara should complete her music degree at the Academy, and during her last year of study, the staff went out of their way to facilitate her as she flew between Munich and Dublin.

In 2011, Tara stunned the German audience when she stepped in to the main role of Romeo in Bellini's *I Capuleti e i Montecchi* at just three days' notice and performed superbly. She received a prolonged standing ovation at the end of the performance, and was lionised as a true rising star. Following further sensational appearances, Tara was bestowed with the prestigious Pro meritis scientiae et litterarum award by the Bavarian government in 2013 in recognition for outstanding contribution to science and the arts. At 26 years of age, she was the youngest recipient and only the fifth musician to receive this honour. 'I couldn't have done any of it without Ronnie and my parents, who are the absolute best,' says Tara. Over the years, Ronnie has attended many of Tara's performances, and watches in delight as her international reputation soars.

Tara Erraught as Romeo in Bellini's *I Capuleti e i Montecchi*

Celine Byrne sang at the inaugural Wexford Festival Opera's artists' development programme in 2005. Ronnie complimented her on her beautiful voice and the two got talking. Celine was just finishing her degree at the DIT Conservatory of Music and Drama and wanted to further her studies. Ronnie suggested that she study for a master's degree at the Academy, but Celine shook her head. The two-year course would be a struggle because she was pregnant, and this was her third child. 'Oh holy God,' exclaimed Ronnie, who warned her female students against trying to combine marriage and motherhood with singing. 'Well, come along to the Academy and we'll see what we can do.'

Celine Byrne

Celine made the daily journey from Naas, County Kildare to the Academy on Westland Row, which was ideally situated for her as it is just around the corner from the National Maternity Hospital at Holles Street. She slotted in her regular check-ups between lessons. On one occasion she was told that her blood pressure was high and that she should be kept in for observation. 'No way,' said Celine. 'I'm singing in a showcase in an hour.' She hurried back to the Academy, sang her heart out and returned to the hospital, her blood pressure sky high.

Deborah Kelleher (whose mother Deirdre had been the administrator for one of Ronnie's competitions) was the accompanist for Celine at many of her classes with Ronnie, and she saw their relationship blossom into one of complete trust and respect. 'Celine has a world-class voice and Ronnie was superb with her. She helped her in every way she could. She was coach, guide, mentor, friend. Ronnie gives three things to her students. The first is time. When they're very young, they might get a lesson a week. It advances to two, three, four lessons until she is really fine-tuning them. The second thing is technique. The third thing is her interpretation and communication – the singer has to be saying something the audience wants to hear. That's the magic.'

At the Conservatory, Celine had studied with Edith Forrest, a friend and former student of Ronnie's, and her technique was excellent. At the Academy she got the push she required for performance. 'You need a kick up the ass!' Ronnie said bluntly. 'You put your two feet on the ground and you get out there and you sing.' Deborah remembers Celine entering for the Geoghegan Memorial Cup at the Feis in 2006 where she was to sing 'Stridono lassù' from Leoncavallo's *I Pagliacci*. 'Ronnie was right there backstage with us and she grabbed Celine's arm and hissed, "Now just remember you're a gipsy bitch!" and thrust her onto the stage. Celine was filled with such energy that she gave a mesmerising performance. It is a piece that ends with an incredible climax and Celine was radiant with brilliance. That's the difference Ronnie makes – the lessons continue right up to the side of the stage if they have to.' Celine is the first to appreciate the difference Ronnie has made:

> Ronnie is a great interpreter of music and when you hear her you know exactly how she is feeling. There are some wonderful singers but they don't touch me, even though I hear the beauty in their voice. What Ronnie did for me and what I've taken from her is the communication element. She touches people when she sings – she hits you right in the heart. She's got a presence. I knew instantly after just meeting her that we had a connection, and we always will. I love

her; I really love her. That's how emotional I am about the woman.

Celine graduated within one year and was honoured with the RIAM award for outstanding achievement in 2007. That same year she received the ultimate accolade for sopranos when she won the First Prize and Gold Medal at the Maria Callas Grand Prix in Athens. Since then, she has performed to great acclaim all over the world, and in April 2015 she sang Cio-Cio San in the Moscow State Opera production of Puccini's *Madama Butterfly* at the Bord Gáis Energy Theatre, Dublin. Ronnie has been to almost everything Celine has appeared in, and both she and Deborah attended her début as Mimi for the 2010 Scottish Opera production of *La Bohème*. Celine remembers that occasion for a very special reason: 'Puccini taught Margaret Burke Sheridan to sing Mimi, Margaret Burke Sheridan taught Ronnie, and Ronnie taught me – it's a lovely connection; a direct musical line.'

The year of 2007 held many dazzling highlights for Ronnie. One of the greatest occurred on 6 April when Patricia Bardon made her debut at the Metropolitan Opera House, New York. Ronnie, Alison Young and Edith Forrest arrived the night before the performance. Judy drove from Boston and they all met up at the Waldorf Hotel on Park Lane.

Celine Byrne as Madam Butterfly in *Madama Butterfly*. Bord Gáis Energy Theatre, 2015

221

The weekend got off to a terrific start when champagne and chocolate-covered strawberries were delivered to each of the two bedrooms as a surprise gift from Tara Erraught. Although it was bitterly cold, over the next two days they took in the sights – Times Square, Macy's, the Empire State Building – and on the boat ride to the Statue of Liberty it started to snow! But the excitement was all about Patricia.

The opera was *Giulio Cesare* by Handel. Patricia sang the role of Cornelia, a woman overcome by emotions of grief and rage, wracked with pain because of her husband's murder. The production was declared 'a staggering masterpiece' by the exacting *New York Times* critic Anthony Tommasini who lavished praise on the 'the rich-toned Irish mezzo-soprano' Patricia Bardon in her 'significant Met debut'.

Patricia had given the small Irish contingent passes to see her backstage after the show. They were directed to a particular entrance and through security and down a warren of corridors before they found the dressing room bearing the plaque *Patricia Bardon – Cornelia*. Patricia and her husband, English tenor Nicholas Sears, greeted them warmly, the champagne was popped, and everyone celebrated Patricia's

Patricia Bardon as Carmen.
Los Angeles Opera, 2013

wonderful success – the first of many on the world's stage.

Ronnie insisted on filling every minute of her New York adventure. They visited Patricia and Nicholas in their rented apartment and when Ronnie discovered that Umberto Giordano's *Andrea Chénier* was going to be performed she exclaimed: 'It's one of my top favourites. I don't care if I have to pay hundreds for the ticket – I'm going!' Edith had never seen Ronnie so exhilarated as at those operas in the Met: 'She was passionate about being there. She knew every note. She was right up there on stage with the character, totally focused and involved.'

Veronica Bernadette Dunne was born on 2 August 1927. She was now eighty years old and it was party time! Ite O'Donovan of the Dublin Choral Foundation came up with the idea of a celebration concert (no hint of 'retirement' this time) that would feature many of Ronnie's exceptional students and former students in an operatic explosion of music.

Cartoon in the programme by former student Nicola Sharkey: Ronnie as Wonder Woman with Cliff, her rescue dog, muttering 'Anything for a quiet life!'

Vivian Coates was delighted to direct and design the show. He has known Ronnie since his days in the College of Music, where he studied with Edith Forrest. He was one of those students lying on the floor in the John McCann Hall, hissing and blowing and exercising his diaphragm. After a spell in England, he returned to Ireland in the 1990s and established Lyric Opera Productions, with Ronnie as its patron.

Suzanne Murphy was the driving force behind the concert. She spent many hours in Ronnie's attic sifting through old photographs and programmes, and put together a remarkable commemorative brochure that included tributes from friends far and wide, and a lively cartoon by Nicola Sharkey that depicts Ronnie as Wonder Woman cracking the whip! In the brochure, President Mary McAleese thanked Ronnie for sharing so generously her talent and dedication to song. The Lord Mayor of Dublin, Councillor Paddy Bourke, commented that Ronnie was an ambassador for the city and the country – a true star long before the idea of celebrity was invented. Judith Woodworth, director of the NCH, saluted Ronnie for her long association with the NCH through her service on the board and for the outstanding performances of her many talented students. In acknowledgement of her unique contribution, Ronnie was appointed an Honorary Silver Friend of the National Concert Hall.

The task of the co-ordinators was not an easy one. Singers were

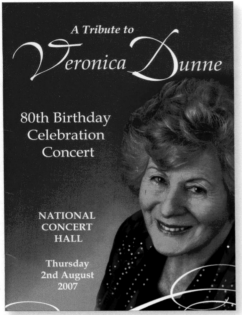

flown in from all over the world, accommodation had to be found, suitable repertoire agreed and positioned on the programme to give variety and cohesion, and solos, duets, trios, quartets and ensemble pieces rehearsed. Deirdre Grier-Delaney, Colette McGahon and Tony Finnegan assisted Ite, Vivian, Suzanne and Angela McCrone with the arrangements.

'A Tribute to Veronica Dunne – 80th Birthday Celebration Concert' took to the stage at the NCH on 2 August 2007. Ite O'Donovan conducted the Orlando Chamber Orchestra and Tony Peacock presented the show. Twenty-eight singers entertained Ronnie's 1,200 friends and supporters to a glorious outpouring of music, opera and joy. Judith Woodworth says it was a terrific occasion: 'The love and respect and admiration for Ronnie in that auditorium was palpable. It was a wonderful expression of gratitude to her. People were there because this was Ronnie's night and they wanted an opportunity to acknowledge this great lady.' Ronnie was persuaded to sing her old favourite, 'Danny Boy', and this time it was not only the men who were reduced to tears.

That concert was not the end of the celebrations. Ronnie thought it would be fun to have a little party at home for her close family and one or two friends. Tara Erraught volunteered the services of her parents, both lecturers in catering. Brianain and Joe readily agreed. They had heard that Ronnie's kitchen was small but a dinner party for about twelve people should pose no problem. However, the idea escalated until suddenly there was a guest list of one hundred and thirty and a huge marquee in the back garden! Delft and cutlery were hired and crates of food and drink were transported by the vanload. Brianain and Joe sweated in the kitchen for a day and a half and Tara's sister Aoife was drafted in as one of the servers. The combined effort of willing helpers produced a banquet fit for Ireland's first lady of song, and the revelries lasted through the night.

An extraordinary year, even by Ronnie's standards, was rounded off on 14 December when she was conferred with an Honorary Doctor of Music by Trinity College Dublin.

Ronnie had a hip replaced in 2010. She was soon back to walking and swimming, but after eighteen years of teaching with the Leinster School of Music she felt it was time to wind down that chapter of her life. At a wonderful party in Griffith College, she asked Diarmuid Hegarty to keep her name on the books, just in case! Far from being less active, however, she now went into the Academy five days a week.

To mark Ronnie's fiftieth anniversary of teaching, EMI Ireland released a three-disc collection of her singing through the years, featuring opera, Celtic and traditional recordings. *Veronica Dunne – The Platinum Collection* was declared CD of the week by Colman Morrissey of the *Irish Times* on 17 December 2010:

> There is much to enjoy here, with notable performances of *O Mio Babbino Caro* (recorded when Dunne was 19) and a rapt singing of *Deh Vieni, Non Tardar* from *Marriage of Figaro*. Irish composers are not neglected, with *I Dreamt I Dwelt in Marble Halls* from *The Bohemian Girl* and *Scenes That Are Brightest* from *Maritana*. However, the real gems of the discs may be the duets from *L'amico Fritz* with the great tenor Nicola Monti. They are a delight to hear, with both singers stylishly expressing the delicate essence of the music.

Ronnie in character as Grandma Tzeitzel. With Vivian Coates backstage at the Gaiety

One of Vivian Coates's regrets is that he never worked with Ronnie in an operatic production, but when he asked her to appear in *Fiddler on the Roof* at the Gaiety Theatre she was thrilled. Vivian directed and inspired his sixty-strong cast in the major musical theatre spectacular, which ran from 16 March to 2 April 2011. Although Ronnie played a cameo role as the ghost of Grandma Tzeitzel, such was her popularity that the advertising strap was 'Fiddler on the Roof' featuring Veronica Dunne'. Tony Finnegan, as Tevye, shared a dressing room and an interest in horses with Ronnie. They swapped racing tips, tall tales and scandalous stories. Vivian visited the pair of them during intervals and was always amused by Ronnie giving out because she had forgotten the odd word in the script. 'But it didn't matter one bit,' he says. 'She has fantastic stage presence and she just made up the words. Everyone adored her.' Despite a long period between Ronnie's appearance and the end of the show, she stayed in costume and passed the time with Sudoku so that she could take the curtain call. Writing in the *Irish Independent* of 20 March, Liam Collins praised the 'superb performance' of Tony Finnegan who was ably supported by Ellen

McElroy as Golde and, he added: 'It is delightful to see Veronica Dunne as Grandma Tzeitzel and the apparition of the three airborne ghosts is one of the many memorable moments in this production.'

After the Gaiety run, Ronnie was back teaching at the Academy when she received great news. Miriam Murphy and Imelda Drumm had both been engaged to star in Wagner's epic opera *Tristan und Isolde*, to be staged at the Bord Gáis Energy Theatre, Dublin. This was a highly ambitious and risky venture for a new Irish opera company, Wide Open Opera, and its artistic director Fergus Sheil.

Miriam had sung Wagner before but she had never performed the role of Isolde. She describes the amount of preparation required for the five-hour opera as 'mammoth'. A year before the production she took out the score, an enormous tome, and started to study the music in London with her teacher and two vocal coaches who specialised in Wagner. While appearing in other operas, Miriam painstakingly learnt the score section by section and gradually built it into a coherent whole; she had to be fully primed for the tight four-week rehearsal period that took place in an old church in the centre of Dublin. Miriam and Imelda had never sung together as students of Ronnie's, but the whole cast were thoroughly professional and Fergus Sheil created a wonderful atmosphere in the rehearsal room that allowed the necessarily intensive work to progress smoothly. The effective production was hired in from Welsh National Opera and was directed by Peter Watson. There were three performances, on 30 September, 3 and 6 October 2012.

Michael Dervan of the *Irish Times* declared: 'Opening night was a

Soprano Miriam Murphy (below), and as Isolde with Imelda Drumm as Brangäne in *Tristan und Isolde*. Wide Open Opera, 2012

triumph all round. Kerry soprano Miriam Murphy was a vocally resplendent Isolde ... Lars Cleveman was a slightly introverted Tristan ... Imelda Drumm's Brangäne was compassionate and concerned ... Fergus Sheil coaxed from the RTÉ NSO some of the finest playing I've ever heard from them in the opera pit. A *Tristan und Isolde* to cherish.'

The event was streamed over the Internet to thirty-five countries. During an interview immediately after the performance, Miriam was thinking 'This is going out live and I'm drenched in sweat!' At that moment Ronnie burst through the door and ran towards her screaming 'Oh God, you were fabulous!' and that went out live as well.

Ronnie loves attending the performances of her singers whenever work, time and finances allow. Early in her career Imelda remembers a happy little troupe of Irish people waving and cheering her on from a balcony at Glyndebourne and not behaving themselves at all. Later, Ronnie spread out the picnic in the grounds amid great hilarity and a good deal of gin! After more than a dozen years of performing all over the world, Imelda returned home to work on a doctoral thesis with Ronnie at the Academy on the effects of performance stress and anxiety on the physiology of female singers.

Deborah Kelleher, whose mother Deirdre had served as administrator for one of Ronnie's competitions, was appointed director of the Academy in 2010. Deborah has long been an admirer of Ronnie and her work. She credits her with developing the répétiteur system in Ireland, teaching and training vocal coaches and accompanists to vocalists. She also believes that Ronnie has transformed the vocal department of the Academy. It now takes its

(Below left) Deborah Kelleher

(Below) Alison Young with Ronnie

place among the finest in the world with its production of highly trained and professional world-class singers. A reciprocal project has been arranged with the Juilliard School in New York and more such projects are envisaged.

Singing students at the Academy are eager to be coached by Ronnie; there is an expectation of success that has been fulfilled time and again. In support of her coaching, facilities have improved beyond all recognition. The Bachelor in Music Performance (Vocal) degree encompasses sight reading, languages, phonetics, acting, movement, song groups, operatic performances, oratorio, master classes – everything that Ronnie fought so hard for in her early teaching days and tried to accomplish on her own! The Academy has its own superb accompanists and répétiteurs, but Ronnie often calls on the services of her great friend Alison Young for extra tuition hours. Over the course of almost forty years Alison has played for all her students.

Sarah Shine (soprano) and Gemma Ní Bhriain (mezzo)

Ronnie's present students include tenors Patrick Hyland, James McCreanor, Robert McAlister and Aaron Doyle, mezzo-soprano Niamh O'Sullivan and soprano Sarah Shine. Sarah and mezzo-soprano Gemma Ní Bhriain started their degree course in 2010, and quickly became the best of friends. Officially they were allocated two hours a week each with Ronnie, but both agree that they received many more. Sometimes they would watch the contestants on *The X Factor* and think: that looks easy, why can't we just sing like that? Now they realise that the training they received from Ronnie will last a lifetime – good for the voice and good for them as performers with long careers. But Gemma recalls those early classes as being frustrating and challenging before the breakthrough that made it all worthwhile:

Up to third year with Ronnie you barely get to sing a song, because it's all technique. Scales, breathing every day, every hour. Over and over. One day she says the voice is too far back in your throat, and you spend six months correcting that, then it's too far forward and that has to be corrected. One day you feel like Maria Callas, the next that you should be working in McDonalds. I think that what Ronnie does is she pulls out every single bad habit you have, whether you sing through your nose, or with your lip in a funny position. For months I had to hold my upper lip out while practising, then I had to hold my lower lip out as well. I was like a beaky bird, and all so that I'd get used to not having my lips on my teeth. Whatever you do she strips it back to nothing but the bare voice that only she can hear; we can't hear it. Then she builds on that again. So for the first three years it's the most frustrating thing ever. Then suddenly it clicks. She says your technique is sorted and she concentrates on arias and songs, which is brilliant. No matter how hard Ronnie is on you, you know it's because she really cares and she wants the best for you, and you know she was right all along!

The end of year recital is a big occasion at the Academy. It is an important element of the performance degree and a chance to sing before family, peers and faculty members in the Katherine Brennan Hall. Sarah Shine says her recital at the end of second year was a turning point. She had postponed her appearance from June to the beginning of the autumn term because of laryngitis. She could not sing all that summer but in September she practised hard every day. Her recital was scheduled for a Wednesday at 2 p.m. On the Monday she felt a niggle in her throat; on the Tuesday she felt iffy and on Wednesday morning she had no voice at all. Ronnie was exasperated. 'Get your music out,' she snapped, 'and sing.' Sarah could only manage a croak. 'That's fine,' said Ronnie. 'There's nothing wrong with you. Go and warm up properly and come back here at one o'clock.' Sarah flounced out, furious that Ronnie was not taking her seriously. When she came back, Kathleen Tynan, head of the vocal faculty, was with Ronnie. Sarah told them that she was just fine. She opened her mouth to sing and a squawk came out. Kathleen was concerned but Ronnie would have none of it.

'It's all in your head, child. If La Scala phoned in the morning, you wouldn't be pulling this stunt! The Academy has paid the examiner to be here and you're wasting everybody's time. You've cancelled the exam once and you're not doing it again. Now go downstairs and get into your dress.'

Sarah grabbed her music, fled from the room in tears, told her accompanist how much she hated Ronnie, got dressed, wiped her eyes and walked on stage as if nothing was wrong. She saw Ronnie at the back of the hall and decided she was going to make her sit through the whole thing and know that she was not lying. She sang her first song as if it was the most beautiful song in the world. Lyrics, pronunciation and acting were perfect, all delivered through an appalling screech. At the end of the piece the examiner said, 'You sound very ill. Do you want to stop?' Sarah looked straight at Ronnie and said she would like to continue. When they agreed she thought: OK, now watch this!

She sang the remainder of her programme using all the resources she possessed. The next day she was told that she had been awarded 69%. It was explained that they could not give her 70% (which would have been a first) because actually she had no voice, but the judges had been very impressed by the way she gave full expression to the songs and continued on in difficult circumstances. Sarah was diagnosed with pharyngitis, a severe form of laryngitis, and had still not forgiven Ronnie when she saw her two days later.

'I'm so sorry,' said Ronnie. 'I knew you were sick; I'm not deaf! But it was just fifteen minutes before your recital and I could not allow you to perform feeling sorry for yourself. If I had sympathised, would you have gone on fighting for your mark like you did? I had to let you be angry with me.'

It was, Sarah says, one of the most valuable lessons she ever learnt. It gave her confidence in her own abilities and taught her what it takes to be a real performer. She has received glowing reviews for student performances and at The Lir Academy in Trinity College Dublin. She was very young when she graduated, just twenty, so she remained with Ronnie for another year to complete a diploma. Sarah will pursue her career at a major opera house in Germany.

Gemma competed in the finals of the Veronica Dunne International Singing Competition in 2013. 'It was fantastic to sing before the home crowd. The audience went wild when I was awarded the prizes for the best Irish singer and the Dame Joan Sutherland Prize for the most promising young singer. And when it was announced that I'd come fourth, people just screamed!' Gemma had a further eighteen months to complete her degree, but her performance made a deep impression on Christian Schirm, director of the Atelier Lyrique of the Opéra National de Paris and one of the adjudicators of the competition, and in 2014 she embarked on a two-year placement at his opera studio. She and Ronnie are in constant communication. 'Ronnie was the first person ever to call me on Facebook Messenger. Viber is one of her favourites, and Little Bird and Dove – you never know when Ronnie is going to pop up on screen.'

Deborah Kelleher is firmly of the opinion that Ronnie's golden era is right now. 'I believe that Ronnie's best students are yet to come. She goes out and finds them, whether it takes a plane trip to Kerry or a drive to Sligo. She is hungry for the next talent she can nurture and by God she's doing it!'

The Veronica Dunne International Singing Competition

*They're ripe, they're ready and they don't get nearly
enough exposure in their home city. These are the voices
that will be winning critical accolades in the years to come –
although it is unfortunately the case that many
of them will be winning those accolades abroad.*

VERONICA DUNNE, The *Irish Times*, 13 May 1991

THE SINGING competition was born of Ronnie's dream to provide well-deserved accolades for the wealth of talented young singers in Ireland, to assist them financially in pursuing their careers, and to give them the opportunity make contact with members of an international jury. The body chosen to turn the dream into reality was the Friends of the Vocal Arts in Ireland, a non-for-profit charitable body.

With the injection of capital from Ronnie's retirement fund, the scope and vision of the FVA was dramatically enhanced. The prime focus of this voluntary group was now directed towards the monumental task of organising and fundraising for a major competition – The Veronica Dunne Bursary.

Ronnie was the figurehead of the ambitious project, but it was accomplished only with the dedicated work of the FVA committee, whose honorary president was Dr Anthony O'Reilly. The chairman was Dr Dermot O'Kelly, Ben McArdle and Ellen Lynch were joint treasurers, and Eilish Fitzgerald was the secretary. The committee members were Frank Coffey, Professor John Fielding,

Leslie Scheps, Richard Stokes, David Wray, Garrett Wren and Ronnie herself. David Wray took on the onerous task of administration.

A fundraising campaign was launched in 1993 and Ronnie went on a charm offensive. The Electricity Supply Board were potential sponsors, and a meeting was arranged between Ronnie and one of its directors, Kevin Donald. As she hurried along Adelaide Road in her highest of high heels, she tried to memorise his last name by association – *Donald Duck, Donald Duck, Donald Duck*. Waiting on the steps of the ESB offices was a handsome man with red hair and a moustache. She walked up, extended her hand and said, 'Hello, Mr Duck!'

In spite of this, the ESB did become a major sponsor of the bursary. In his programme article for the final of the competition, P.J. Moriarty, chairman of the ESB, wrote that the Board was 'honoured to have the opportunity to support our great lady of music, Dr Veronica Dunne, in her mission to develop Irish singers to the highest of world standards'. The other major sponsor was Radio Telefís Éireann. Its chairman, John P. Sorohan, noted:

> Ireland is now producing more world-class singers than at any time in her history. It can be no coincidence that this upsurge in the quality of Irish singing has coincided with the teaching career of Doctor Veronica Dunne. After a sparkling and brilliant career on the opera stage, she has devoted her life not simply to teaching young singers but into inspiring them with a love and a respect for their art.

With Joan Sutherland

Following two years of intensive planning and fundraising, the competition was launched in January 1995. Ronnie had kept up her friendship with Dame Joan Sutherland and her husband, the conductor Richard Bonynge, and was delighted when Dame Joan agreed to become an adjudicator for the competition, together with Diana Mulgan of the IMG agency in London and Heinrich Bender, director of the Bavarian Opera Studio. The experienced and knowledgeable non-voting chair was Jane Carty, Senior Producer-in-Charge, FM3 Music in RTÉ.

At the same time as the final hectic preparations for the competition were taking place, Cork-born coloratura soprano Cara O'Sullivan contacted Ronnie for advice. She was keen to pursue her career abroad and wondered how she could maximise her chances at auditions. 'We'll ask Dame Joan,' said Ronnie. 'She'll give you a master class when she's in Dublin!'

It seemed impossible, but one Sunday morning Cara was woken by the sound of the phone. The caller said, 'Hello? This is Joan Sutherland.' Her voice was very slow and distinctive. Cara thought it must be her sister playing a joke.

'Em, actually no. It really is Joan Sutherland. I'm ringing from Switzerland and I want to talk to you first because I am concerned. I have never given a master class before. What do you want from it?'

'I want a job in Welsh National Opera,' Cara blurted. 'I know how to sing; I just need to find a way of getting the job. Can you help me, please?'

'Yes,' came the reply. 'I can do that.'

At the arranged time, a very nervous Cara O'Sullivan arrived at the presidential suite of the Conrad Hotel overlooking the NCH on Dublin's Earlsfort Terrace. With her was her accompanist, Mairéad Hurley.

Dame Joan received them very graciously but she confessed that she, too, was nervous. 'I don't know how to do this,' she said. 'I stopped singing eighteen months ago and I just can't sing anymore. I find it most distressing.'

One of the most famous singers in the world, renowned for delivering fiendishly difficult arias with extravagant displays of vocal pyrotechnics, was able to sing no longer! All Cara could think of saying was, 'You've given so much pleasure throughout your life; perhaps it's your voice's opportunity to have a rest.'

'That could be it,' was the thoughtful response. 'I didn't think of that.'

For the next hour and a half the three musicians worked on the arias that Cara had brought, particularly 'Bel raggio lusinghier' from Rossini's opera *Semiramide*. Cara sang a phrase or two, Dame Joan stopped her to fix something; Cara sang on and was stopped again. In this way the piece was broken up and put together again without Dame Joan singing a note. As they finished, the great lady complimented Cara, but she refused any payment, saying, 'My first master class – absolutely not!'

Later that year, Cara sang 'Bel raggio' for Carlo Rizzi at Welsh National Opera, who declared that he had never heard it sung so clearly, so efficiently and so quickly. She got the job.

Television producer Anne Makower was another visitor to the presidential suite. Anne was in charge of the live television broadcast of the final of the competition and was there to record a piece that would be screened during the interval. 'Joan Sutherland was a lovely lady, so accommodating. She didn't mind a bit that the floors were all draped in cables and things, and she gave me a very good interview.'

The competition was open to young singers in training who were Irish or had Irish parents. They were free to choose their own repertoire within guidelines that ensured proficiency in a variety of musical styles and languages. The prize money was substantial: £7,000 first place; £2,000 second place; £1,000 third place; a prize of £500 from RTÉ FM3, and two prizes of £500 each presented by Edwin FitzGibbon, Ronnie's former student. There was a special trophy for the most promising singer (not necessarily a finalist) presented by Dame Joan Sutherland. Thirty-six singers made it through to the last two heats held at the RTÉ Radio Centre in Donnybrook, where they sang with piano accompaniment.

On 19 January 1995, the six finalists performed on the stage of the NCH with the RTÉ Concert Orchestra, conducted by Proinnsías Ó Duinn. The auditorium was filled to capacity with dignitaries, people from the music world, and friends and families of the singers. It was the scariest, most important night in the lives of young singers Johanna Byrne, Julia Canavan, Bridget Knowles, Orla Boylan, Imelda Drumm and Miriam Murphy.

Miriam Murphy won the trophy for the most promising singer, and the first prize went to twenty-three-year-old soprano Orla Boylan, who studied at the DIT College of Music with Mary Brennan and Mairéad Hurley. Orla had the honour of meeting her heroine, Dame Joan Sutherland, who came up to her at the end and said in a gentle Australian accent, 'Marvellous breath control – how do you do it?' Orla looked at her and said, 'I can't believe *you're* asking me that!'

Chatting with Orla Boylan, winner of the 1995 competition

In 1997 the event was renamed the Veronica Dunne Singing Competition. The entrance regulations were relaxed so that, as Ronnie said: 'In this, the 150th commemoration year of the Irish Famine, we may bring all our grandchildren home.' As President Mary Robinson presented the finalists' awards on 27 January she echoed this sentiment by remarking that she loved the 'great-grandparent clause as it really widens the sense of Irishness'. Franzita Whelan from County Offaly was awarded second place and received the Johannes Brahms Centenary

Ronnie, President Mary Robinson and Dame Joan Sutherland at the 1997 Veronica Dunne Singing Competition

Award – a stepping-stone to a successful international career. The .stunning singing of French soprano Norah Amsellem, whose ancestors can be traced to Limerick and Donegal, captivated the international jury. She scooped the first prize of £10,000 and has become one of the world's top singers.

Eighty hopefuls gather in Dublin for the week of the competition. Members of the FVA and other opera enthusiasts welcome the competitors into their homes, ensure that they are comfortable, transport them to knockout rounds and are there to ease the tears of sorrow, and share the tears of joy. Margaret Quigley became one of these hosts in 1999. As a child, Margaret had adored singing and opera. In the late 1940s she moved from Carlow to Dublin to study at University College Dublin. Night after night she paid a shilling to ascend to the gods of the Gaiety Theatre where she immersed herself in all the DGOS productions. It was then that she first saw the young Irish star Veronica Dunne. She quickly became one of her greatest fans. 'I used to go to everything she did. She had a beautiful voice, and she was a gorgeous-looking lady. I collected all her reviews, which I still have. Veronica Dunne – a diva.'

Over the ensuing years, Margaret Quigley's love of opera continued, a love she shared with her husband Tony, whom she met in the 1980s. Tony was immensely knowledgeable and passionate about all things operatic. As often as work permitted, the couple travelled to Milan, Vienna, Munich, London, New York – wherever there was great opera, there too were the Quigleys. Margaret and Tony's guest for the 1999 competition was soprano Byung-Soon Lee from South Korea. In the final, Australian soprano Rebecca Nash was placed second, and Anthony Kearns and Imelda Drumm were placed third and fourth. Byung-Soon Lee soared into first place with an exquisite rendering of Zerbinetta's aria from Strauss's *Ariadne auf Naxos*. Shortly after this, Ronnie invited Margaret to serve on her committee. Margaret is now the major sponsor of the competition.

President Mary McAleese was patron of the competition from 1999 until she left office in 2011. In 2003 the event was named the Veronica Dunne European Union Singing Competition. All the rounds in 2003 took place in the Mahony Hall at the Helix Theatre, Dublin. Miriam Murphy was one of the finalists, and the overall winner was Italian soprano Stefania Spaggiari.

Diarmuid Hegarty became chairman of the Friends of the Vocal Arts in 2004. He soon realised that the competition had become too big and too important to be administered purely by members of a voluntary group. Ronnie asked the advice of Ann Fuller, artistic

Dearbhla Collins

director and administrator of the Dublin International Piano Competition. Ann suggested that a professional be engaged, and she mentioned Dearbhla Collins, who had organised the Hugo Wolf Festival in Dublin in 2003. Dearbhla was the vocal coach to many of Ronnie's students at the Academy. Although she had plenty of other commitments on hand, she jumped at the chance of being involved and in 2004 was appointed artistic administrator of the competition.

With the backing of Ronnie, Diarmuid and the committee, Dearbhla assembled a firm structure around the running of the competition. It was agreed that it should be held on a triennial basis and take place during the second half of January. The website has been improved. An on-line system has been developed to enable contestants to enter their particulars and send sound recordings, and clear timeframes are indicated for entering and hearing back from the organisers. Initial selection is based on submitted recordings that are judged 'blind', and auditions for the preliminary rounds are held in the United States and Europe. In this way, up to two hundred entries are whittled down to the eighty who travel to Dublin. A welcome package is provided for each contestant with useful information and maps. A public relations company handles promotion and publicity for the competition.

Annual events organised by the FVA at Dublin Castle and Killruddery House in County Wicklow not only provide much-needed

funds, they also raise the profile of the competition and give the young singing stars of the future an opportunity to shine. In Killruddery, the Orangery forms a glittering arena for Ronnie's students and former students who love the elegant surroundings, the gorgeous garden and the appreciative guests. Diarmuid and his wife Susan are always entranced by the quality and poise of the singers and the magnificent sounds that reverberate around the room and into the very soul. The evening concerts in Dublin Castle have a charm and grandeur all their own.

In 2007 the competition became truly international with the lifting of the entrance criteria regarding Irish descent. The 5th Veronica Dunne International Singing Competition took place from 19 to 25 January, with the finals in the NCH. Margaret Quigley sponsored the first prize of €10,000 in memory of her husband Tony. Geraldine McGee, the singing teacher from Dundalk, presented the second prize of €5,000. A prize of €3,000 for the best male singer was sponsored by Anthony Kearns, which on this occasion was won by Dante Alcalá from Mexico. Alison Young presented a prize in memory of her husband William Young for the best performance of an aria by Handel, and this was awarded to Celine Byrne. Much has already been written about this competition, in which Tara Erraught was placed second. The winner, soprano Mari Moriya, continues to delight audiences in Europe, the United States and her native Japan.

Contestants who enter distinguished singing competitions are committed artists who wish to pursue their careers on the worldwide

With Diarmuid Hegarty (left), chairman of the Friends of the Vocal Arts, John O'Donoghue, Minister for Arts, Sport and Tourism, and Dearbhla Collins, 2004

Dieter Kaegi

stage. Jane Carty has been chairman of the jury for all but one of the competitions. She is scrupulous about never revealing how decisions are reached within the jury room. All she will say is that jurors take their responsibilities extremely seriously and it is always an open vote. 'In a competition we usually know within the first bar or two if there's a voice there. Sometimes, as the singer is singing, suddenly, inexplicably, I feel tears coming into my eyes, and that's when I know something special is happening.'

There are many factors to be considered when assessing the merits of the contestants. Dieter Kaegi was a member of the jury in 2003 and he knows what a difficult task it is:

For myself, the singer has to have the whole package, physically, mentally, artistically. There is no use in promoting someone who cannot take the pressure of performing, of learning, of delivering an artistically expressive and deeply felt role. They must convey the meaning of the words and make an emotional connection with the audience. The knockout stages of a competition put competitors under a certain amount of pressure, but nothing to what they will face later on. I look for people who can, and will, cope. They have to deal with nerves. When they are young that may be easier – they have everything to gain and nothing to lose. It gets harder when they have made it onto the big stage, yet still they have to audition for each part. There are so many good singers, and a finite number of big companies with big roles.

The competition in 2010 attracted contestants from twenty-five countries, including China, Iceland, Thailand and Russia. The competitor from Romania was soprano Gabriela Istoc, who had lived in Bushy Park for two years while studying with Ronnie at the Academy. The finals took place in the NCH on 26 January with the RTÉ National Symphony Orchestra conducted by Laurent Wagner. The finalists were Irishmen Dean Power and Benjamin Russell, American Christopher Magiera and Russian-born Anna Viktorova, but it was the two sopranos from South Africa who stole the show, and both were graduates of the Royal College of Music in London. Sarah-Jane Brandon from Johannesburg was placed second, and she also received the two Wil Keune prizes of €1,000 each for the best song performance and the best performance of a Mozart aria. These two prizes were presented by Jane Carty in memory of her husband, Dutchman Wilhelmus Keune.

The first prize of €10,000 was awarded to Pumeza Matshikiza, who began life in a township on South Africa's Eastern Cape. Pumeza has

achieved international recognition for her operatic performances, and in 2014 over one billion people worldwide viewed her rendition of 'Freedom Come-All-Ye' at the opening ceremony of the Commonwealth Games in Glasgow.

The National Concert Hall and Ronnie are complementary – they each have played a large part in the other's career, and the NCH has been generous in its support of many of Ronnie's endeavours. Judith

With Martin McAleese, President Mary McAleese and Diarmuid Hegarty, 2010

(From left) Pumeza – 2010 winner of the competition, with Dearbhla Collins, Sarah-Jane Brandon, Mairéad Hurley and Dean Power

Woodworth was director during the time that Ronnie served her third term on the board, and she has overseen six of the singing competitions. 'Ronnie is the most difficult person in the world to say no to, because one loves and admires what she's trying to do, and even if you feel you can't do it, you end up doing it anyway!'

Generally the first rounds now take place within the NCH complex where rehearsal rooms are readily available. A huge amount of organisation is required to ensure that the performance in the auditorium runs smoothly for the audience. There is a continuity person interacting with the stage manager; as one performance finishes, the next competitor should be ready to come on. There are pianos in the dressing rooms for the competitors to warm up. They have to walk from their rooms down a corridor of about sixty metres to an anteroom where they can watch a video link to the stage. The master of ceremonies talks for a few moments to give time for the singer to prepare close to the stage; they must be ready to perform from the second they go on.

President Michael D. Higgins became patron to the competition in 2013. Richard Bonynge served on the jury with Jane Carty and six other eminent adjudicators who attended the first three rounds and then the final on 31 January. Once again, the competition welcomed singers from as far afield as Australia, New Zealand, Korea, South Africa and the United States to join their counterparts from Europe and Ireland. In his programme notes, Diarmuid Hegarty made a point of thanking the sponsors whose generosity makes the event possible. He added: 'We all acknowledge that the driving force that inspires us is Ronnie's exuberance, energy and enthusiasm.'

Gemma Ní Bhriain was one of the finalists in the 2013 competition. She remembers a lovely lady called Enid backstage who did everything she could to look after them and keep them calm. The six contestants had shared so many rounds and experiences that Gemma felt as if they were not competing against one another, it was more as if they were giving a concert together, and they all enjoyed performing with a full orchestra behind them – the RTÉ National Symphony Orchestra under the baton of Patrik Ringborg from Sweden. The singers who joined Gemma on stage were soprano Aoife Miskelly from Northern Ireland, tenor Simon Chambers from New Zealand, baritone Szymon Komasa from Poland, soprano Nadine Sierra from the United States and baritone Insu Hwang from South Korea. Nadine Sierra, who was awarded first prize, was outstanding. As Michael Dervan commented in the *Irish Times*: 'The voice is as clear as a mountain stream .... She's a communicative singer, who knows how to engage her listeners fully on her own

Margaret Quigley and Brid Collins at 2013 launch of competition

terms.' After the evening's celebrations, Nadine gave an early morning interview on RTÉ radio before flying to another engagement and on to a dazzling career.

From modest beginnings in 1995, the Veronica Dunne International Singing Competition has become an Irish musical event of international standing, which offers a global stage for the encouragement and development of Irish and international vocal talent. A glance at the names of singers who have participated in the competition and subsequently enjoyed phenomenal careers is testament to its significance in the lives of young performers.

In 2011 the competition became a member of the Federation of World Competitions. It continues to develop and flourish with the support, hard work and commitment of the FVA.

A partnership has been forged between the competition and the celebrated Wexford Festival Opera. As part of this alliance, Wexford Festival Opera will host one of the audition heats, the Orchestra of Wexford Festival Opera will be the orchestra for the final of the competition in the NCH, and the winner will be given an opportunity to perform at the Wexford Festival in 2016.

The FVA committee – chairman Diarmuid Hegarty, artistic director Dr Veronica Dunne, artistic administrator Dearbhla Collins, and Mary Brennan, Enid Chaloner, Martin Coonan, Mairéad Hurley, Margaret Quigley, Caitriona Shaffrey and Kathleen Tynan – are anticipating their next big adventure, the 8th Veronica Dunne International Singing Competition, in January 2016. The audience will again have the pleasure of listening to some of the finest young singers in the world.

Nadine Sierra, winner of 2013 competition, with President Michael D. Higgins

There is an intangible moment of silence after performing when the singer stops breathing; waiting for the judgement of the harshest critics they will face that night, the audience. The applause builds; the singer breathes again.

DIETER KAEGI

27 *A lifetime of achievements*

Once upon a time there lived in Ireland a bonnie wee lass called VERONICA and when she was young, it became very evident that she was blessed with a quite exceptional, beautiful voice. So after initial training in her own country she was sent to study in Italy. There, apart from learning how to sing, she also learnt how to protect herself from bottom-pinching Italians and in due course returned to Ireland, prepared to start a vocal career which was eventually to lead her to Covent Garden (the opera house, not the market!)

It is impossible to list her success, nor shall I attempt to do so. Apart from her glorious voice, she was blessed with a warm and generous nature, always willing to spread sunshine around.

When the years passed and she retired from the concert platform, she was able to imbue her pupils with these qualities, and there is evidence of her success in this field in many of the opera houses in Europe.

I was lucky to have been her partner early in her career and to have joined in the pleasure she gave to her fans. Now her pupils carry on that pleasure to a new generation of listeners – singers such as Suzanne Murphy, Angela Feeney and many others. She will live through them.

God bless you, Ronnie.

HAVELOCK NELSON, 28 June 1992

THE SENTIMENTS expressed by Havelock Nelson are as true now as they were when he paid his personal tribute to Ronnie in the programme for her 'retirement' concert. The only change today would be the names of many more students, some of whom you have met in the pages of this book, who now enjoy careers as performing artists or as teachers themselves, and whose lives continue to be enriched by Ronnie's friendship.

Ronnie has garnered many honours for her unique contribution to the vocal arts in Ireland, including: an honorary DMus in 1987 by the National University of Ireland; honorary life membership of the Royal Dublin Society in 1988; an Honorary Fellowship by the Royal Irish Academy of Music; a Professional Excellence Award from Griffith College in 2005; and in 2006 a degree of Doctor of Laws (*Honoris Causa*) from the Higher Education and Training Awards

Council, Ireland. The citation on this award concluded:

> Ronnie's students of all generations will attest that she is a hard taskmaster. Talent alone is not sufficient. To this must be joined musicianship and most important, commitment. Where Ronnie has found this combination she has nourished it with the passion that she expects from her protégés. Her heart has become theirs just as her home so often has. Her dedication and generosity are so often referred to by students, as is the confidence she inspires. If we are to emerge as a musical nation worthy of our reputation it is down to individual commitment and few epitomise that better than does Ronnie Dunne.

These awards, together with her academic achievements, mean that Ronnie is a doctor twice over and has an impressive list of letters after her name, but she is known throughout the opera world, at home and abroad, as Ronnie! She has been patron of several organisations, including Lyric Opera, Dublin Choral Foundation, Lismore Music Festival and Saint Agnes's Music Project, Crumlin, and is a keen attender of all the events at the National Concert Hall.

Simon Taylor, chief executive of the National Concert Hall, decided with his board members that Ronnie should be presented with the greatest honour they can bestow, the Lifetime Achievement Award, to mark her distinguished operatic career and more than five decades of inspiring and selfless teaching. The event was celebrated with a gala concert. Tickets for the occasion were sold out within four hours of going on sale.

Sunday, 21 September 2014, 8pm. Ronnie's children Peter and Judy and her nephews Kevin and Aidan joined the throng of expectant friends in the auditorium and then hushed as the RTÉ Symphony Orchestra tuned up under the baton of Robert Houlihan. To the front of the stage were several smart armchairs; at the back the pipes of the magnificent green and gold organ gleamed under the spotlights. The host for the evening, Bryan Dobson, introduced Ronnie amid a prolonged wave of enthusiastic applause, and they took their seats. Thereafter, he guided her adroitly through a career spanning more than seventy years. Several friends were asked to say a few words – Suzanne Murphy, Tony Ó Dálaigh, and John O'Conor, who threw himself at her feet in homage! There, too, were her students whose glorious singing was living proof of her greatness as a teacher. Tara Erraught, who flew in from Munich, wowed the audience, and flew out the same night; Anthony Kearns, with his warm personality and lyrical voice;

THE NATIONAL CONCERT HALL
Lifetime Achievement Award 2014

Dr. Veronica Dunne
A SPECIAL GALA EVENING CELEBRATING ONE OF IRELAND'S NATIONAL MUSICAL TREASURES

Sunday 2 September 2014, 8pm

Bryan Dobson host • Celine Byrne soprano
Miriam Murphy soprano • Tara Erraught mezzo-soprano
Anthony Kearns tenor • RTÉ National Symphony Orchestra
Robert Houlihan conductor

Tickets from €25.
On sale from 6 August (or 1 August for Friends of the National Concert Hall).
This special evening is supported by the Friends of the National Concert Hall.

www.nch.ie 01 417 0000

RTÉ NATIONAL Lyric Orchestra   NATIONAL CONCERT HALL
                                      CEOLÁRAS NÁISIÚNTA

Sarah Shine and Gemma Ní Bhriain with a delightful duet; Miriam Murphy who brought the house down with Isolde's 'Liebestod' from *Tristan und Isolde*; Patrick Hyland, whose aria from *La Bohème* recalled Ronnie's days at Covent Garden; Celine Byrne with her gorgeous delivery of 'Un bel dí' from *Madama Butterfly* – the aria that Ronnie's father had adored and which instilled in her a love of singing and opera.

It was a jewel of an evening, illuminated with love and gratitude and respect for a woman who gave pleasure to thousands and who has changed the lives of hundreds for the better. As Ronnie says, she is now teaching the grandchildren of her first students. President Michael D. Higgins presented Ronnie with the Lifetime Achievement Award, which was almost too heavy for the both of them to hold!

Peter and Judy admit that growing up with the extraordinary woman who is their mother was not always easy. The house was often overrun with students; endless scales and 'shrieking' emanated from the front room morning, noon and night; overnight guests became year-long lodgers; furniture mysteriously disappeared and then reappeared after a performance; meetings were missed and important personal events were subsumed by professional engagements. On the other hand, they never wanted for anything. They were taken to fine restaurants and the best of theatre. They were brought to London, Rome, Paris and the south of Spain. Authors, musicians, composers, friends from the racing and business world, eccentrics and intellectuals all dined at the house. The children were encouraged to engage in conversation and to respect the opinions and lifestyles of others.

In later life Peter pursued his love of horses and became a notable amateur jockey. Following his marriage to Sandra Mullins in 1978, the couple eventually established their own stud farm in County Kilkenny. In 2001 the Association of Irish Racehorse Owners nominated Peter as its representative on the board of Horse Racing Ireland, a position he held for four years, and he chaired the Foal Levy committee. Peter and Sandra have bred and trained winning racehorses.

Having graduated as a nurse, Judy moved to Texas where she met her husband, Richard Gaughan. The couple have two children, Kevin and Aidan. After they relocated to Boston, Judy completed a Masters degree in Nursing Leadership. She is a member of a small development team that set up a pioneering programme in 2008 to help children with chronic pain. That programme is now established at the Mayo Family Pediatric Pain Rehabilitation Center at Boston Children's Hospital, and is recognised as a national and international referral centre for children and adolescents who are physically and emotionally disabled owing to conditions such as musculoskeletal

pain and chronic neuropathic pain disorders. Judy and Richard's sons lived with Ronnie while attending universities in Dublin – Aidan at Griffith College and Kevin at the Royal College of Surgeons.

Mother, grandmother, exceptional singer, celebrated teacher and hard taskmaster: generous, warm, dedicated and passionate. Ronnie is all these, leavened by a delicious sense of the ridiculous. Her laughter is legendary and her friendships enduring. She has had many loves in her life, some of which have surprised her. Her brother Billo, her father William, her dog Rex, her two ponies and, ultimately, her mother Josephine; most surprisingly of all, perhaps, her sister May. Her teacher Hubert Rooney. Monsignor Hugh O'Flaherty. Her husband Peter; her children Peter and Judy. Her grandsons, who never cease to surprise. The artists with whom she has performed. All the students who have come and gone and yet remain close. The people who have helped her and those whom she has helped. Colleagues in the music world who have become true companions. Ronnie's heart is big, her reach wide.

The success story of Ronnie's life in music lies in her own superb performances, and in the singers she has nurtured and then launched: the singers with international careers; the singers who continue singing for the joy of it; and the singers who have become teachers to the singers of the future. The tree extends outwards.

The Lifetime Achievement Award, 2014, at the National Concert Hall with (left) Bryan Dobson, RTÉ, and Simon Taylor, NCH CEO

Veronica Dunne's
Art of Beautiful Singing

MY **WONDERFUL TEACHER**, Hubert Rooney, instructed me in the art of bel canto singing, a technique that had been passed on to him by the great Polish tenor Jean de Reszke. As a child, I could not really understand what Mr Rooney was telling me; I just did what I was told and absorbed the method so naturally that even he was impressed by how much my voice progressed. It was only when I started to teach that I recalled his words, and I came to appreciate what a wise and sensible method I had been fortunate enough to learn.

The bel canto tradition was introduced into Italy in the fifteenth century with the communal plain chant of Benedictine monks from Spain. Over the next three hundred years the technique was developed and refined, largely influenced by the fluidity of the Italian language, with its rolling vowel sounds that resonate in the facial structure. This, coupled with the advent of trained soloists in the seventeenth and eighteenth centuries, led to an appreciation among opera enthusiasts of solo virtuoso singing – the art of singing a beautiful melodic line with great sensitivity and expression, as in the antique arias of Monteverdi, Scarlatti, Vivaldi, Pergolesi and Gluck. Bel canto flourished in the nineteenth century with the Italian operas of Rossini, Donizetti and Bellini.

The singing technique is characterised by a smooth production of sound throughout the entire vocal range. Like a bow being drawn across a stringed instrument, there is no jerkiness, but a lovely legato line that allows for great flexibility and seemingly effortless flights of dexterity. This cannot be taught in any book, but is passed on to the student by a teacher, preferably one who has performed professionally, who understands the difficulties experienced by many singers and who knows how to overcome them.

It is not possible to distil forty years of teaching practices into a few short paragraphs, but I will set out a few key elements that I always consider with my students.

IF YOU KNOW HOW TO BREATHE, YOU KNOW HOW TO SING

In conversation, you do not gulp in air to speak. To do so repeatedly would separate and damage the vocal chords, those two little flaps stretched across the larynx that vibrate when you speak or sing. You open your ribcage and air flows in automatically. It is the same with singing, but now you learn to hold that air in the ribcage and release it gradually so that you may sustain a note. The muscles that control the weight and flow of air are the diaphragm muscles. These muscles need to be strengthened and developed. A useful exercise is to lie flat on the floor, draw up both your legs and slowly lower them while hissing through your mouth. Gradually

247

increase the time this takes. Another is to stand, expand the ribcage, let the air settle down in the lungs and hold out the ribcage for forty-five seconds or longer. Your lungs are not muscles, they are sponges. Give them the space to expand within the ribcage and then practice releasing the air and the voice simultaneously. Think of the straight column of smoke rising from a cigarette on an ashtray; now visualise the air being inhaled and exhaled through your mouth; there must be no obstructions.

KNOW HOW SOUND IS CREATED

Air flows from the lungs with sufficient pressure to vibrate the vocal chords. Sound is produced which is adjusted by the larynx and filtered and articulated by the tongue, palate, cheeks and lips. This sound resonates off the bone structure of the mouth and head, particularly in the space between the mandible and the temporal bone. This is the area which experiences pressure as an aeroplane comes in to land. To unblock it, you yawn. You will feel the two bones glide against each other and open. This is the space in which vowels resonate; therefore the jaws must be loose.

Imagine opening your mouth to bite an apple: the cheekbones rise, the top part of your mouth goes forward, your bottom jaw goes back into your neck. This is the perfect position for singing. Lifting the cheeks lifts the uvula at the back of your throat and allows more space for the voice to resonate upon the bone structure in your mouth for a clear, bright sound. The neck must be completely relaxed, allowing the head free movement. Think again of the straight column of air rising from the depths of your body and into your mouth.

The ringing of a church bell is heard for miles. Why? Because sound caused by the strike of the clapper against sides of the bell reverberates back and forth within its chamber. Your head is like a bell and the clapper is the vowel sounds resonating off your facial and cranial bones. When using the bel canto technique, there is no necessity for a singer to project the voice outwards or to use a microphone. The strength of the sound is controlled by the weight of air from the diaphragm and the voice is produced within the chamber of the head. Every member of the audience can hear a well-trained singer over a full orchestra. Consider the violin, how it makes itself heard with one thin string resonating within its body.

THE VOWELS

The five classic Italian vowels of a (ah), e (eh), i (ee), o (oh) and u (oo) form the basis of bel canto singing. These pure vowel sounds allow for specific mouth, face and throat positions. The most important instrument in your mouth is the tongue. The tip of your tongue will always rest at the back of your bottom teeth; if it goes back, it obstructs the air from your throat. To say 'a,' your tongue will rise slightly in the middle and the sides will touch your molars on the top, so it will flatten. The 'u' is right up, touching the soft palate at the back of the roof of your mouth, and the bottom lip is tightened. To say 'o', you tighten your top lip. The 'i' is a marvellous vowel for it hits the top of your mouth, raises the cheekbones and opens the throat.

Exercises that improve the flexibility of the tongue are important, such as specific movements within the mouth and the repetition of tongue twisters. The same principles are applied to vowels in any language.

When studying a score for the first time, practise by singing only the vowels. Instead of articulating the word truck, for example, sing only the 'u' to the music. Be conscious of where the tongue goes and the placing of vowels on the bone structure. Sustain the vowels within the mouth. Then learn the libretto by intoning the words to yourself over and over. Only then draw music and words together.

KNOW YOUR BODY

Professional singers are mindful of their health and well-being. Their instrument cannot be packed in a case after a performance, put in a safe place and forgotten for the night. Their voice is the instrument they live with, day in and day out. It is intensely personal. Problems with the voice cannot be blamed on poor workmanship or bum notes; they have to be fixed from within, and a trusted vocal coach is not a luxury, she or he is a necessity.

Singers need an enormous amount of stamina to carry them through just one performance, let alone a series of performances spanning many months and in several different countries. The practice of Yoga can be done anywhere, at any time. It is wonderful for relaxing the mind and improving strength and mobility within the body, and it promotes correct posture and breathing.

MUSICIANSHIP

All singers require excellent sight-reading and musicianship. You must be able to quickly adapt to any orchestra and conductor. Productions are expensive, and anything that wastes time costs money. A conductor may correct you once, or even twice. After the third time he will say nothing, but when you come looking for another job, he'll say no thanks. You should learn all the operatic roles that are suitable for your voice so that you are prepared for any engagement. In these days of digital recording, familiarise yourself with different productions, different interpretations.

Listen to the great singers. There is one recording that I would urge everyone to obtain: *Tosca* live from Parma, 21 January 1967, with Corelli, Gordoni, D'Orazi, Carbonari and Majonica, conducted by my old friend from Rome, Giuseppe Morelli, on the Bel Canto Society label (2 CDs). Franco Corelli is in absolutely fantastic voice, never more so than in 'E lucevan le stelle' where the phrase 'disciogliea dai veli' is sung with such a gorgeous diminuendo in a breath that lasted for twenty-two seconds! The audience were stunned – you can actually hear them gasp.

Challenge yourself. When practising a run of ten bars in, say, a Handel aria, repeat the last two bars again and again – see how far you can go on that one breath. I like to take my students one third above and one third below their natural singing range. This gives them great security when aiming for very high or very low notes – they know they have done it before, and have gone even further. But in rehearsal, preserve your voice for the performance. This is a lesson I had to learn the hard way.

I was singing Mimi in a live broadcast for Granada Television of *La Bohème*, a role I had sung countless times before. The tenor Richard Lewis and I had been rehearsing all day with Sir John Barbirolli and the Hallé Orchestra, and I was exhausted. At the end of Act One I had to hit top C, and I cracked. It was mortifying, but afterwards people were very kind – it can happen. It took me a long time to regain my confidence on the top notes. So, know your range and exceed it, and conserve your voice for when it really matters.

COMMUNICATION

I have saved the best until last. You can be the most technically assured singer, you can know your music inside out, you can look fabulous and sound wonderful, but if you cannot communicate with the audience, you are missing a fundamental aspect of performance.

I have adored many singers in my time and learnt so much from all of them. Maria Callas had it all. I admired Renata Tebaldi, one of the first sopranos I heard in Rome, for her magnificent voice and technique. Magda Olivero, how beautiful she was and how very expressive. Dear Kathleen Ferrier with her gloriously rich tone that captured every heart.

When you sing, you draw everyone in. You must be sincere in what you are saying and what you are singing. Get in character; know the role. Know what the situation was before the song takes place. If you love what you are singing and are enjoying it, you are relaxed; the audience relaxes with you and is receptive. You will transport them to another world.

Always think of beautiful sounds. When I am singing something sad, something like 'As I Sit Here Remembering You', I think of my mother, and how she used to make me do my piano practice and how she loved to listen to me singing. Thinking of a very personal memory means you sing from your heart. I just love 'Danny Boy'. I remember singing to 7,000 people in the Royal Albert Hall:

> *And I shall hear tho' soft you tread above me*
> *And all my grave will warmer sweeter be*
> *For you will bend and tell me that you love me*
> *And I shall sleep in peace until you come to me.*

'And I shall hear ...' and when I sing 'hear' I use a lovely pianissimo. I remember doing that pianissimo so much that it was almost silent. It was like the elevation at the Mass when the priest takes up the host – reverential, that's how I felt when I sang that. And I felt the stillness in the audience; they were in the palm of my hand. It's amazing how you create sound, how you paint a particular word in a phrase. You may be the greatest singer in the world, but you still have to tell a story.

CATALOGUE OF PERFORMANCES BY VERONICA DUNNE
1947 – 2011

This list is by no means complete. The publishers would be delighted to hear from anyone with additional information which may be included in later reprints.

1947
Operatic arias, Sala Borromini, Rome, with students of Contessa Soldini Calcagni. 6 Jun.

1948
Irish songs, St. Patrick's Church, Rome. 17 Mar.
Irish songs and operatic arias, Radio Éireann, Dublin. Mar.
c. Dermot O'Hara, Live radio broadcast.
The Children of Lir, Harty. Phoenix Hall, Dublin. Live radio broadcast.

1949
Mass in D Major, Pergolesi, Loreto College, Dublin. Jun.
c. Edward Appia. Radio Éireann Symphony Orchestra and Choir, with Eva Tomshon.
This Is Ireland, ECA, Telecine Radio, Paris, Dec.
with Patrick Thornton and Joseph McNally.

1950
Army No. 1 Band Concerts in Connacht. Feb. and Mar.
c. J.M. Doyle.
Requiem, Verdi, Phoenix Hall, Dublin. 21 Apr.
c. Jean Martinon. Radio Éireann Symphony Orchestra. Patricia Lawlor, Joseph McNally, Michael O'Higgins, Our Lady's Choral Society.
Carmen, Bizet (Micaëla). Gaiety Theatre, Dublin. DGOS. 29 April, 1,3 May.
c. Vilém Tauský. Patricia Black, Frans Vroons/Ken Neate, Bruce Dargaval, Josephine O'Hagan, Barbara Lane.
Recital, Gaiety Theatre, Dublin. 30 Apr.
with Frans Vroons, Bruce Dargaval, Jeannie Reddin (piano).
Bach arias. 'Organ, Violin and Song' with Robert Johnston. Radio Éireann, Dublin, Jun.

1951
Verdi arias with Francesco Calcatelli. Chiesa Nuovo, Rome. 15 Mar.
Solo Recital. Arias by Bach, Brahms, Duparc, Debussy, Handel, Pergolesi. Rome. Apr.
Giorgio Favaretto, piano.
Requiem, Verdi, Capitol Theatre, Dublin. 4 Nov.
c. Francesco Mander. Radio Éireann Symphony Orchestra. Michael O'Higgins, Joseph O'Neill, Maura O'Connor, Our Lady's Choral Society.
Carmen, Bizet (Micaëla). Gaiety Theatre, Dublin. DGOS. 3,8,12,19 Dec.
c. J.M. Doyle, with Patricia Black, Frans Vroons/Ken Neate, Alfred Orda/Roderick Jones, Josephine O'Hagan, Jean Healy, Sam Mooney, Martin Dempsey.
Faust, Gounod (Marguerite). Gaiety Theatre, Dublin. DGOS. 4,6,8 Dec.
c. J.M. Doyle. James Johnston/Rowland Jones, Bruce Dargaval, Patricia Lawlor, Anne Bishop, Ralph Morris.
Messiah, Handel, Capitol Theatre, Dublin. 23 Dec.
c. J.M. Doyle. Radio Éireann Symphony Orchestra. Our Lady's Choral Society. Owen Brannigan, Joseph McNally, Maura O'Connor.

1952

La Bohème, Puccini (Mimi). Gaiety Theatre, Dublin. DGOS. 29 Apr. 1,3,7,10 May.
c. Karl Rankl. Giuseppe Zampieri, Sandra Baruffi, Giulio Fioravanti, Gino Belloni, Arturo La Porta, Brendan Cavanagh, Joseph Flood.

Don Pasquale, Donizetti (Norina). Gaiety Theatre, Dublin. DGOS. 17.19,13,14 May.
c. Vilem Tausky. Ronald Stear, Ivan Cecchini, Bruce Dargaval, Barry O'Sullivan.

Radio Éireann Promenade Concerts. Dublin and Sligo. May.
Radio Éireann Symphony Orchestra.

La Bohème, Puccini (Mimi). Teatro Nuovo, Milan. Concorso Lirico Milano. From 13 July (6 perfs.).
c. Ugo Rapalo. Gianni Piluso, Bruna Boccalini, Lino Puglisi.

Faust, Gounod (Marguerite). Gaiety Theatre, Dublin. DGOS. 2,4,6 Sept.
c. J.M. Doyle, with James Johnston, Howell Glynn, William Edwards, Betty Sagon.

Concert. Abbey Cinema, Drogheda. 29 Sept.

Der Rosenkavalier, Richard Strauss (Sophie), ROH Covent Garden, London. 29 Oct. 7,11 Nov.
c. Peter Gellhorn. Sylvia Fisher, Constance Shacklock, Howell Glynne, Anthony Marlowe, Barbara Howitt.

La Bohème, Puccini (Mimi), ROH Covent Garden, London. 19,24 Nov. 5,13,22 Dec.
c. John Barbirolli. John Lanigan, Ronald Lewis, Jess Walters, Inia Te Wiata, Geraint Evans, Andrew Sellars, James Jones, Kathryn Harvey.

L'amico Fritz, Mascagni (Suzel). Gaiety Theatre, Dublin. DGOS, 3,8,10,12 Dec.
c. Giuseppe Morelli. Alvinio Misciano, Arturo La Porta, Brendan Cavanagh, Noel Reid, Maura Mooney.

Concert with Frans Vroons. Olympia Theatre, Dublin. 7 Dec.

1953

La Bohème, Puccini (Mimi). ROH Covent Garden, London. 15,26 Jan.
c. John Barbirolli. James Johnston, Jess Walters, Inia Te Wiata, Geraint Evans, Andrew Sellars, James Jones, Kathryn Harvey.

Orpheus, Gluck (Euridice). ROH Covent Garden. London. 3,6 Feb.
c. John Barbirolli. Kathleen Ferrier, Adele Leigh, Covent Garden Opera Chorus, Sadler's Wells Ballet.

La Bohème, Puccini (Mimi). ROH Covent Garden tour of 9 cities. 16 Feb to 24 Mar.
c. Emanuel Young. John Lanigan, Jess Walters.

The Marriage of Figaro, Mozart (Susanna). ROH Covent Garden tour, including Edinburgh, 24 Feb.
c. James Gibson. Veronica Dunne/Adele Leigh, Joan Sutherland, Geraint Evans, Jess Walters.

Messiah, Handel. Tour of Ireland: Cork, Limerick, Waterford, Dublin. Apr. (ending Dublin 25 Apr.).
c. John Barbirolli. Hallé Orchestra. Kathleen Joyce, William Herbert, Marian Nowakowski, Our Lady's Choral Society.

Schéhérazade, Ravel, Capitol Theatre, Dublin. 11 Apr.
c. Eimear Ó Broin. Radio Éireann Symphony Orchestra.

Radio Éireann Promenade Concerts. Gaiety Theatre, Dublin. Oct.
c. Milan Horvat. Radio Éireann Symphony Orchestra.

1954

Radio Éireann Promenade Concerts. Gaiety Theatre, Dublin. 25 Oct. and Nov.
c. Milan Horvat. Radio Éireann Symphony Orchestra.

La Bohème, Puccini (Mimi). Gaiety Theatre, Dublin. DGOS. 29 Nov. 1,3,8 Dec.
c. J.M. Doyle. Walter Midgley, Elizabeth Fretwell, Jess Walters/Roderick Jones, William Dickie, Kenneth Stephenson, Bernard Hooton.

Carmen, Bizet (Micaëla). Gaiety Theatre, Dublin. DGOS. 14,16,18,21 Dec.
c. Milan Horvat. Marianna Radev, Brychan Powell, Jess Walters/William Dickie, Josephine O'Hagan, Betty Sagon, Bernard Hooton.

1955
Carmen, Bizet (Micaëla). ROH Covent Garden, London. Autumn (1 perf.)
Irish Festival Singers Tour of Canada and the United States of America. Jan to Mar.
including Carnegie Hall, New York: 28 Jan. *Ed Sullivan Show*, Chicago: 13 Mar.
c. Kitty O'Callaghan. The Irish Festival Singers.
Pagliacci, Leoncavallo (Nedda). Gaiety Theatre, Dublin. DGOS. 26 Nov. 2,5,8,14,16 Dec.
c. Stanford Robinson/J.M. Doyle. Antonio Annaloro. William Dickie, William Edwards, Brendan
Cavanagh.
Faust, Gounod (Marguerite). Gaiety Theatre, Dublin. DGOS. 28,30 Nov. 3,7,10 Dec.
c. J.M. Doyle. Brychan Powell, Michael Langdon/David Ward, William Edwards, Celine Murphy.
La Bohème, Puccini (Mimi). Gaiety Theatre, Dublin. DGOS. 12,15,17 Dec.
c. Bryan Balkwill. Joan Stuart, Charles Craig, Arda Mandikian, Frederick Sharp/Ronald Lewis,
Harold Blackburn, Peter Glossop/John Probyn.

1956
Concert. Gaiety Theatre, Dublin. 29 Jan.
c. Milan Horvat. Radio Éireann Symphony Orchestra.
BBC Home Service radio broadcast. 4 Mar.
c. Stanford Robinson. Helen Watts, Ian Wallace, Winifred Davey, Peter Gellhorn.

1957
Symphony No 4, Mahler, Gaiety Theatre, Dublin. 17 Feb.
c. Milan Horvat, with the Radio Éireann Symphony Orchestra.
La Bohème, Puccini (Mimi). ROH Covent Garden Opera tour. Mar to Apr., including Gaumont
Theatre, Cardiff: 9,14,16 Mar. Palace Theatre, Manchester: 23,30 Mar. Gaumont Theatre,
Southampton: 2,6,13 Apr.
Four Last Songs, Richard Strauss. Gaiety Theatre, Dublin. 4 Jun.
c. Éimear O'Broin. Radio Éireann Symphony Orchestra.
The Tales of Hoffmann, Offenbach (Antonia). ROH Covent Garden, London. 9 Jul. (4 perfs.)
c. Edward Downes. James Johnston, Dermot Troy, Ronald Lewis, Barbara Howitt, Mimi Coertse,
Forbes Robinson, David Tree, Marie Collier.
Tancredi e Clorinda, Monteverdi, Phoenix Hall, Dublin. 27 Sept.
c. Carlo Franci. Radio Éireann Symphony Orchestra.
The Tales of Hoffmann, Offenbach (Antonia). Gaiety Theatre, Dublin. DGOS. 20,25 Nov. 9,14 Dec.
c. Peter Gellhorn. Edgar Evans/Brychan Powell/James Johnston, Barbara Howitt, Margaret Nisbett,
Joyce Barker, Bruce Dargaval, Nevan Miller.
The Tales of Hoffmann, Offenbach (Antonia), ROH Covent Garden, London. Nov. and Dec.
With Michael Langdon/Forbes Robinson, James Johnston/Edgar Evans, Otakar Kraus/Forbes Robinson.

1958
The Carmelites, Poulenc (Blanche) ROH Covent Garden, London. Jan. (also tour of England).
c. Rafael Kubelik. Joan Sutherland, Jess Walters, Sylvia Fisher, John Lanigan.
Concert, Gaiety Theatre, Dublin. 17 Mar.
c. Dermot O'Hara. Radio Éireann Light Orchestra. Deirdre O'Callaghan, Martin Dempsey, Richard
Cooper.
La Bohème, Puccini (Mimi). ROH Covent Garden, London. 3 Apr. (8 perfs.)
c. Emanuel Young. Jess Walters, Oreste Kirkop, Joseph Rouleau, Robert Allman, Rhydderch Davis,
James Jones, Marie Collier, Afan Davies, James McCluskey.
Carmen, Bizet (Micaëla). ROH Covent Garden, London. Aug. (2 perfs.)
Requiem, Verdi. Hereford Cathedral, England. Three Choirs Festival. 9 Sept.
c. Hugh Maguire. London Symphony Orchestra and Chorus. Valerie Heath-Davies, Charles Craig,
Owen Brannigan.

1959
Requiem, Verdi. Usher Hall, Edinburgh. Edinburgh University Orchestral Concerts. 25 Feb.
c. Henry Havergal.
Lily of Killarney, Benedict (Eily). Limerick. Nov.
Lily of Killarney, Benedict (Eily). Mars Theatre, Kilrush. Kilrush Operatic Society. 10 to 17 May.
c. George Minne. Dennis Noble, Janet Howe, Kenneth MacDonald, Jack McGrath, Thomas
Moloney, Michael Howard, Gerry Clancy, Jack Culligan, Eileen Lynch.
Symphony No. 9, Beethoven, Phoenix Hall, Dublin. 29 May.
c. Milan Horvat. Radio Éireann Symphony Orchestra. Radio Éireann Choral Society.
Samson; Messiah; Solomon; Jephtha: Handel. Cork, Dublin, Galway, Limerick. 28 Sept. to 17 Oct.
c. Frederic Jackson. Douglas Cameron Orchestra. Flora Vickers, David Galliver, Helen Watts,
William Young, Roger Stalman, Culwick Choral Society.

1960
Messiah, Handel. Rosary Hall, Galway.
c. Frederic Jackson. Douglas Cameron Orchestra. Roger Stalman, Helen Watt, David Galliva.
La Bohème, Puccini (Musetta). Sadler's Wells Company, London. 2 Feb.
c. Warwick Braithwaite.
Lily of Killarney, Benedict (Eily). Olympia Theatre, Dublin. Glasnevin Musical Society. 22 Feb. (6
perfs.).
c. Miss Terry O'Connor. Dennis Noble, John Carolan, Bernadette Greevy.
Symphony No. 4, Mahler, Phoenix Hall, Dublin. 4 Mar.
c. Milan Horvat. Radio Éireann Symphony Orchestra. Anne Edwards, William Aiken.
Aida, Verdi (Aida). Gwyn Hall, Neath, Wales. 10 Mar.
c. Gwilym Roberts. Morgan Lloyd Orchestra. Valerie Heath-Davies, Rowland Jones, Gerwyn
Morgan, Redvers Llewellyn.
Belfast Festival Concert. Queen's Hall, Belfast. Mar.
Exsultate Jubilate, Mozart; *A German Requiem*, Brahms. St. James Church, Belfast. Mar.
c. Havelock Nelson. BBC Studio Orchestra. Eric Hinds, Evan John (organ), Ulster Singers.
The Bohemian Girl, Balfe (Arline). Mars Theatre, Kilrush. Kilrush Operatic Society. 8 to 15 May.
c. Capt. R.B. Kiely. Veronica Dunne/Estelle Valéry, Dennis Noble, Jack Culligan, Brychan Powell,
Gerry Clancy, Janet Howe.
Das Marianleben, Hindemith, Phoenix Hall, Dublin. 1 Nov.
c. H.W. Rosen. Radio Éireann Symphony Orchestra. Radio Éireann Choral Society.
Concert. Phoenix Hall, Dublin. 23 Dec.
c. J.M. Doyle. Radio Éireann Symphony Orchestra. Austin Gaffney.

1961
Tannhauser (part Act 2) **and** *Die Meistersinger* (Act 3), Wagner. Phoenix Hall, Dublin, 21 Feb.
c. H.W. Rosen, with Radio Éireann Symphony Orchestra.
Symphony No. 9, Beethoven, Olympia Theatre, Dublin. 25 Mar.
c. Tibor Paul. Radio Éireann Symphony Orchestra. Helen Watts, James Johnston, Roger Stalman,
Radio Éireann Choral Society.
Faust, Gounod (Marguerite). Mars Theatre, Kilrush. Kilrush Operatic Society. 14 to 21 May.
c. Captain R.B. Keily. Veronica Dunne/Josephine Scanlon, John Carolan/Tano Ferendinos, Stanislav
Pieczora, Russell Cooper, Patricia Lawlor.
The Gipsy Baron; Die Fledermaus, Johann Strauss (arias). St. Francis Xavier Hall, Dublin. 30 May.
c. H.W. Rosen. RTÉ Symphony Orchestra. Radio Éireann Choral Society.

1962
Elijah, Mendelssohn, St. Francis Xavier Hall, Dublin. 11 Sept.
c. Tibor Paul. RTÉ Symphony Orchestra. Bernadette Greevy, Adrian De Payer, Hervey Alan, Our Lady's Choral Society.

L'amico Fritz, Mascagni (Suzel). Theatre Royal, Wexford. Wexford Festival Opera. 21,23,25,27 Oct.
c. Antonio Tonini. Radio Éireann Symphony Orchestra. Nicola Monti, Bernadette Greevy, Paolo Pedani, Derick Davies, Adrian de Peyer, Laura Sarti.

Manon, Massenet (Manon). Gaiety Theatre, Dublin. DGOS. 28,30 Nov. 3,7 Dec.
c. Charles Mackerras. Edward Byles, Russell Cooper, Edwin FitzGibbon, Noel Mangin, Bryan Drake, Hazel Williams, Beryl Brier, Christine Palmer.

1963
Carmen, Bizet (Carmen). Mars Theatre, Kilrush. Kilrush Operatic Society. 26 May to 2 Jun.
c. Capt. R.B. Kiely. Veronica Dunne/Bettina Jonic, Nasco Petroff/Brychan Powell, June Barton, Michael Maurel, Frederick Bateman.
La Bohème, Puccini (Mimi). New Theatre, Cardiff. Welsh National Opera. 7,9 Oct.
c. Bryan Balkwill. Robert Savoie, Stuart Burrows, David Gwynne, Jenifer Eddy.
Le nozze di Figaro, Mozart (Countess Almaviva). Gaiety Theatre, Dublin. DGOS. 2,5,10,12 Dec.
c. Tibor Paul. Peter Behlendorf/Derek Davies, Ingrid Paller, Hans Otto Kloose/Rudolf Jedlicka, Cora Canne-Meier/Frances Bible, Edouard Wollitz, John Kentish/Hans Blessin, Edwin FitzGibbon.

1964
Te Deum, Bruckner, Gaiety Theatre, Dublin. 23 Feb.
c. Tibor Paul. RTÉ Symphony Orchestra. Radio Éireann Choral Society.
Stabat Mater, Rossini, National Stadium, Dublin. 26 Mar.
c. Tibor Paul. RTÉ Symphony Orchestra, Bernadette Greevy, Edwin FitzGibbon, Harold Gray, Our Lady's Choral Society.
Tosca, Puccina (Tosca). Mars Theatre, Kilrush. Kilrush Operatic Society. 17 to 24 May.
c. Nicholas Braithwaite. Veronica Dunne/Victoria Elliott, Gwyn Griffiths/Geoffrey Chard, David Parker/Edward Byles, Michael McCann, Evan Thomas, Tegwyn Short.
La Bohème, Puccini (Mimi). New Theatre, Cardiff. Welsh National Opera. 7 Oct. (4 perfs.)
c. Bryan Balkwill. Stuart Burrows, David Gwynne, Robert Savoie, Michael Maurel, Tegwyn Short, Malcolm Williams, Jenifer Eddy, Gordon Whyte, Ivor Phillips.
Der Rosenkavalier, Richard Strauss (Sophie). Gaiety Theatre, Dublin. DGOS. 1,3,5,7 Dec.
c. Napoleone Annovazzi. Elizabeth Thoma, Margarethe Sjostedt, Erich Winkelmann, Rudolf Knoll, Ann Moran, Erich Klaus, Edwin FitzGibbon.
Les Pêcheurs de Perles, Bizet (Leila). Gaiety Theatre, Dublin. DGOS. 8,10,12 Dec.
c. Napoleone Annovazzi. Rowland Jones, Raimund Herincz, James Pease.

1965
Tosca, Puccini (Tosca) Grand Theatre, Swansea. Welsh National Opera. 17 Mar. (4 perfs.)
c. Bryan Balkwill. Rowland Jones, Otakar Kraus.
Bartered Bride, Smetana (Marenka). New Theatre, Cardiff. Welsh National Opera. Autumn. (4 perfs.)
c. Vilém Tauský. Robert Thomas, John Holmes, Malcolm Williams, Elizabeth Vaughan, Delme Bryn Jones, Anne Pashley.
Four Last Songs, Richard Strauss. St. Francis Xavier Hall, Dublin. 19 Mar.
c. Éimear O'Broin. RTÉ Symphony Orchestra.
Stabat Mater, Rossini, National Stadium, Dublin. 14 Apr.
c. Tibor Paul. RTÉ Symphony Orchestra.

Never to have lived is best, Bodley. World Première. St. Francis Xavier Hall, Dublin. 11 Jun.
c. Tibor Paul. RTÉ Symphony Orchestra.
Mass, Stravinsky; *Mass in E Minor*, Bruckner. Liberty Hall, Dublin. 25 Nov.
c. Seóirse Bodley. Culwick Choral Society, Hazel Morris, Richard Cooper, Frank Patterson, Gerald Duffy.
La Bohème, Puccini (Mimi). Gaiety Theatre, Dublin. DGOS. 1,3,11,13 Dec.
c. Harold Gray. Charles Craig, June Barton, John Hauxvell, James Pease, John Rhys Evans, Raymond Farrell, Terence Conoley.
Don Giovanni, Mozart (Donna Elvira). Gaiety Theatre, Dublin. DGOS. 10,14,16,18 Dec.
c. Myer Fredman. Forbes Robinson, Elizabeth Rust, Robert Savoie/Richard Golding, Edmond Bohan, Ann Moran, James Pease/Richard Golding.

1966
Orchesterlieder, Vogel. Irish Première. St. Francis Xavier Hall, Dublin. 29 Jan.
c. Tibor Paul. RTÉ Symphony Orchestra.
Don Giovanni, Mozart (Donna Elvira). New Theatre, Cardiff. Welsh National Opera. 14 Mar. (4 perfs.)
c. Bryan Balkwill. Forbes Robinson, Kenneth Bowen, John Gibb, Patricia Reakes, David Kelly, David Rhys Edwards.
The Bartered Bride, Smetana (Marenka). New Theatre, Cardiff. Welsh National Opera. 22,26 Mar.
c. Eric Weatherell. Stuart Burrows, Malcolm Williamns, Anne Pashley, David Gwynne.
A Terrible Beauty is Born, Boydell. World Première. Gaiety Theatre, Dublin. 11 Apr.
c. Tibor Paul. RTÉ Symphony Orchestra. Bernadette Greevy, William Young, Our Lady's Choral Society.
Concert. Holst, Delius, Boydell, Brahms, excerpts. Royal Dublin Society, Members Hall. 14 Apr.
c. Seóirse Bodley. Culwick Choral Society, Gerard Shanahan (piano), Sheila Cuthbert (harp).
Requiem, Verdi, St Mary's Cathedral, Limerick. 29 Apr.
c. Tibor Paul. RTÉ Symphony Orchestra. Bernadette Greevy, Edwin FitzGibbon, Joseph Dalton.
A Terrible Beauty is Born, Boydell. St. Francis Xavier Hall, Dublin. 8 Jul.
c. Tibor Paul. RTÉ Symphony Orchestra.
Voyelles, Victory. World Première. St. Francis Xavier Hall, Dublin. 27 Jul.
c. Colman Pearce. RTÉ Symphony Orchestra.
Te Deum, Kodály. St. Francis Xavier Hall, Dublin. 11 Nov.
c. Colman Pearce. RTÉ Symphony Orchestra, Limerick Choral Union.

1967
Naughty Marietta, Herbert (Marietta). Cork Opera House. Jan.
St. Patrick's Day Festival Concert. Royal Albert Hall, London. 16 Mar.
With Kathleen O'Connor (piano), John Jackson (organ).
War Requiem, Britten, St. Patrick's Cathedral, Dublin. 5 Apr.
c. Tibor Paul. RTÉ Symphony Orchestra. Kenneth Bowen, Peter McBrien, Radio Éireann Singers and Choral Society.
Don Giovanni, Mozart (Donna Elvira). Grand Theatre, Swansea. Welsh National Opera. 25 Sept to 14 Oct.
c. Frank Doolan. Forbes Robinson, Stuart Burrows, Patricia Reakes, Kenneth Bowen, David Rhys Edwards, John Gibbs, D.Kelly/D.Gwynne.

1968
Glagolitic Mass, Janáček, Savoy Cinema, Dublin. 26 Apr.
c. Ľudovít Rajter. RTÉ Symphony Orchestra, Mary Sheridan, William McAlpine, Patrick McGuigan, Limerick Choral Union.

The Water and The Fire, Milner. Irish Première. St. Francis Xavier Hall, Dublin. 1 Nov.
c. H.W. Rosen. RTÉ Symphony Orchestra. Radio Éireann Choral Society.
Symphony No. 4, Mahler. Gaiety Theatre, Dublin. 24 Nov.
c. Colman Pearce. RTÉ Symphony Orchestra.

1969
Harawi, Messiaen. Harty Room, Queen's University. Belfast Festival. 26 Nov.
Havelock Nelson (piano). Recorded by BBC Radio 3.
Songs, Humphrey Searle. Harty Room, Queen's University. Belfast Festival. 27 Nov.
Havelock Nelson (piano).

1970
Don Giovanni, Mozart (Donna Elvira). Irish National Opera tour of Ireland.

1971
Never to have lived is best, Bodley. St. Francis Xavier Hall, Dublin. Festival of Music. 8 Jan.
c. Pierre Michel Le Conte. RTÉ Symphony Orchestra.
Seven Irish Songs, Wilson. Ded. to V. Dunne & H. Nelson. World Première. Goethe Institute,
Dublin. 4 Mar.
John O'Conor (piano).
Mass in F Minor, Bruckner. St. Francis Xavier Hall, Dublin. 19 Jun.
c. H.W. Rosen, RTÉ Symphony Orchestra, Guinness Choir.

1972
Four Last Songs, Richard Strauss, St. Francis Xavier Hall, Dublin. 26 Feb.
c. H.W. Rosen. RTÉ Symphony Orchestra.
The Táin, **Wilson**. Ded. to V. Dunne. World Première, Trinity College Dublin Exam Hall 29 Jun.
Jeffrey Cosser (percussion), Courtney Kenny (piano).

1975
Fand and *The Táin*, Wilson. St Canice's Cathedral, Kilkenny. 26 Aug.
Veronica McSwiney (piano), John Fennessy (percussion), Doris Keogh (flute).

1978
The Táin, **Wilson**. First perf. of orchestral version. St. Francis Xavier Hall, Dublin. 30 Aug.
c. Colman Pearce. RTÉ Symphony Orchestra,
Concert. Royal Dublin Society. Kevin Hough Productions. 8 Dec.
Geraldine O'Grady (violin), Havelock Nelson (piano).
Pierrot Lunaire, Schoenberg, Kilkenny Arts Festival. Aug.
John O'Conor (piano), Thérèse Timoney (violin), Deirdre Brady (flute, piccolo), James Daley
(clarinet)

2002
The Queen of Spades, Tchaikovsky (Countess). Gaiety Theatre, Dublin. Opera Ireland. 17,19,21,23 Nov.
c. Alexander Anissimov. Viktoria Kurbatskaya, Peter Svensson, Vassily Savenko, Sam McElroy,
Tatyana Kaminskaya, Galia Ibragimova, Kathleen Tynan.

2011
Fiddler on the Roof, Bock and Harnick (Grandma Tzeitzel). Gaiety Theatre, Dublin. Lyric Opera.
16 Mar. to 2 Apr.
c. Aidan Faughey. Tony Finnegan, Ellen McElroy, Des Manahan, Vladimir Jablokov.

INDEX

Major operatic roles performed by Veronica Dunne are indexed. Images are indicated by italics.